From
PRIVATE
to
General

From PRIVATE to General

An African American Soldier Rises Through The Ranks

Major General Jerry R. Curry
(U.S. Army Retired)

BELIEVE BOOKS
Life Stories That Inspire
WASHINGTON, DC

FROM PRIVATE TO GENERAL
By Major General Jerry R. Curry, U.S. Army Retired

ISBN: 0-9787428-9-3

Library of Congress Control Number: 2006933289

Cover design: *Jack Kotowicz, Washington, D.C., VelocityDesignGroup.com*
Layout design: *Annie Kotowicz and Jen Anderson*

Believe Books publishes the inspirational life stories of extraordinary believers in God from around the world. Requests for information should be addressed to **Believe Books** at www.believebooks.com. **Believe Books** is a registered trade name of **Believe Books, LLC** of Washington, D.C.

Printed in the United States of America

To the loving memory of my mother, the Reverend Marion Mercer Curry; and my father, Jesse Aaron Curry; and to my very loving and vibrant helpmate, Charlene Elaine. Without my parents, I would not have life and without Charlene, life would not be worth living.

Contents

ACRONYMS AND MILITARY TERMS

ACLU — *American Civil Liberties Union*

ARVN — *Army of the Republic of Vietnam (South Vietnamese).*

AVICE — *Office of the Assistant Vice Chief of Staff of the Army*

CGSC — *Command and General Staff College*

CP — *Command Post, or military headquarters*

DMZ — *Demilitarized Zone*

FAA — *Federal Aviation Administration*

FB — *Fire Base*

Gunships — *Helicopters armed with rockets, 40 mm grenade launchers and machine guns.*

KMAG — *Korean Military Advisory Group*

LP — *Listening Posts*

MDW — *Military District of Washington*

MP — *Military Police*

NAACP — *National Association for the Advancement of Colored People*

NPI — *The National Perspectives Institute*

NVA — *North Vietnamese Army*

PFC — *Private First Class*

R & R — *Rest and Recuperation*

Slick — *A helicopter that is only armed by a machine gunner in each back door.*

TECOM — *The U.S. Army's Test and Evaluation Command*

VC — *Viet Cong. Guerilla fighters for the North Vietnamese.*

1

Praying for Wisdom

It was the end of the day. The bloated bodies of the dead Vietnamese soldiers baked under the cruel equatorial sun. They littered the jungle hillside surrounding Captain Larry McNamara's position like rotting clumps of jellyfish cast up on a hot sandy beach. Larry was a U.S. Advisor to a South Vietnamese Army Battalion. He and his American sergeant and about 40 Vietnamese soldiers were surrounded and trapped.

Miles away, at the command post, their fellow South Vietnamese soldiers sprawled or squatted Oriental style, behind dug-in M-60 machine-gun or M-16 assault rifle positions. The guns were surrounded with a protective wall of tightly tamped down sand bags. Those sand bags would hopefully stop bullets or shrapnel in an attack. Some of the soldiers smoked cigarettes while others told rough jokes or engaged in soldier horseplay. A few slept. They were the smart ones.

It was a typical command post. Light bulbs, powered by nearby generators, dangled from two-strand electric wires that had been hurriedly looped over ten-penny nails pounded into the wooden support rib that held up the rusted tin roof. The naked light bulbs tried unsuccessfully to chase away the onslaught of darkness that crept up on the 41st ARVN (Army of the Republic of Vietnam, South Vietnam) Infantry Regimental command post.

Beyond the post's barbed wire perimeter, a line of two-man Listening Posts was spaced at irregular intervals extending out into no man's land. Each man, in his Listening Post—or LP as the soldiers called them—waited and watched for any sign of an enemy attack. Close to the scrub trees and bushes the men had carefully dug foxholes, painstakingly spreading the dirt in the natural creases of the reddish earth and under the lush vegetation so that, hopefully, their location would not be detected by the feared North Vietnamese military.

Suddenly, the radio inside the barbed-wire enclosed command post barked to life. Captain McNamara's muffled but recognizable voice cut through the heavy static. "Can't hold on much longer," he said, his voice urgent, but controlled. "They're killing us with 82-millimeter mortars and B-40 rocket-propelled grenades!" These were not light weapons. The mortar shells weighed over six pounds and fragmented on impact.

The command post radio operator was a senior U.S. Army infantry sergeant, a hard man, six-four in his stocking feet wearing run-down-at-the-heels jungle combat boots. The ARVN feared and respected him. They had cause. He sat hunkered down in a gray metal chair facing fold up wooden campaign tables, which supported a plethora of military radios. Abruptly, without turning his head or body, he swiveled his right arm up and back over his shoulder to signal me.

Reaching out, I grabbed the extended radio telephone handset and mashed down hard on the push-to-talk switch. "Larry," I said, in what I hoped was my calmest, most professional, most reassuring voice, "just hold on . . . we need a little more time to get you out of there."

With a heavy heart, I laid the handset on the wooden campaign table and averted my eyes so that no one, especially not the sergeant, could tell that I had no idea how to extricate Larry and the ARVN soldiers he was advising, from the clutches of the encircling North Vietnamese Army.

On the other side of the command post, a large tactical map was smoothed out on top of two campaign tables placed end-to-end. The ARVN artillery officers stuck a red-capped pin at the spot where they guessed Larry and the ARVN soldiers might be trapped, but they were only speculating. The fighting had been so intense that Larry hadn't been able to verify his coordinates. Earlier, I had tried to get a fix from him, but had failed.

"Larry," I had said, "I know you're under a lot of pressure, but you've got to take out your compass and shoot some magnetic azimuths. It's imperative that we know your exact geographical location."

"I'm laying flat on my face in the dirt," he shouted back at me over the din of battle. "Both my arms are over my head. My compass is in the pouch on my pistol belt. To get it, I have to work my arms down to my waist.

"Across the clearing from me is a .51 caliber machine-gun with a North Vietnamese Army (NVA) soldier hanging on the end of it. When I try to move my hands down to my belt, my shoulder blades rise up and that bastard fires a string of machine-gun bullets right down my back . . . Got any other suggestions?"

All of us in the headquarters had desperately searched for solutions, especially the 41st ARVN Regiment's, Colonel Vy, but we could find none. Each time Vy or an ARVN officer came up with a suggestion, one of my U.S. advisors pointed out some fatal flaw in it. When one of us Americans came up with a counter proposal, the ARVN officers reciprocated.

Finally, there was nothing left to propose or discuss. With daylight swiftly fading, it would soon be dark and impossible to land helicopters and try to extract Larry and his ARVN soldiers. There was no way a relief column could fight its way to them on foot before morning, and morning would be too late.

"We've lost them," Colonel Vy sadly concluded. Suddenly, it was dark.

From painful experience, we knew that slowly, methodically, persistently, the NVA soldiers would work their way closer and closer until they were able to surge forward and overrun Larry's position. Numbers, time, and darkness were on their side. Larry and his pathetic remnant of ARVN soldiers were outnumbered by more than four to one and Larry was no longer just advising. He was fighting for his life.

By default, he had had to assume command of the ARVN soldiers. It was an obstacle all U.S. advisors faced in Vietnam at one time or another. They were forbidden to assume direct control of South Vietnamese troops; they were only supposed to make suggestions. However, sometimes U.S. advisors were forced to assume direct command in clear violation of those directives, or simply stand by and watch leaderless ARVN units disintegrate and be slaughtered under enemy fire.

Larry's situation seemed hopeless.

If only this were a video game or a movie, I mused. *We'd simply call for the fighter bombers or fire the artillery. All the bad guys would fall down dead, and the good guys would walk away unscathed.* But it didn't work that way in real combat.

Sick at heart, I stepped out of the rusty, corrugated tin command post into the open air. Glancing up at the radio antennas bristling against the moonlit sky, I leaned back against the rough bark of a palmetto tree.

Shafts of yellow light spilled out from around the command post door and windows, filtering through holes in the canvas curtains. Strangely, it reminded me of returning home after dark and seeing the light in the distance filter through the curtains of our home outside the small town of Liberty, Pennsylvania, where I grew up. Every evening, my mother would stand in the kitchen doorway and call us children in from play or farm chores to listen to a Bible reading followed by prayer.

"Jerry," Mom used to say, "There will be situations in your life that you won't know how to handle. When those times come, if you pray, God will surely give you wisdom." Mom was right. If ever there was a time to pray for wisdom, this was it.

Near the command post, dug into the clay-like earth, was a sleeping bunker I had borrowed from another U.S. Advisor who was currently on R & R in Bangkok, Thailand. It was there that I went to pray.

Ducking under the dusty burlap curtain that separated the combination office and sitting room from the sleeping area, I un-buckled my pistol belt. The weight of the holstered Colt .45 auto-matic spiraled the belt from around my waist like peeling the skin from an orange.

I knelt on the concrete bunker floor and prayed that somehow God would give me wisdom. I asked Him to show me a way to save Larry and his men. How long I knelt there I don't know, but finally I felt inside that everything was somehow going to work out and I thought I knew how.

Calmly now I stood up, secured my equipment and purposeful-ly strode from the bunker. As I headed back toward the command post, the light filtering out from the windows again reminded me of my parent's home in Liberty.

2

First Things

When you grow up in a town named Liberty, you often think of the meaning of the word, not just for the present or future, but what liberty has meant throughout history.

One of my favorite Bible stories is the story of Queen Esther and her nation's quest for freedom and liberty, and when our church decided to present it as a musical, a cantata, I was overjoyed.

I got to sing the role of Mordecai the Jew. I loved singing Mordecai's lament, "Woe is me, for the devices of the wicked prosper. Israel for thee, for thee do I tremble."

The cantata tells the story of how Haman the Agagite schemes with his friends to kill all the Jews in the Babylonian empire. But God used Mordecai and Queen Esther to foil Haman's plans and to deliver the Jews from the hatred of their enemies. The story concludes with Haman's execution.

As a teenage baritone, I had never been in finer voice.

Perhaps the Old Testament prophet's costume helped, or was it that I was trying so hard to please my mother, who was sitting in the front row of the audience? I certainly wanted to impress the girl sitting next to my mother, the auburn-haired, freckle-faced Charlene Elaine Cooper.

Most operas are written with the tenor role dominant, but not this version of Queen Esther's story. This night, the male star was an accomplished operatic baritone who had been imported from Pittsburgh to sing the role of King Ahasuerus, and to lend an air of professionalism to the church production.

The year was 1949. It marked the high point of the Golden Age of music at Bethlehem Baptist Church. Reverend Clarence M. Long, Jr. and his gracious wife, Laverne, grandly presided over Bethlehem's renaissance. Together they brought balance, dignity, high moral purpose and tone to the colored community of McKeesport, Pennsylvania. They were refined, highly educated, energetic, success-oriented people who set and demanded high standards. For the most part, the congregation measured up.

These were heady days at Bethlehem and the music helped set the tone for godly worship, as it does in so many churches and synagogues. Our church was blessed with Gertrude Johnson as choirmaster. Imperious and dictatorial, Trudy, as she was called, brought a decade of classical music, cantatas, opera singers, organists, harpists, and pianists to the church. She was a classically trained operatic soprano and had on occasion sung on the concert stage with the contralto Marion Anderson.

Shortly after her appointment as choirmaster she declared that, "Gospel music is nothing more than noise and emotionalism." With that statement, she banished gospel music and gospel choirs from the church. For more than a decade, Bethlehem's worship music was "high church."

The year before I sang in the Queen Esther cantata, I had heard my first operatic aria, a scratchy '78 era recording of Enrico Caruso singing *Vesti la Giubba* from *Pagliacci*, played on an old Gramophone. For some inexplicable reason the aria resonated with something deep inside me. I didn't understand or remember the words, but hummed the tune for weeks, driving everyone around me crazy, especially my mother. Unknowingly, opera had become a part of my life.

Not long afterwards, one of the local theaters ran a black and white film adaptation of the opera *Rigoletto* for one week. For hours, I sat in the third row of the nearly empty theater enraptured.

Later that summer a touring African American opera troupe performed *La Boheme* in Pittsburgh. Mrs. Johnson encouraged choir members to attend and, of course, I was among the first to volunteer. This beautiful and inspiring production reinforced my growing operatic addiction.

Under my mother's influence, the spiritual dimension in my life also grew. Her father and my grandfather, Edward Lee Shiflet, was an ordained Baptist minister who had greatly influenced her own Christian development. But she had learned her theology from her grandfather, Edward Lee Eubanks, who for many years had been the leading deacon in a local Baptist church at the southern end of Virginia's Shenandoah Valley.

During the years of the Great Depression, work was so scarce in the southern Shenandoah that my parents migrated north looking for work and a way to feed their family. Dad finally found a job working in a steel mill in western Pennsylvania.

The steel town of McKeesport, Pennsylvania lies upstream from Pittsburgh at the confluence of the Monongahela and Youghiogheny Rivers. Running parallel to the Monongahela is Fifth Avenue, once McKeesport's main thoroughfare, now just another narrow, forgotten street in the nation's rustbelt.

McKeesport's other main thoroughfare is Walnut Street, which roughly crosses the north end of Fifth Avenue at a right angle. From there it stretches west for two miles before slicing through the suburb of Christie Park.

At 421 27th Street in Christie Park, I was born at 4 A.M. on September 7, 1932. Doctor Matthew Ralph Hadley did the honors with his nurse wife, Rubye, assisting.

"Doctor," my mother said after the pains of childbirth had passed, "you and your wife have been so wonderful to me that I'm going to give my son your middle name, Ralph."

"The honor is mine, Mercer," the tall, distinguished Hadley replied, washing his hands in a basin of water. "He's a fine looking baby, perfect in every respect. I'm sure he'll grow up to be a blessing to you and a credit to our nation."

The house, a small white clapboard, sits back from the street and the other houses. Today, though renovated, it still looks insignificant.

Those of us born in the early 1930s entered a ragged American society that was economically depressed, spiritually tormented, and racially segregated. It was a turbulent, terrible, fascinating, and challenging time in which to be born and grow up.

Back then, the Greater Pittsburgh area was known as the land of "Big Steel." People congregated in diners and ethnic social clubs, they talked and drank at picnics, back slapped, and bet on semi-pro baseball or sand-lot football games. Everyone was expected to go to a church or synagogue, but many worshipped at other altars, which were neither Protestant, Catholic, nor Jewish. Their altars were named "Bessemer" and "Open Hearth"—what were then "high tech" ways to refine steel.

The Big Steel plants carried names of the towns and cities where their altars were erected, names like Clariton, Duquesne, Homestead, Irvin, Youngstown, and Steubenville. Above each steel mill's entrance, huge painted letters framed the plant's pedigree in words such as, "United States Steel, McKeesport Plant."

On brooding nights the flaming breath of the fiery furnaces lit up the soot- and smog-laden sky. The flames threw long, eerie shadows which brought with them a feeling of wealth and well-being.

"Look at that beautiful red sky, children," mothers said, interrupting the nightly chores and school homework while herding them outside. Approvingly, they all stared upward at the reflections from the brightly colored flames, which leapt hungrily heavenward.

The omnipresent by-product of this bounty, a foul particulate akin to the mythological sulphur and brimstone of dragons, filtered down through the layers of thick air to darken the sky in summer and to brown the snow in winter. Yet, to the workers and their families, the pollution was a welcome sign of divine favor and blessing.

"Be thankful your father has work," mothers snapped when children complained about soot-covered bushes or flowers. Even the filthy dust from the wood and coal-burning stoves, which heated their homes and over which women cooked, was counted as good fortune. Even when work shoes ground black grime into the wooden floors and irreversibly soiled rugs, no one complained. No windows dared display white curtains in the steel gods' smog-browned valleys.

In their hearts, these women were not thinking of the glow from the miniature aurora borealis that clawed low against the darkened sky. This was the Great Depression, so they uttered thankful, silent prayers to God that their husbands' and lovers' jobs were secure. They thanked God that their men had enough money to stop at the local bars, which were strategically placed near the entrances to the steel mills and foundries.

There were stand-up bars for the hard men who tapped the mouths of the furnaces and poured and chipped, welded, machined, and polished the steel. Six inches above the floor a burnished brass foot rail ran the length of the dark wood bar. Large brass cuspidors, polished until they gleamed, stood at either end of the rail.

The workmen wore overalls with bone or metal-buttoned jackets cut off at the waist and plaid flannel shirts, cotton in summer, wool in winter. Each carried a black or gray metal lunch box, with a thermos snapped securely in the hump-backed lid.

The bartenders knew what each man drank and could set up the entire work shift without a word passing between them. A nod of the head or a meeting of the eyes told them all they needed to know to fill each order.

So long as the steel furnaces brightened the night sky, the men knew their bills would be paid and, should they choose, they could register their children for parochial school. They could afford to buy their daughters white, or pale pink, or pastel blue confirmation dresses accented by brand new patent leather shoes with matching purses.

Less than an hour's car ride from McKeesport and its furnaces, men burrowed deep into the earth to get at the rich deposits of coal. When they returned to the surface bearing the black gold the earth had grudgingly shared, they looked up into the brown-red sky, and were satisfied.

"Where does all this iron and steel go?" I once wistfully asked my mother.

"Oh, to places like Illinois, Detroit, Saint Louis, Atlanta, Boston, Seattle, and California . . . all over the world I guess," she replied, pushing a strand of black hair out of the way.

I was impressed with Mom for many reasons. She seemed to have answers for everything. All I had to do was ask, and she told me wonderful stories of far away places.

My father, Jesse Aaron Curry, a steel worker and part-time farmer, was one of God's original eccentrics. He was gifted with exceptional natural intelligence, and he thought and acted as if it was divinely mandated for the entire world to adjust to him. Occasionally, the world did.

Brown skinned, standing five-eight and weighing 150 pounds, Dad had narrow hips and medium-sized, meatless shoulders and chest. Despite his small bones and slight stature, he was strong and wiry. He would rather fight than eat. When he was born, his father, who was a deacon in the Baptist church, gave him two biblical names: Jesse for the tribe of Judah and Aaron for the tribe of Levi.

Until his death, he maintained his eccentric independence, no matter how often or severely life pummeled him. Even his terminal illness was forced to adjust to Jesse's own peculiar way of dying.

In the summer of 1989, when a CAT scan revealed that Dad's bones were riddled with cancer, he called a doctors' conference. After they explained his condition and presented him with two options, chemotherapy or radiation, he chose neither.

He discharged himself from the hospital, after asking for and receiving a pocketful of pain killers. Then, he drove himself home to die, which he did a year later, after the real pain had been hard upon him for five months.

Dad was born in Glasgow, Virginia on September 12, 1905. His father, Hubert Anthony Curry, was kind and gentle by nature, even though he was descended from the Nash family, which gave birth to many hard, cruel, and even dangerous people who hurt others. They welcomed physical confrontation, occasionally killed people, and held grudges for life. They could move from a state of quiescence to uncontrollable rage in a millisecond.

Dad's mother was Rosanna Campbell, a regal, gracious, warm and wonderful woman who always maintained a sense of dignity and decorum. She was in her mid-eighties when she stopped dyeing her long, thick black hair and, for the first time, allowed the gray to show. Both Rosanna and Hubert were of African descent, with a large measure of American Indian mixed in.

Marion Mercer Shiflet Curry, my mother, was born in the heart of the Shenandoah Valley at Steeles Tavern, Rockbridge County, Virginia, on September 29, 1911. She brought excitement to every man who looked at her.

Her father, Edward Lee Shiflet, was a tall, fine, strong-featured man. Mom used to say again and again, with a faraway misty look in her eyes, that her dad "was one of the most wonderful men in the world."

Ed Shiflet was an ordained Baptist minister, a graduate of Howard University's School of Theology, who spoke with an Irish brogue. He loved a good "visit" and enjoyed social gatherings of all kinds, as long as the laughter was hearty and the conversation fast and stimulating. He was addicted to art, music, words, women, books, fine things, horses, and a "good time," in no particular order.

Mom's mother was Rose Anna Eubanks, the first wife of Edward Lee Shiflett. Rose Anna Eubanks was the daughter of Edward Eubanks and Mary Sue Hughes. Mary Sue's mother was Leticia Jane and her father was Hezekiah Hughes. Both were born in Massy's Mill, Nelson County, Virginia.

Hezekiah's father was the white plantation owner's son; his mother was an African slave. It was a love relationship and at birth, Hezekiah's father acknowledged that the child was his own son and gave him his "Freedom Papers" at the age of 10.

Hezekiah earned his living, even during the bitter years of the Civil War, by traveling about west-central Virginia working as a cooper—barrel maker. He married Leticia Jane Hughes. Her father was an American Indian, tribe unknown, and her mother was African.

Leticia Jane was born a slave at Massey's Mill. When, toward the end of the Civil War, the Emancipation Proclamation was signed, all the slaves in Nelson County were freed. They were given the choice of staying on the plantations where they had been slaves and working for wages or leaving.

The day following the proclamation of freedom, Leticia Jane came upon the white son of Hezekiah's father and the eldest of her own children, a 12-year-old daughter, passionately kissing and fondling each other—even though they were half uncle and niece.

Next morning before daylight, she bundled up her four children and, carrying on her back a few meager possessions, struck out west across the Shenandoah Mountains on foot. Some days later, she found her husband Hezekiah hard at work making barrels near the town of Vesuvius.

"Leticia Jane," he cried out in horror, "what have you done? Why did you run away? Don't you know what they'll do to you and the children when they catch you?"

"Haven't you heard, Hezekiah?" she laughed, hugging and kissing him. "We are free! We are free!"

At least once during each visit to the old family homestead, near the town of Vesuvius, Mom would draw me aside, point east and exclaim, "That's the mountain Leticia Jane crossed, Jerry. Right over there."

3

Living in Liberty

From the center of McKeesport, if you drive west along Walnut Street, turn right at 15th Street, and cross the bridge to the far side of the river, the roadway swings sharply to the left and then splits like a pair of scissors. The right blade of the "scissor" points directly up toward the town of Port View. The left drops sharply down into a "holler," wanders around a bit then climbs steeply up a hill to Liberty, the small town where I grew up and spent my childhood.

Houses still line both sides of Liberty Way, the main street, just as they did then. All of the old houses facing the street had front porches. When I was a boy, the locals sat on those porches in wicker chairs or rockers; the women hooking rag rugs or crocheting, and men chewing tobacco and snuff or sucking on corncob pipes. It seemed you could leave in the middle of a conversation, return a year later and pick up right where you left off.

"Now, how you been getting on?" one would ask the other.

"Not too good," the visitor might reply, dropping wearily into a chair.

"You put on a little weight I see . . . you got to get that off," would be the unsolicited advice.

"I was here for a visit yesterday, but couldn't climb up the front steps . . . felt a little peaked," the visitor might continue. "I stood down there below and looked up for a while, then pulled out and come on home."

"You should have hollered some," the other would admonish.

"Almost did, but I was too weak."

"Uh-huh, next week if we have a pretty day, I'd like your boy to come over here and cut the grass." About then one or both of the men would arch a spit of tobacco juice up over the porch railing, a few drops dribbling onto the gray painted, weather-beaten, wooden porch floor.

A mile past the porches and the old men, a hard right turn put you onto Washington Boulevard, then a dirt and cinder road. The potholes were many and deep, the ruts worn wide. In the 1930s there were no utility poles or power lines, which meant no running water, electricity, or streetlights.

In 1937, Dad worked in McKeesport's Tin Plate Mill alongside Jim Mickolic. I still have Dad's mill identification card. Jim was a kind-hearted, hard-working man who had emigrated from Hungary. They both shared rural backgrounds and longed to move out of the city into the country.

Also working at the Tin Mill was Jim Harrison who lived just outside the small rural town of Liberty. Harrison said he knew where there was land for sale. It was owned by the Brinkman family, but no one lived on it. It was also 12 years in arrears for payment of back taxes.

The property was being handled by the Wilkins Real Estate Company with offices in McKeesport. Since the nation was still in the grips of the Great Depression, few people were buying land or any kind of property.

So the agent, Lynn Hart, said, "Mr. Curry, if you and Mr. Mickolic can come up with enough cash to pay off the taxes and throw in two hundred dollars for the real estate fee, you can split the property between you and both have free and clear titles."

"You got yourself a deal," they said, shaking hands.

The sale was made without anyone in Liberty knowing about it. But now came the tricky part. Over the years one colored family had lived in Liberty, and one of their children had even attended the all-white grammar school for a year. But the experience was less than satisfactory for all concerned, and the family moved away.

Essentially, our family would be integrating the town of Liberty. The townspeople had recently gone on record saying that colored families were unwelcome and that they would physically prevent any who tried to move into the area.

Dad and the two Jims conspired to circumvent the townspeople's objections. The Jims decided that if Dad secretly took possession of the land, it would thwart local efforts to prevent our colored family from locating to Liberty. They bided their time. One day, Dad heard that there was a construction company tearing down old houses. He contacted them and obtained the company's permission to scrounge the site for used lumber.

Early on a Saturday morning in May, Dad and the two Jims borrowed a truck, picked up timbers and siding at the construction site and, by nightfall, had constructed a huge, one-room tarpaper shanty on our property.

Before daylight the next day, May 9, 1937, household goods were in place and the Curry family had "taken possession." There were loud complaints from the white Liberty residents, but no physical effort was made to evict us.

For light, we used kerosene lamps. We had a potbellied coal stove for heat and a woodstove for cooking. Dad dug an outhouse.

He often told us, "Living in a tarpaper shack may be hard, but it's fair." I still don't know what he meant by that. I'm not sure he understood it himself, but when he said it, it sounded profound.

My parents' decision to relocate to the country was a good one. Within a year we were growing all sorts of vegetables as well as raising ducks, chickens, pigs, and goats—all of which we sold.

"I'll dig a foundation for the house right away, and before winter we can move our stuff into it," Dad said, smiling. "The living will be a little close, but we'll be warm and dry."

"And next spring, we'll build a house over the existing cellar," Mom added.

But by early July of that year, Dad still hadn't gotten around to digging the foundation. Over and over Mom nagged him, "Jesse, the children can't survive a cold Pennsylvania winter with all its wind, snow, and freezing temperatures huddled in this tarpaper shack. You've got to start building a house!"

Dad did nothing. So on July 4th, a hot sunny day, Mom selected a mattock and shovel from the makeshift toolshed, tossed them into a wheelbarrow and pushed it over to two green saplings, each of which sported three or four thin, green-leafed branches.

"Here's where we build the house, children," Mom announced with a finality born out of desperation.

With the pick end of the mattock, she traced a square in the dirt, a good distance down the hill from the two saplings. Digging up a shovel full of earth, she threw it into the wheelbarrow, followed by another, and then another. Years later, the saplings grew into giant elms which were cut down in 1991, after a long and fatal encounter with Dutch elm disease.

Digging a foundation for a house by hand is easier started than finished. At first Mom had to pry loose rocks, roots, and stubborn lumps of earth with the spade end of the mattock. When a wheelbarrow load was piled high with dirt and debris, Marjorie and Rose, my older sisters, along with Jesse, my older brother, helped Mom push it up and over the hill to a dump site.

By the time Dad arrived home from work that evening, a good start had been made. Sullenly, silently, he took the mattock from Mom and started digging. Rapidly the excavation deepened. Perhaps my youthful enthusiasm boosted Mom and Dad's morale a bit, but that was about all I contributed that summer. The next year I helped a little more, but not much.

Dad was a hard worker. Every night and weekend he labored mightily, digging and pushing the wheel barrow until it was so dark that it was dangerous to swing a pick. A white friend he made in Liberty, Lawyer Bishop, came out and helped him dig.

Now Mom turned her attention to other matters, but still found time to tactfully supervise Dad's construction efforts. She was careful not to bruise his overly large ego and never let him know that she, not he, was calling the shots.

Because of her persistence and encouragement, Dad made more progress with house building than expected. Not only did he finish the cellar by winter, but he also framed in the first story walls and shingled the roof.

Now, Mom was confident we would be able to endure the bitterly cold winter that was predicted. Somewhere Dad located a used coal-burning furnace and installed it in the basement while on the first floor Mom tended both a potbellied stove for heat and a wood-fired stove for cooking.

We moved in the day before Thanksgiving. After spending the summer and fall in a one-room, rambling tarpaper shanty, our small unfinished house seemed like a palace. The following day dawned bitter and cold and snow began to fall. We killed the old red rooster, *literally*, and feasted sumptuously. The Currys had a lot for which to be thankful.

In the spring, a representative from the McKeesport Bank came out, inspected Dad's progress and loaned us enough money to finish the construction. One of Dad's white friends put in the plumbing, another ran the electrical wires. Dad cemented red brick walls over the tarpaper-covered used lumber, and soon the Curry house was finished.

That year we children looked forward to the first traces of snow because the previous year we learned that when it snowed, giant cooking pots were rolled out, and set up on large stones. Soon a fire roared under those pots. Men from the surrounding area, including my father and Jim Mickolic, moved as a team from farm to farm slaughtering livestock, gutting, skinning, and butchering. It seemed that the local farmers, unlike some of the townsfolk, didn't have a problem with colored people owning property next to them. The smell of apples boiling themselves into apple butter filled the fall air for miles, as did the smell of preserves and crackling rind.

Too soon for us children, the fete was over; the next year's meat salted and hung in attics, while smokehouses cured other cuts. Fruits and vegetables were canned, preserved, or wrapped in newspaper by Mom and the girls. My older brother, Jesse, and I cut, carried, and laid in the winter's supply of firewood.

This was Pennsylvania coal country with veins of coal running just under the surface of the ground. Toward the back of our property, Dad sunk a vertical mine shaft by hand, about 20 feet deep. Many days my older brother, Jesse, and I climbed down a series of handmade ladders to the horizontal coalface. With pick and shovel, we dug coal and hoisted it to the surface in metal buckets and wicker baskets using chain, block, tackle, and an A-frame constructed of trimmed tree trunks.

These were the years where we learned to resolve life's many challenges through hard work, patience and persistence. This physical and mental toughening was preparation for things to come, though at the time I had no idea what lay ahead.

4

Eagle Scout

"You're only 11 years old, Jerry. That's awfully young to hold down a regular job, but I think you can do it," Mom said. "It's sweeping floors in a dress store in McKeesport, emptying trash, washing windows, that sort of thing. There's no heavy lifting."

So from that time until I graduated from high school, I had an evening and weekend job. Unfortunately, this left little time for sports and after school activities.

"Mondays, instead of riding the bus back home after work," my older brother, Jesse, suggested, "why not stop by the church? The Boy Scout meeting is over at 7:30 and afterward we can walk home together." Jesse was five-ten, a stocky 165 pounds, and like my father, took himself much too seriously.

In the 1940s, civic and social life was segregated along racial lines. Having a Boy Scout meeting at Bethlehem Baptist Church for Jesse to attend was, in itself, a minor miracle.

It started when one of the men, Dan Snyder, rhetorically asked the adult men's Sunday School Class at Bethlehem Baptist Church this question: "Isn't it time we colored folks in McKeesport provided the same opportunities for our young people that white folks routinely provide for theirs?"

Dan was a strong, serious man with a well-developed sense of humor. He stood six feet tall, weighed 220 pounds and was a carpenter and cabinetmaker by trade. He was also a community stalwart, one who believed that each of us should pay back something to the community that nourished us. He and his wife, Alameda, were childless. That may be why he was so concerned about the well-being of other people's children, especially boys.

"I propose," Dan continued, "that we start a Boy Scout Troop!"

"Scouting is for white people," objected "Brownie." His real name was Paris Brown, a short, no-nonsense, driven man who worked as a legal clerk for the Allegheny County judicial system. Most of the men in the Sunday school class nodded their heads in agreement. "Who ever heard of a colored Boy Scout?"

"So what?" Dan retorted. "You never know how a thing will turn out 'til you try it." His eyes fiercely swept across the class telling all present to agree or be silent.

"All right, Dan," Brownie finally agreed, rising to his feet. "If you're crazy enough to try, I'm just stupid enough to help you."

"It's settled then. Let's apply for a charter." There had never been a colored Boy Scout Troop in McKeesport and the request must have caused the local Boy Scout Council more than a little concern. However, the application finally came back approved. Boy Scout Troop 25 was official, with my brother Jesse as one of its charter members.

So on Mondays after work, even though I was too young to officially join the Scouts, I would watch my older brother and the other novice scouts memorize the Scout oath and laws, learn how to tie knots and complete merit badge requirements.

The Boy Scout oath became my personal credo, "On my honor I will do my best to do my duty to God and to my country, to obey the Scout law. To help other people at all times, to keep myself physically strong, mentally awake, and morally straight." The Boy Scout law also became a personal guide. "A Scout is: trustworthy, loyal, helpful, friendly, courteous, kind, obedient, cheerful, thrifty, brave, clean, and reverent."

When the Boy Scout Council approved Troop 25's charter, no one was thinking about summer camp. As spring of the second year approached, the white scout leaders realized that they were going to have to decide: would the local Boy Scout camp be segregated? No boy of color had ever gone to summer camp.

In McKeesport both the YMCA and the YWCA were segregated by race, as were country clubs, fast food restaurants, and churches. So why should Boy Scout summer camp be any different?

Thankfully, the council president disagreed. "Summer camp is a major part of scouting," he contended. "All year long our boys look forward to camp. Aren't the colored kids in Troop 25 our boys, too? Don't they deserve to go to camp alongside our white scouts?"

By this time I was old enough to officially join the Scouts, so each summer, until I finished high school, I attended Boy Scout camp. The interaction with other boys, the positive influence of the Scout counselors, and the warmth and support showered upon me by the families of black and white scouts alike, helped me better define how I would face and handle life's challenges.

Summers at Camp Aliquippa quickly propelled me along the path toward Eagle Scout. But I had one seemingly insurmountable obstacle to overcome. To complete the last merit badge, I had to pass the Red Cross Lifesaving swimming course.

As a young boy, I had taught myself to swim in the local swimming hole, as did most farm children. But that wasn't good enough for scouting. Scouting required formal training and lots of practice. The training I got at summer camp, but practice had to come during the winter months.

Once again, America's racist and segregationist policies stood in the way. In McKeesport the only indoor swimming pool belonged to the YMCA. Unlike the Boy Scouts, the Young Men's Christian Association was unwilling to make an exception for a young colored boy trying to become an Eagle Scout. Even the intercession of the Scout Council failed to persuade them.

"I'm sorry," Dan Snyder confessed. "I've done all I know to do, and for the first time in my life, my best isn't good enough. Jerry, you've done your part. All you need is a Lifesaving Merit Badge and you'll be an Eagle Scout, the first colored Eagle Scout in our city, perhaps in western Pennsylvania. Brushing aside tears he continued, "But there's no place in the McKeesport area for you to swim this winter."

Then Brownie offered me a carrot. "There's an indoor swimming pool at the colored YMCA in Pittsburgh in the Hill District. That's probably too far a distance for you to travel as often as you'd need to go. It's called the Center Avenue YMCA. If you'd like to try, I can set it up even though you're not a member of the 'Y'."

"Thanks," I said doubtfully. "But I'll need my parents' approval before I can make a commitment like that."

Dan nodded, "We understand. Don't feel too disappointed if your parents say no. It's a long trip and the transportation costs a lot of money. Besides, the Hill District isn't the safest place in the world for a young boy to go alone. It's pretty rough over there. There are a lot of muggings and killings."

To my surprise, Mom immediately agreed, and then coaxed my father into saying "Yes." He was willing, provided I pay the bus and streetcar fare out of my meager earnings.

A half-mile walk from our house along Washington Boulevard brought me to Liberty Way and the bus stop. It took the bus, picking up and discharging passengers along the way, about half an hour to wend its way from Liberty down to the corner of Walnut and Fifth Avenue in the center of McKeesport.

There, every half hour or so, Street Car Number 56 passed by on its journey to downtown Pittsburgh. The trip took a bell clanging, swaying, and jerking hour. Once in Pittsburgh, I changed over to the Central Avenue Street Car. Twenty minutes more took me to the front door of the Center Avenue Y.

Its indoor pool was usually empty or nearly so by the time I got there, and I swam until exhausted. It would have helped to have had a coach, but that was not to be.

The following summer at Camp Aliquippa, I completed my Lifesaving Merit Badge. That fall, my application to be an Eagle Scout was approved. In February 1949, at the annual Scouting Banquet held at McKeesport's Penn McKee Hotel on lower Fifth Avenue, a red-, white-, and blue-ribboned Eagle Scout Badge was hung around my neck.

Though scouting taught me to welcome difficult challenges and to persevere, it was my mother who taught me to meet life with dignity, honor, and humor. "Don't think more highly of yourself than you should," was her constant, biblical admonition. From my father, I learned a strong work ethic.

Under the tutelage of the Boy Scouts I learned and refined my leadership skills. At church, I was intellectually and musically challenged. But there had been earlier encounters, neither uplifting nor pleasant, which also helped cast and define the content of my childhood and later my character.

Some of my white classmates at Liberty Grade School taught me what it meant to grow up colored in a white dominated society. I had to learn to deal with these challenges without the benefit of the help, support, or sympathy of the federal government, NAACP, America's liberal establishment, or television cameras and the news media.

We Curry children were not welcomed at Liberty's all-white grammar school. Fortunately for me, my brother and two sisters went to school without me that first year. They bore the full brunt of racial bigotry. Another two years passed before I was enrolled in Liberty's first grade.

It was my siblings who endured the real racial hatred directed against our family. For example, a popular children's book at the time was the story of *Little Black Sambo*. Sambo was portrayed as being something of a fool, having black skin, huge red lips, overly large eyes, and exceptionally kinky hair. The story was viciously racist.

A recording of the story had been purchased by one of the school teachers. It was played and passed from class to class. While the record was playing, the white children pointed their fingers at my brother and sisters and snickered.

One of the teachers, a Miss Moon, seemed to be a major instigator. She made the school days of the Curry children as degrading as possible. One day, Jesse stole the record and broke it into pieces. No one ever figured out who had done it.

Finally, things became so intolerable that Mom went to visit Miss Moon personally to see if the situation could be remedied. Miss Moon ignored her. Mom grabbed her by the shoulders, spun her around and shook her until her "teeth rattled," as the saying goes. This physical confrontation, as unpleasant as it was, nevertheless seemed to help.

But what really made the difference was Margaret Barth, the no-nonsense principal of Liberty Grade School. Miss Barth was a fair-minded, decent person who was opposed to prejudice of any sort and let all the teachers know that she would no longer tolerate the continued race baiting and harassment of the Curry children. Teachers who could not accept that edict were encouraged to leave. Two years later, Miss Moon left.

Conversely, my first grade teacher, Miss Taylor, loved all children, regardless of their racial background. She, like Miss Clark, the fifth grade teacher, couldn't have done more to make us feel welcome.

Several times that first year I remember running home from school crying in humiliation, anger, and despair after being forced to pass through a gauntlet of white children who lined both sides of the street throwing rocks and shouting racial epithets at me. My face still bears the scars from one of those rocks. Fortunately, these few tormentors did not represent the majority of white students who were decent and helpful.

For his part, Dad tried to visit each white family and talk to the father of each tormentor that we could identify. It took a few years, but things did finally cool off, and we were eventually accepted as a solid American family that contributed much to the town of Liberty.

My fellow white students weren't evil; they were simply acting out—childishly, insensitively, cruelly—what they had been taught by their parents. Though our family earned grudging community acceptance, a few years later Liberty was again stirred to hate when two Jewish families chose to make Liberty their home.

Like us, the Jewish families were forced to run a gauntlet of prejudice and bigotry. "Why?" I asked my mother. "Why do people hate Jews?"

"It is spiritual," she responded. "The Jewish people gave the world Jesus. The devil hates Jesus and the devil is the one that motivates people to persecute the Jews and, unfortunately, they will do so until the end of time." There may be a better answer, but at the time this one made sense to me.

Like us before them, the Jewish families eventually gained acceptance, but it wasn't easy. I often thought, *It must be nice to be a white, non-Jewish family and to move into a community and be welcomed and respected without having to fight to earn that respect.*

* * *

One of my happiest memories and probably the most important day of my childhood happened on a sunny spring day when I was 13 years old. The wind was rustling the leaves and chasing white cotton candy clouds across a bright blue sky.

Charles Cooper, a friend of my father and a coal miner who lived in McKeesport, drove out to the Curry homestead with his very young son, George, in tow. They came to plant a garden on our land. More importantly, Mr. Cooper brought with him his copper-tressed, freckle-faced, ten-year-old daughter, Charlene. When she stepped down from the car and shyly looked around, I thought that she was the most beautiful girl in the world and decided that I would one day marry her.

While the grown-up Coopers and Currys talked about gardens and politics, labor unions, and the price of bricks, sheetrock, and lumber, I got acquainted with the two Cooper children. That is to say, with Charlene.

Before the sun went down, the grown-ups had plowed the soil and planted a garden with their hands, and had solved the problems of the nation and the world with their words. George had found new friends who were to be a great influence in his life and I had fallen head over heels in love with Charlene.

Like mine, Charlene's background was multiracial: French Canadian, American Indian, and African American. Her great-grandparents, the LaRues, had migrated down to Pennsylvania from Quebec. Being good Frenchmen, they arrived with grape vine seedlings originally from France. One of the first orders of business was to plant a small vineyard. For years they bottled their own wine.

Her father worked as a motorman in the Sutersville bituminous coal mine. He drove the locomotive that pulled the coal carts in and out of the mine. His mother, a seamstress, died when he was a little boy. Until the time of his death, at age 91, he grieved her loss.

My political education began during my high school years under the tutelage of the American Legion. The summer between my Junior and Senior year in high school, the local Legion Posts paid the expenses for me and a half-dozen other boys to attend "Boys' State." The white Legion Post paid the white boys' expenses. The colored Post paid mine.

Boy's State was located at Indian Town Gap Military Reservation, near Harrisburg, the Pennsylvania State Capitol. We boys were quartered in old wooden World War II Army barracks. Each building was designated a city, and the occupants of each building elected a student to be mayor. It was here that I was elected to my first political office—mayor of our "city."

This was followed by selection of a chief of police, fire chief, city manager, sanitation department director, superintendent of schools, and school board—as well as every other administrative job that a real-life city government should have.

Next, several cities were grouped together to form a county government. Finally, state representatives and senators were voted into office. Then a state government was set up, complete with governor, lieutenant governor, and attorney general.

We learned that America's republican form of government requires leadership, integrity, and a willingness to consider the other person's point of view. Honest, intelligent compromise is the linchpin of civil intercourse, the graphite that quiets the inherently competing frictions of a democracy.

In high school, I pursued college preparatory courses in hopes of becoming a college professor. My father, who dropped out of grade school in Virginia to work on a highway construction gang, insisted that I study medicine.

Why, he never said, but he was adamant, at times even emotional about it. Perhaps it was because all his life he had admired and respected those men and women who were successful in professions such as dentistry, law, and medicine.

Dad didn't often have conversations with us children. Usually, he spoke and we obeyed. If one of us demurred or showed signs of resistance, it immediately became a confrontation, sometimes a violent confrontation. One area of confrontation was my reluctance to study medicine, which one day culminated in an ultimatum.

"If you refuse to study medicine," he shouted at me, "I'll not pay a penny of your college expenses."

I didn't study medicine, and he kept his word. However, when I graduated from high school, he did get me a job working alongside him in the Pittsburgh Steel Foundry as a welder and scarfer—I used an acetylene torch to burn defects out of 20 ton steel castings. The foundry had a union shop, so I automatically became a member of what is now the AFL-CIO.

For eight months I worked hard, saved my money, and watched the goal of attending college inch toward reality. The Korean War changed everything. Along with many other patriotic young men, I enlisted in the Army as a private.

5

You're in the Army Now

June 6, 1950, I graduated from McKeesport High School. Nineteen days later, at 3:30 in the morning, Communist North Korean military forces crossed the 38th parallel, the internationally agreed upon border between North and South Korea.

Quickly and efficiently, they slashed through the South Korean Army and raced toward Seoul, South Korea's capital city, just 30 miles south of the 38th parallel. Seoul was then a dirty, sprawling, chaotic city surrounded by rice paddies, not the delightful, modern city it is today.

The United Nations Security Council asked member nations to provide military assistance to South Korea. Fifteen nations did. By September 5th, three months after my high school graduation, the North Koreans had driven the South Korean and United Nations Forces into the tiny southeast tip of the Korean Peninsula called the Pusan Perimeter.

General Douglas MacArthur, the United Nations Commander, cut the North Korean Army in half by making a strategic end-run around the North Korean Army, landing his army at Inchon on Korea's west-central coast. What was left of the North Korean army fled north with MacArthur's troops in hot pursuit. On October 25, 1950, at the Yalu River, North Korea's border with China, the

Communist Chinese intervened on the side of the North Koreans. By early January, the Chinese and North Korean military forces had recaptured Seoul.

Our government put out an urgent, nationwide call for volunteers to enlist in all branches of the armed services. Along with thousands of other patriotic young Americans, I answered the call. On March 5, 1951, at the Armed Forces Recruiting Station in Pittsburgh, Pennsylvania, I, along with a half-dozen other volunteers, raised my right hand and repeated:

"I, Jerry R. Curry, do solemnly swear that I will support and defend the Constitution of the United States against all enemies, foreign and domestic; that I will bear true faith and allegiance to the same; and that I will obey the orders of the President of the United States and the orders of the Officers appointed over me, according to regulations and the uniform code of military justice. So help me God!"

I didn't suspect then, when I put on the Army uniform, that I would wear an army uniform for nearly 34 years of active military service. Like all important decisions in my life, the decision to enlist was made after much prayer. My mother was surprised, and a little shocked. My father was proud.

The United States Army seemed double-minded when it came to the subject of race. Every soldier was expected to succeed. But colored soldiers were not supposed to succeed too much.

Years earlier, my mother had gently, philosophically explained the racial realities of American life to us Curry children with a touch of humor. She took the high road while doing it, as she did with most things.

Conversely, Dad went for the jugular. His version was as follows: "White people make the rules," he said, "and define mainstream values and acceptable codes of conduct. They worship success, thrift, and a work ethic. If you work hard and try to cooperate, white folks will encourage you to think that you will get a fair chance to compete and share in the rewards of the American dream. Occasionally, that will actually happen.

"In reality, you are a member of a minority group, so no matter how hard you work and try to adapt to mainstream American life, look out when you approach the finish line. Somehow the goal posts get yanked back or moved to one side. Or you find some new obstacle or qualification has been added to prevent you from breaking the winner's tape. And if you don't compete, even with the rules biased against you, you are doomed to living on the fringes of economic failure—or worse—you are condemned to accepting permanent underclass status.

"If you exert superhuman effort, America's white society might let you realize 75 percent of your potential, perhaps even 80. Yes, it's unfair to be prevented from going as far as you can in life, but that's the way it is and neither of us has the power to change that. Still, 75 percent is a whole lot better than 30 or 40.

"Don't forget, humans are not all the same. There are variations in all our actions. Some white people mean you well, and will even give you a fair deal. Others won't. And when white people are running in a pack, most won't give you the time of day. Life in this country hasn't seen fit to be fair to your mother and me, and it's not about to be fair to you."

My mother's comment was, "Those who think the government owes them something are in for a rude surprise. Each of us has to stand on our own feet. There comes a time in life when we become responsible for our own lives and futures regardless of the obstacles we face and the nation's preoccupation with race. Race isn't just a handicap; it's also a challenge. Those who think of themselves simply as victims will become losers."

Living means facing challenges, taking risks, making choices, and accepting responsibility for the outcome. While we may be free to pursue life, liberty, and happiness, we are not and should not be free from the responsibilities and penalties that come with that pursuit.

As a young man, I was determined to endure and persevere above the cruel slights and unfairness of the racial curse that American society had pronounced over me. But I resented having to do so.

I subscribed to Patrick Henry's approach toward the British. There were limits beyond which my patience would not go. There were times when I would not turn the other cheek. As a warrior, it is preferable to die on the field of battle than to surrender one's personal freedom and dignity.

Early in the morning of March 6, 1951, after a pleasant overnight ride from Pittsburgh in a Pullman sleeping car, a half-dozen of us new U.S. Army privates arrived in Louisville. There in the Bluegrass State of Kentucky, the place that supplies half of the world's bourbon and where it is said that men take poker, politics, and horse racing equally seriously, we disembarked from the train and began our military careers.

Eight weeks later, on the first Saturday in May, at Churchill Downs, the world's best three-year-old thoroughbreds would compete in the Kentucky Derby's one-and-a-quarter-mile "Run for the Roses," just as had happened every year since 1875. Unfortunately, the Army's plans for us recruits did not include watching the Derby.

At the train station, we were greeted by a corporal who seemed to be the meanest man in the Army. That conclusion was overly optimistic. We were soon to learn that the meanest man was the sergeant for whom the corporal worked. He was awaiting our arrival at Fort Knox, Kentucky.

I later discovered that the sergeant had only pretended to be mean. As he asked probing questions designed to fill in the gaps in our skimpy, newly-constructed personnel records, I could tell that he was genuinely interested in each of us. He concluded my interview by saying, "One day you'll be an officer. Climb as high as you can, as fast as you can, for as long as you can."

Then he added, "Oh, by the way, you're the only colored recruit who came in today."

Abruptly, he stepped to the door and motioned in a private first class, who had been waiting just outside. The private was white, a small soldier with a twinkle in his eyes and a cocky spring to his step. The creases in his starched, wet-pressed fatigue trousers were razor sharp.

"Yes, sergeant," he barked in that clipped military affectation I was now getting used to hearing.

"At ease, soldier," the sergeant replied. The private relaxed—barely. That is, his hands no longer pressed hard against his sides, but were now clasped behind his back.

"This is Private Curry. Arrived this morning. You know the routine?"

The private nodded, "Colored 'cruits don't process with white 'cruits. White 'cruits go through in a group, filling out papers, giving blood, and drawing clothing and equipment. Colored 'cruits process separately."

"That's right. Now take charge of Private Curry here and get him processed. He's assigned to Baker Company, 765th tank battalion." This was three years after Truman signed an order integrating the Army, but the news apparently had not yet reached Fort Knox.

Somehow, I felt like a VIP rather than someone who was being discriminated against. The white soldiers were herded from place to place in large bunches and continuously harassed. On the other hand, I had a private aide who escorted me smoothly from processing station to processing station. In addition, he cut in and put me at the head of each line because he didn't feel like waiting.

Not bad, I thought. *It's about time there was some benefit to this racial segregation stuff.* But within a few days the processing was over, the VIP treatment concluded, and I was lumped in with all the white guys. Seems there was a down side to racial integration after all.

I don't remember much of the training, except frigid late winter weather that refused to turn into spring. Sleeping on the frozen ground, wrapped only in a woolen Army blanket, I caught pneumonia and almost didn't recover in time to graduate with my class.

As countless others before and after me discovered, life in the military doesn't make a man or woman "bad" or "good." The pressures and tensions associated with military life simply act as a catalyst. They speed up the normal maturation process. Essentially, one quickly becomes the kind of person he or she already is.

I learned many lessons at Fort Knox. One of the most amusing centered on my years of singing classical music under the tutelage of Trudy Johnson.

Shuffling out of the communal shower in my rubber flip-flops one day, I was stopped by a tall, raw-boned recruit who spoke such an odd strain of Carolina Waxhaw Mountain English that I scarcely understood him.

He had a square-cut face with dark straw-yellow hair and cool blue eyes, "That you singing in the shower just now?" he inquired.

"Uh-huh," I said.

"You want to sing with our band?" he asked.

"Not particularly, but thanks anyway," I said, brushing him off.

Not easily discouraged, he followed me down the hall. "You got somethin' against Hank Williams?"

"Hank who?"

"Williams, Hank Williams. You haven't heard of Hank Williams?" he asked, agitated.

"No, and I don't care to," I said, tossing my toilet kit onto the bunk bed.

He scratched the back of his neck with a big knuckled hand, "How 'bout comin' down to the Service Club tonight around seven?" His voice rose on the last syllable.

"We're rehearsin'. Our lead singer got hisself transferred. Now I'm countin' on you, ya hear?"

He ambled off, switched hands, and continued to scratch his neck.

At first, I ignored the invitation. But as the afternoon moved toward evening, my curiosity overrode my reservations. Besides, it isn't every day that an operatic baritone is invited to sing with a "country" band.

It was quite an evening. I don't think Hank Williams felt that his career was threatened. In fact, most of the soldiers at the club seemed to think there wasn't much hope for me. But from then until I graduated, each Wednesday night I sang with the band. By the time basic training was completed and I was transferred, I'd learned to swallow word endings and sing with a bit of a nasal twang, though not very impressively. But more importantly, I developed a liking for country music, which has stayed with me.

After graduating, the Army didn't ship me off to fight in the Korean War, for which I had volunteered. Instead, my entire basic training class was sent to WWII occupation duty in West Germany.

It seems too many experienced soldiers had been transferred from Europe directly to Korea as replacements for losses in combat units. So in order to refill the vacuum created in Europe, one entire basic training class was diverted to West Germany.

Crossing the stormy North Atlantic in the World War II "Liberty Ship" S.S. *Simon B. Buckner* was awful. Most of the four or five thousand soldiers on board were seasick. Even worse, I was billeted on "F" Deck, in the belly of the ship, and given a hammock that abutted the throbbing engine-room bulkhead. Because of the pounding engine noise, the seasick groans and the sour smelling air, I tried to spend as much time as possible topside. But during the stormiest days, topside was closed to all but the crew. We soldiers were confined below decks.

Eleven days later we docked at Southampton, England. A few soldiers disembarked; most stayed aboard. Next morning, the ship sailed on to Bremerhaven, Germany.

Crossing the Atlantic, all soldiers, colored and white, shared the same troop compartments. But as soon as we touched German soil, we were again separated according to race.

White soldiers boarded troop trains going to white processing camps. Colored soldiers were put on trains going to colored processing centers. Ours went to Sonthofen in the Austrian Alps, previously a Hitler Youth training camp.

I was amazed at America's schizophrenic preoccupation with race: first came the integrated train ride from Pittsburgh, then came the segregated processing at Fort Knox followed by integrated basic training, this was followed by a racially integrated ocean crossing, then a segregated personnel processing in Germany, followed by an assignment to an all Negro unit. If it hadn't been so humiliating, vile and confusing, it might have been humorous.

6

The End of the "Colored" Army

During processing, we were told that colored soldiers were not well educated. All new colored soldiers were given academic aptitude tests. Those scoring above a specified level were trained to be school teachers. We were not allowed to ask questions; we were told.

I was assigned to the 7744 Educational Training Unit headquartered in Munich. In those days, Germany was still struggling out from under the rubble of World War II. Large areas of the city, still covered with debris from World War II bombing, were placed off limits to us.

In Munich, I was trained as a grammar and high school teacher, and then assigned to the all Negro 373rd Armored Infantry Battalion. The battalion was a cavalry unit stationed in remote Wildflecken, West Germany. The word *Wildflecken* means "wild spot," and it was indeed a wild spot. Our mission was to screen, patrol, and secure the East German border.

The name of the place seemed to describe my situation. I had enlisted in the U.S. Army to fight in the Korean War. The Army had sent me to Germany. I wanted to be a combat soldier; the Army had trained me to be a school teacher. *It was wild!* Being assigned to a place named Wildflecken seemed to fit perfectly.

Monday through Friday, I taught English and U.S. History to selected soldiers in my battalion at the Army Education Center. In my off time, and on weekends, I traveled around Germany, once venturing as far as the opera in Munich.

The constabulary uniforms that we wore were gorgeous: olive drab wool trousers with "Ike" jackets cut off at the waist and cinched tight by yellow pistol belts. Combat boots were polished until they gleamed. Our glossy olive drab helmet liners had a big yellow "C" centered on the front. A lightning bolt pierced the "C." On special occasions, we wore yellow ascots. Even as a teenager I'd been partial to ascots. Soldiers of other units called us the Circle "C" Cowboys.

I behaved myself, worked hard and got promoted from Private to Private First Class to Corporal, and I had my sights on making Sergeant.

Senior educational training sergeants regularly evaluated the academic proficiency of the soldiers we taught by administering and grading exams. One day as they were passing back an English exam on the "parts of speech," a soldier asked, "Sergeant, Corporal Curry taught us that a noun is the name of a person, place or thing. Is that right?"

"Certainly it's right," he replied, looking at the soldier much as a robin regards an earthworm.

"Well, Sergeant, you marked one of my answers wrong. You wrote that the word "yellow" is a noun, but it doesn't fit the definition. So what makes this word a noun?"

The sergeant replied, "Young man, it's a noun because I said it's a noun." The U.S. Army even had the power to change English grammar.

One day as I walked past the old German Army building that served as battalion headquarters, a first lieutenant yelled out of a window, "Corporal, come in here at once!" My short experience in the Army had taught me that when an officer yelled at you for any reason, something bad was about to happen. So, expecting the worst, I reported as directed.

"Corporal," the ramrod-stiff lieutenant said, peering out from under thick, bushy eyebrows, "Have you ever considered applying for Officer Candidate School?" He was tall, beige-skinned, with a thick, black mustache and few illusions.

Being young and still very much a country boy, I asked, "Sir, is being an officer better than being promoted to sergeant?"

He laughed, "Corporal, we have an old saying in the Army, go as high as you can, as quick as you can, for as long as you can. Yes, being an officer is better than being a sergeant." He patted me on the shoulder and motioned me to a chair beside his desk.

For the better part of half an hour, he explained the advantages of going to Officer's Candidate School, or OCS as they called it, and becoming an officer. What he didn't say was that the 373rd had never had an enlisted man accepted into OCS, and the battalion commander was determined to change that. He also didn't mention that so many second lieutenants had been killed in the first year of the Korean War that the Army was desperate for replacements. *Second Balloons* they were called, but we enlisted men called them "cannon fodder."

Before the interview was over, the lieutenant had convinced me that OCS was my racial and national duty. I agreed to apply without delay. A few months later, I had assembled the necessary documents, taken a physical exam, and sent in the application.

That winter, 1951–1952, while I was waiting to hear from OCS, the Army ended *de facto* racial segregation in Europe, three years after Truman signed an order integrating our nation's military forces.

One day, we were directed to form up by companies in the German cobblestone streets in front of our billets. The battalion sergeant major, a tall, stocky mean man with fat cheeks and a thick, wrinkly neck, then read a startling message over the public address system:

"Listen up, troops. The chief of staff of the United States Army has directed that all Army units in Europe be racially integrated not later than one month from now. That includes the 373rd." His big head swiveled around slowly on his massive, immobile shoulders, and his eyes seemed to individually connect with the eyes of all six hundred of us.

"That means that a month from now, there won't be any colored units in Germany. Do you understand me?"

"Yes, Sergeant Major," we shouted back.

"Good. Now, First Sergeants have your companies count off by fours," he directed.

"One," the first soldier in each rank screamed.

Next to him another soldier counted, "Two."

"Three."

"Four."

Then the next soldier counted, again starting at the number "One." So it went until every soldier standing in ranks was designated by a number from one through four.

When the battalion finished counting off, the sergeant major commanded, "All soldiers numbered four take one step forward." Simultaneously, 150 men stepped forward.

"All right, you who stepped forward will remain in this unit. Numbers one through three will be transferred to white units and be replaced by white soldiers. There are no questions! First Sergeants, take charge of your companies and record the names of those staying and those leaving!"

A few weeks later, racial integration of the United States Army Europe began. Being a number four, I stayed put. The change went smoothly. Soldiers changed, sergeants changed, officers changed. The 373rd did not change.

In May, 1952, I said goodbye to Germany, and crossed back over the Atlantic on another crowded troopship. At Fort Benning, Georgia, I reported to Infantry Officer Candidate School.

Once again America's schizophrenic preoccupation with race rose like a Phoenix. I thought I had left it behind in Germany, but I was wrong. On arrival at OCS, one of the first orders of business was a haircut. In Wildflecken, all soldiers and officers went to the same barbershops.

Not so at Fort Benning; the Army's Post Exchange System ran the barbershops. They had one barbershop for white soldiers and another for colored. At the main post bus station, there were "colored" and "white" waiting rooms, restrooms, and water fountains, each with its own neatly printed sign.

But racial discrimination and hatred was not limited to signs. There were so few of us that all the colored officer candidates in the class could have fit into one taxi. One day a white classmate from Tennessee said to me, "Segregation of the races is here to stay. That's the way it is and always will be. Face it. You Negroes are inferior to white people. My pappy taught me that and I intend to teach it to my children. People like you are always going to ride in the back of busses, because that's where you belong."

I nearly decked him, but fortunately concluded that he was just another ignorant, poor white who couldn't hope to compete with candidates like me on his best day. His opinions weren't worth spit. I unclenched my fists, spun on my heel, and walked away. A month later, he washed out of OCS due to academic deficiencies.

Harassing minorities was a favorite sport of some of the white instructors. They made life quite difficult hoping that minorities would become discouraged and drop out. Some did.

For me there was little chance of that. I knew from experience that I could outperform just about anyone in the class. It was possible for an instructor to shave points off my exams or to downgrade me in personal evaluations, but not enough to cause me to fail outright. Though the Army system was biased against minorities, it was not grossly corrupt. It was struggling to decide how much integration was enough. For the most part, I coped with what was being dished out at OCS without losing my temper.

One day we candidates watched a "made in Hollywood" movie entitled *Rugged Rangers*. After the film, a barrel-chested major named "Bull" Simons paced back and forth across the stage like a caged Bengal tiger. He told us of the challenges and benefits of being a Ranger, the American equivalent of a British Commando. As soon as I heard about the Rangers, I wanted to be one just as I had wanted to be an Eagle Scout when I was a boy.

Then Simons suggested that if any of us were interested in finding out more about the program after we graduated, we should sign the paper at the rear of the room. I signed along with a dozen other candidates.

A few weeks later, another officer swaggered about the same stage telling our class how wonderful it was to be airborne qualified and to wear paratrooper wings on our uniforms. There was also "jump pay" to look forward to because an airborne assignment was considered hazardous duty, so extra money was included. He too suggested that those of us wanting to find out more about jump school sign the paper at the rear of the room. I signed.

Still later, there was a presentation about the joys of being an Army Aviator—flying airplanes and helicopters. Again all we had to do was sign the ever present paper at the rear of the room. Since I was on a roll, I signed that one, too.

In September, I celebrated my twentieth birthday. Three months later, on December 19, 1952, I pinned on the gold bars of a second lieutenant of Infantry. Of the 237 soldiers who had started OCS, 88 of us graduated, including some who "washed" back to our class from other classes.

After graduation, I learned that my cavalier signing of all those sheets of paper at the back of the room had a payoff. Over the next two years, I attended all three schools: Ranger, Airborne, and Army Aviation.

7

Jerry Loves Charlene

The U.S. Army Ranger School was structured to push the minds and bodies of its student victims far beyond the normal limits of mental and physical stress and endurance. It succeeded. At the same time, I was slowly growing accustomed to being the only, or one of the few, colored students in each military class.

In mid-January, toward the end of the first week of training, all of the Ranger students were huddled close together for warmth in an open bleacher on the banks of the Chattahoochee River. A crust of snow and ice covered the frozen ground, while a bitter cold wind whipped our faces.

Hard along both banks, dirty gray ice reached out into the water for about a meter and a half. Farther out, thin, windowpane sized sheets of ice floated down the river.

We were taking a course entitled, "Field Expedient River Crossing Techniques." Two assistant instructors stripped down to their underwear, crossed two M-1 rifles to form an X on a rubberized poncho, rolled up the sides of the poncho to form a small square shaped raft, threw their clothes and boots into it, and launched the raft out into the river. Then they jumped into the freezing water and using their webbed Army belts as a tow rope, swam the makeshift raft across the river.

"Now," said the captain, "all students pair into groups of two, disrobe, construct poncho rafts as you've seen demonstrated, and swim them across the river!"

Ranger School, I decided, was not going to be much fun. Hank Small, an OCS classmate of mine who later became a general, agreed with my assessment. Quickly, he and I built a poncho raft, jumped into the freezing water and towed it across the Chattahoochee.

The Jungle Training phase of Ranger instruction was run by Bull Simons, a man whose exploits in later years included the Son Tay raid into North Vietnam to rescue imprisoned U.S. flyers. From a military point of view, the raid was a success, but it failed because when Simons got there, the American pilots had been moved to another prison. After retiring from the Army, Simons planned and led the successful rescue of H. Ross Perot's men from an Iranian prison. The men had been captured by dissidents who assaulted the American Embassy in Tehran during the latter part of President Carter's administration.

"Anyone can kill an enemy soldier with a rifle at a hundred meters," Simons groused during our training. "But it takes a real man to throw down his weapon, draw a knife, and go out there and gut the enemy face to face."

A few weeks later, near Dahlonega in the North Georgia mountains, one of the students fell off a slick, muddy rope while trying to rappel down a rain-soaked cliff. His limp body lay where it had fallen; face down on some rocks at the base of the cliff.

The short, compact colonel commanding the Ranger School had motored up from Fort Benning to witness the mountain climbing phase of instruction. He seemed indifferent to everybody and everything except training, about which he was a fanatic.

His World War II combat experiences had taught him how extreme were the demands placed on those who daily have to fight fear, death, and the enemy. In North Africa he had been twice captured by Rommel's forces, but had escaped each time.

He sauntered across the slippery, jagged rocks to where the fallen officer lay. With the toe of a booted foot, he partially rolled him over to get a look at his face. Then turning to one of the instructors, he asked, "Isn't this the same officer who fell off the rope bridge crossing the river?"

"Yes, Sir," the captain replied.

"Drop him out of the course." He paused, and then almost as an afterthought, quietly called, "Medic."

There was little color in the gray sky. A sickly paleness indicated the general location of the sun and the rain slanted down diagonally. The colonel picked his way back across the slick rocks to the waiting Jeep; he slung himself onto the wet canvas passenger's seat and motioned to the driver. The Jeep lurched elliptically back toward the muddy road.

After completing training and graduating, I was assigned to the 7th Armored Division at Camp Roberts, California. But first, I had an appointment to keep back in McKeesport.

It was spring of 1953 and Charlene Curry would soon graduate from high school. Now she was sitting beside me on the lipstick-red couch in her parents' living room. A coal fire glowed in the small fireplace. I slipped to one knee in front of her and asked, "Will you marry me?"

Without hesitation, she said, "Yes."

Next, I asked Charlene's father for permission to marry her. He also said "yes." Mission accomplished, I tossed my belongings back into my gray 1950 Chevy, picked up Route 66 and headed west.

During the drive, I often thought of how few Americans realized what a giant, magnificent country we live in. For example, in Europe the driving distance from London to Moscow is about the same as driving from Boston to Kansas City. And best of all, in the United States you don't have to change currencies and languages and go through customs five times.

At Camp Roberts, I was assigned to a leadership school teaching the commando skills I had mastered at Ranger School. Since

Ranger School had just been restarted after its deactivation at the end of WWII; there weren't many graduates.

In fact, I was the only Ranger-qualified officer at Camp Roberts. Also, I was the only minority officer assigned to the leadership school. In many subtle but unmistakable ways, the white officers didn't let me forget it.

Duty with the 7th Armored Division didn't last long. Three months later I was ordered to return to Fort Benning to attend Airborne School. Again, I detoured through McKeesport.

Charlene graduated from high school on June 2, 1953, and four days later she floated down the carpeted stairs at the parsonage of the Bethlehem Baptist Church. She was wearing a mid-calf, lacy white wedding dress and veil, carrying a small bouquet of yellow roses with fragile baby's breath on top of a white Bible. Standing at the foot of the stairs to receive her, I caught my breath. I hadn't expected her to be so dressed up for our little family-only ceremony. Lieutenant and Mrs. Jerry Ralph Curry sounded exactly right.

For the adventurous Charlene, growing up in McKeesport had been stifling. She longed for new places, new things to do, and new worlds to conquer. Fortunately for us both, being an Army officer's wife would more than meet her longing for adventure.

A week after the wedding, we packed our luggage in my Chevy and started south toward Fort Benning, Georgia. Charlene had never been south of Pennsylvania, and was not prepared for the culture shock.

America's wonderful interstate highway system hadn't yet been built and as we motored along two lane roads through rural Virginia, North and South Carolina and then Georgia, she was appalled by the unpainted, weather ravaged sharecropper shacks with the ever present rusted farm machines and wrecked or derelict autos abandoned in their yards.

"Jerry, surely this isn't how you expect me to live?"

"No, dear," I said, laughing, "we won't be living like this."

In central Virginia, we stopped for gas. A sunken-jawed, vacant-eyed attendant about 30 years old, wandered out of the shack that passed for a gas station.

"Fill her up?" he asked, his face registering poverty of mind and spirit.

"Yes, and where's your bathroom?"

He looked from me to Charlene several times, and then gestured, "Around the side."

Quickly Charlene came back. "It's locked," she said.

I told the attendant, "We need the key."

He snickered, "It's locked to keep your kind from using it. We don't have no colored toilet."

His snicker twisted into a silly grin, "She'll have to go in the woods." He was really enjoying himself.

Topping up the tank, he held out his hand for payment.

"Let me see if I've got this right," I said. "My money's good enough for you to take, but we can't use the restroom?"

"About the size of it," he concluded, fishing in his pocket to make change.

My new bride, Charlene, had grown up in a multi-racial, multi-ethnic neighborhood and had experienced little racial discrimination. This experience was like being wakened out of a sound sleep by having a bucket of ice-cold water dowsed on her.

"What's wrong with these people?" she asked. "Don't they have any sense of decency?"

"Welcome to the South," I said.

From then on, when we pulled into a gas station, the first thing I asked for were the keys to the toilet. If they refused, we didn't buy gas there but drove on to the next station.

About one out of every four stations was more eager for money than advancing the cause of white supremacy. They reluctantly surrendered their keys as part of the barter. Occasionally though, we hit a string of clunkers and then we were forced to stop alongside the road and take a trip to the woods.

Eating was a problem we decided not to experience. We just didn't have the time or inclination to drive around trying to find a colored section of some impoverished southern town where we could sit down to a meal. Instead, we hit the local grocery store and ate in the car or at a roadside table. The critters didn't seem to object to our company.

Finding a place to sleep was out of the question, so we slept in the car. By the time we arrived in Columbus, Georgia, we'd decided on a strategy. We asked directions to the colored section of town. There we selected the largest church and asked for the Pastor.

"My wife and I need to rent an apartment for about a month while I'm attending Airborne School at Fort Benning. Can you help us find a place?" I asked. He and his secretary were pleasant, friendly, and helpful. Within an hour, they had located a place for us that was clean, comfortable, and furnished.

In Columbus, as in other southern towns, there were "colored" and "white" signs ad nauseam, "colored" and "white" water fountains, bathrooms, dining rooms, public building entrances, and bus stations, to name a few.

Neither of us was reared or prepared to docilely accept being so humiliated and demeaned. Obviously, we needed to stay out of the South before we both ended up in serious trouble.

From that moment on, avoiding racist practices and confrontations became a major driving force in my military career. From then on we tried to only get assignments in the North, unless it was possible for us to live on a military installation.

The decision was somewhat career limiting since the best jobs for infantrymen like me were in the south at places like Benning, Fort Bragg, North Carolina, or Fort Hood, Texas. But to us, the benefits were not worth the price.

Each day, I departed for Jump School early in the morning and arrived home to Charlene well into the evening. It was physically exhausting running through the Georgia sand all day, taking calisthenics, and learning how to jump out of airplanes while wearing steel helmets and carrying rifles, packs, and other heavy, cumbersome combat equipment. It wasn't much of a honeymoon.

There is an old joke told by instructors at the Airborne School at Fort Benning. It says that the first week of school you separate the men from the boys. The second week you separate the men from the idiots. The third week the idiots jump.

One mid-July day in 1953, the brass sun stepped over the eastern Georgia horizon and marched toward its zenith high overhead as the temperature shot up from warm to hot. We "idiots," who had successfully jumped, graduated.

It was an awesome, inspiring sight to see the soldiers and officers parade past the reviewing stand in their stiffly starched khaki uniforms. Newly sewn on our caps were distinctive Airborne unit identification patches. Proudly affixed to our breasts were silver Paratrooper Wings.

Next, Charlene and I were assigned to the First Battalion of the 503rd Airborne Infantry Regiment stationed at Fort Campbell, Kentucky. The Regiment, part of the 11th Airborne Division, was called "The Rock" because toward the end of WWII, when U.S. Forces liberated the Philippines, it had made an extremely dangerous but successful airborne combat assault on the rocky island of Corregidor in Manila Bay.

Like many newlyweds living on base at Fort Campbell, Charlene and I couldn't afford much. Rooms devoid of furniture were the norm. Fortunately, the government partially furnished the apartments with some basic items, a few overstuffed chairs, lamps, stoves, and refrigerators—but not washers and dryers. As you would expect, our first purchase was a bed.

We were assigned to an old, wooden World War II Army barracks which had been converted into family quarters. Eight families shared the building. Four families were clustered around each of the two stairwells. The four households in our stairwell were like one big family. We didn't swap husbands and wives, but swapped practically everything else, including children.

Once a month, we had what we called a "G.I. party." In a group, husbands and wives scrubbed and cleaned from one apartment to another, until every room in the stairwell was spotless. There were no on-base Laundromats in those days, so by hand, khakis and fatigues were scrubbed on wash boards, starched in bath tubs, and then ironed damp so that the board-stiff trousers, with their razor-sharp creases, could almost stand up on the floor by themselves.

Washing clothes by hand in metal tubs was hard work. And Charlene soon tired of the drudgery, as well she should have. One morning as I left for work, she insisted that we buy a washing machine. Being in a hurry and also in a bit of a playful mood, I jokingly handed her a 10 dollar bill and suggested that she get one.

That evening, when I returned home from work, a Sears' delivery truck was parked in the street outside our quarters. Inside, an overall-clad serviceman had just finished installing a new Kenmore washing machine. Charlene had discovered that Sears was having a washing machine sale that day. The terms were five dollars down and so much a month from then on—probably for life.

Quickly, my new bride had signed the contract. When she saw me that afternoon, with a great deal of satisfaction she handed me a five-dollar bill and said, "Here, darling, is your change." Never again did I underestimate her resourcefulness, nor Sears' for that matter.

Social life at Fort Campbell was fun, and Charlene took to it naturally. There were books for her to read on etiquette and classes to attend on entertaining. The Officers' wives had numerous coffees and teas, with bridge clubs and cocktail parties thrown in for good measure.

Late in my military career, Charlene would tire of these diversions. But for a teenage wife newly escaped from McKeesport, her role as an officer's wife was joyous, exciting, and adventurous.

In Clarksville, Tennessee, just across the Kentucky state line, Charlene got her driver's license. Clarksville was closer to Fort Campbell than Hopkinsville, the nearest Kentucky town. It was named after General George Rogers Clark and was known for its dark-fired tobacco market.

Ever since then, Charlene has had a romance with cars and driving. Unfortunately, living most of her young adult life in Europe taught her to scoot down the highway rather rapidly. I remember one day in 1976 when a Mercedes salesman took her on a demonstration ride in a 450 SLC, a car she later purchased. At 75 miles an hour they motored along the Frankfurt-Stuttgart Autobahn driving in the right lane, with normal German traffic whizzing past them on the left.

The salesman drummed his fingertips on top of the dashboard as though trying to break through to the glove compartment. Finally, he could stand it no longer. "Frau Curry," he snapped irritably, "This is a Mercedes you are driving, not a Fiat.

"When you drive a Mercedes you get into the left lane, you turn on your lights, and you go-go-go-go! You do not let inferior cars pass you!"

Even today when driving in the United States, there are times when Frau Curry gets that *ubermensch* gleam in her eyes, swings her Mercedes into the left lane, turns on the head lamps, and floors the gas pedal. When the urge passes, she retreats back down to the posted speed limit, hopefully without the aid of a state highway patrolman.

We had been at Fort Campbell for nearly a year when a letter arrived in the mail ordering me to primary flight school. I would be taught to fly airplanes at Gary Air Force Base near San Marcos, Texas.

We said goodbye to our many friends and the excitement that belonging to an elite military unit brings. We piled what we could into the Chevy and shipped the rest of our household goods by freight motor carrier, at Army expense.

It was a joyous departure, because we had an extra passenger. Charlene was expecting our first child.

8

Flying

We left just after sunrise driving southwest. The land lay black and indefinable before us. From the east a pale, almost spiritual hint of dawn crept over the earth, dragging along behind it an unbalanced gray sky.

Soon we crossed into Tennessee, and then Arkansas and Texarkana. A day later we skirted Dallas, and halfway between Austin and San Antonio we drove into San Marcos, Texas. It was a small, rural, hot, dusty, sleepy, Mexican American town with a few paved streets and a state teachers' college.

Gary Air Force Base, where I would undergo U.S. Air Force primary flight training, was located a few miles outside of San Marcos. It had no military housing for students. Either we located a decent place to live off base, or Charlene would have to return to McKeesport.

Slowly, we drove around checking out the town, such as it was. There were quite a few "for rent" signs posted. Evidently, the local landlords were anticipating the arrival of new military students.

In the middle of one of the best sections was a large house that had been separated into three apartments. A phone call to the number on the sign and a short drive brought us to the owners' house, two elderly, gray haired, spinster sisters.

"Yes, young man," one of them began clearing her throat and smoothing the front of her dress with a hand, "what can I do for you?"

"We're looking for a place to rent while I'm going to flight school at Gary Air Force Base," I explained, motioning toward Charlene who had stayed outside in the car.

"Is it the large wooden house with gigantic trees all around?" the other sister clarified.

"That's the one . . . but I don't want there to be any misunderstanding. My wife and I are colored." Because both of us were light skinned, we were often mistaken for white.

Charlene and I found the necessity of engaging in such conversations demeaning. But experience had taught us that in the end it saved a lot of hurt, humiliation, and confusion.

"We only rent that house to military," the first sister agreed. "Military don't mind livin' next to colored. Apartment's yours, provided you got the money."

Her sister nodded, "Sure is . . . besides, it was beginnin' to look like those apartments weren't goin' to get no renters this time around."

I paid in cash, took the keys and immediate possession. "Well, well," I said to myself, "once again money wins out." But deep inside I knew it was an answer to much prayer. What I didn't know was that the two sisters who were willing to take us as tenants would become busy trying to persuade their other tenants, my fellow classmates, to avoid socializing with us "negras."

Gary Air Force Base was as unimposing as the town. However, unlike the town it was neat, clean, water-sprinkler-green, and well run. Most officers and their wives, including Charlene and me, spent their leisure time at the base.

At the student orientation, the colonel in charge of Gary Air Force Base welcomed us students warmly. He was a confident man, who moved easily and seemed well satisfied with life.

"Turn your head and look at the person on your right," he said, making a prescient observation. "Now look at the person on your left. When you graduate, those people won't be here."

During training, due to a dramatic shift in wind patterns, I became involved in an airplane crash. Aircraft crashes are often followed by raging fires. So we student pilots were taught to get away from the aircraft as fast as possible. Hanging upside down in the wreckage, I quickly released my shoulder straps and seat belt, just as I had been taught, and fell on my head nearly breaking my neck. The instructors had failed to mention that part.

Toward the end of flight qualification training, a coordination competition was held. The instructors graded each student based on his ability to make power off landings in the single-engine Piper Super Cubs we were flying.

First you fully leaned the mixture, shut off the master switch, and then stopped the prop just short of stalling on downwind. Each student was awarded points based on whether the aircraft's wheels touched the runway short or long of an area marked by colored panels. Points were added for a solid, no-bounce, three point landing on the bull's eye, and deducted according to the distance the aircraft was short or over. If you were going to be too long, you could compensate by putting the aircraft into a sideslip, and if you were short you could stretch your glide by pulling on some flaps and pushing the stick forward. I received the highest number of points and won the competition. It was no big deal, only a game. I didn't suspect that later it would save my flying career.

After successfully completing Air Force primary training, Army pilots were posted to Fort Sill near Lawton, Oklahoma for Advanced Flight Training. Fort Sill was also the home of the U.S. Army's Artillery School and where the Army conducted all helicopter training. After successfully completing the "Sill" phase of training, we officers would be awarded silver Army Aviator Wings.

So after graduating from Gary, Charlene and I shipped our household goods, loaded up the car, and headed north to Fort Sill.

We student pilots completed advanced training in Cessna L-19s, single engine planes slightly larger than the Supercubs I had learned on. Then we moved on to instrument training, the final phase of instruction. My instrument instructor was a fat, slovenly character from Corpus Christi, Texas.

"Lieutenant," he sneered after our first flight together, "you are rougher on the controls than any student I've ever instructed. I'm surprised they let you slide through advanced training."

I said nothing. After each flight he made a similar comment and marked on my records, "This student lacks good coordination!"

One day the Senior Flight Instructor took me aside and said, "Jerry, I'm sorry, but you seem to lack good coordination and as much as I'd like to see you graduate, I can't let them pin silver wings on an officer who just can't cut the mustard. Too bad we didn't pick this up in your earlier training."

"May I make a suggestion?" I asked.

"Certainly," he replied.

"Phone Gary Air Force Base and ask them about my coordination. If they agree that my flying in Primary was rough and uncoordinated, I'll resign. You won't have to wash me out!"

He nodded.

I put away my flying gear and left for the duplex Charlene and I occupied at Fort Sill on Snow Road in Artillery Village. "Well, Char," I said, "it looks like the bad side of white America has struck again, but I've appealed to the good side. Let's pray that the good side wins." We did.

Next morning when I reported to the flight line, there was a notice tacked on the bulletin board directing a change of instructors for several students. My name was among them.

"Need I say more?" the Senior Flight Instructor asked while walking me to the flight line.

"No, Sir," I said, "and thank you."

"Good luck," he called over his shoulder as he strode toward a cluster of waiting students.

Soon October came, and with it, graduation. Above the parachute wings on my left chest pocket were now pinned the silver wings of an Army Aviator. I would wear them for the next 30 years and would still be a fully flight qualified Master Army Aviator on the day of my retirement from the Army.

Charlene had an accomplishment of her own to celebrate a few weeks earlier, when she gave birth to our first child, daughter Charlein Dyanne, in the military hospital at Fort Sill on October 2, 1954. Charlene's mother flew down a week before the birth to help us out. Both mother and daughter came through in fine shape. Come to think of it, Grandmother and I didn't do too badly either.

Upon graduation, I was directed to report to the 10th Infantry Division at Fort Riley, Kansas. The division had helped push the German Army out of Italy during WWII. While we were en route, the Division was selected by the Army to participate in a new overseas rotation program code named "Operation Gyroscope."

In the summer of 1955, the 10th Division was ordered to depart Fort Riley for multiple locations in West Germany. There it was to replace the "Big Red One," officially known as the First Infantry Division. The Big Red One would rotate back to the United States.

Upon arrival at Fort Riley, we learned that I had been further assigned to the 86th Infantry Regiment. The officers and wives of the regiment opened their arms, hearts, and homes to us. We became part of a warm, friendly, extended Army family.

Kansas was unusually frigid and bleak that winter of 1954–1955. Several times storms raged across the western plains, blowing snow before them and causing the temperatures to plummet. I was thankful that I had traded my parachute for an airplane with a warm heater.

The division operations officer who scheduled me to fly my first operational mission, "Pappy" Wagers, was an old World War II Army Air Corps pilot who had flown C-46 cargo over the "hump"—the Himalayas—to resupply engineers building the Burma Road. Pappy was a slender, decent, careful man who looked and talked like the small southern farmer that he was. Solid, stable, and slow talking, he always called things as he saw them.

He leaned his left elbow on top of a dented, paint scarred, olive-drab steel filing cabinet that was left over from WWII, and he watched me assiduously. After I finished the elaborate flight planning procedure I had learned from my Air Force instructors, he grinned at me and asked, "That what they teach you fellows in flight school these days?"

I nodded.

"All that navigation stuff can wear a man out," he said casually. "If I was you, I'd take off to the west, turn south and pick up route 40. Then go east through Topeka and Lawrence. Just before you get to Kansas City you turn left on State Route 7. If you aren't sure of the turn, fly down low and read the route sign. The road'll take you directly north to Fort Leavenworth." Then he added almost absently, "The air field's on the right. You'll spot it down by the Missouri River."

Putting away my navigational chart, plotter, and E6-B computer, I took the Texaco road map he offered, picked up a parachute, fired up the engine, and headed east. Pappy was right, Route 7 ran directly through Leavenworth, and I found it without having to drop down and read the road sign.

Two years later near Wuerzburg, Germany, a single-engine Cessna L-19 that Pappy was flying crashed and burned. There were no survivors. The entire division mourned his loss.

At Riley, Charlene began her first serious house decorating and social entertaining. While growing up, she had seldom ventured far from the town of McKeesport. Socializing, except at church and county fairs, was never high on her parents' agenda.

Within two years of marriage, she would be living in a foreign country, ordering a household and supervising servants. She took to it naturally.

The Korean War had recently ended and the armed forces were directed to significantly reduce the size of the officer corps. In most cases, regular army officers were retained and reserve officers were forced out of the Army or into the enlisted ranks.

Young reserve officers like me were told to go to night school and earn a college degree or to get out of the Army. After much discussion and prayer with Charlene, I opted for night school. Because Kansas State University maintained a branch campus on base, it was easy to enroll and attend classes at Fort Riley.

A year later, our entire division was ordered to Germany. Summer came quickly and with it my little family and I left Riley and motored to New Jersey by way of McKeesport. At Bayonne, New Jersey, we turned in our new Chevy for ocean shipment, and then flew to Europe in a triple-tailed Super "G" Lockheed *Constellation*. The "Connie," as it was called, was sleek and smooth, with two prop engines on each wing.

The trip was not short. We refueled in Iceland and then again at Shannon, Ireland. It was close to midnight when we arrived at Rhein Main Air Base in Frankfurt, West Germany. We finally arrived in Schweinfurt close to 3:00 in the morning, exhausted and irritable after a harrowing, foggy, late-night bus ride by way of Aschaffenburg and Wuerzburg to drop off other military families. Schweinfurt was the new home of the 86th Infantry Regiment. Our infant daughter, Charlein, didn't share our aggravation. She blissfully slept through the entire ride.

Waiting up for us in Schweinfurt were our designated sponsors, Gail and Moon McKenzie. They greeted us with open arms, a home cooked meal, dishes and glasses on the shelves, food in the cupboards and fridge, and a turned down bed. No one has ever been more kindly received and graciously treated than we were.

That summer of 1955, West Germany had finally come out from under the rubble of World War II. In the Northern Bavaria area surrounding Schweinfurt, stucco and dark wood-framed houses and chalets were being refurbished and everywhere flowers sprouted from window boxes. Charlene called the chalets "gingerbread" houses. The *Deutsche Volk* were starting to live again.

During our rare vacations, we toured as much of Europe as possible, including delightful trips into Scandinavia, the Low Countries, Austria, Switzerland, and Paris. In those days, prices were set by hard bargaining between buyer and seller and Charlene loved getting out into the German communities with their town squares, marketplaces, and bazaars where she could haggle over prices with the local German merchants and housewives.

The University of Maryland had an extensive overseas campus program, so shortly after our arrival in Schweinfurt, I began attending college classes in the evening. My days were filled with military duties, so Charlene decided to enroll in the university so we could be together at least some of the time. She mostly took German language courses.

We did manage to have some free time together because a year later Charlene informed me that we were going to have another addition to our family. Early one morning, she awakened me and said, "Jerry, I think it's time. The labor pains are strong and regular."

"OK," I said, "I'll let the maid know that we're going to the hospital, and ask her to take care of little Charlein when she wakes up."

Quickly we dressed. I bundled Charlene down to the car and we set out over the narrow, twisting country roads that led from Schweinfurt to the U.S. Army Hospital at Weurzburg. That early in the morning, with little traffic, it was less than a half-hour's drive.

The stars had faded and day was breaking, another sullen German sky of unbroken gray. I longed for a colorful, good old

American sunrise. By the time we arrived at the front gate of the hospital, the birth pains had all but stopped. A nurse helped Charlene slip into a wheelchair, while I completed the omnipresent paperwork.

Judging from previous experience, we expected that the baby would choose to be born sometime within the next 48 hours. Back in those days, fathers were not in the labor rooms with their wives, so I turned Charlene over to the excellent care of the hospital, and calmly drove back to Schweinfurt for what I knew would be another routine day's work.

Just as I unlocked the door of our four-bedroom apartment at 17C Maplestrasse and stepped inside, the phone rang. Congratulations, Lieutenant Curry," the nurse said. "You and Mrs. Curry are the parents of a fine, healthy baby boy!"

After telling our maid, Amy, the good news, I got back in the car and drove to the hospital. Proud Charlene and son, Jerry Charles, were radiant, well—and waiting for me.

The first year of my three years in Schweinfurt was spent flying training and liaison missions over most of West Germany. My commanding officer was Ben Hacket, a first-rate aviator and commander. This was followed by a year split between being the executive officer of Company A and the company commander of Company C, First Battalion, 86th Infantry Regiment. Then it was back to flying for the final year.

Captain Gene Marder, a Korean War veteran and a great American, was Company A commander. He never tired of helping me learn the profession of an infantryman. He and his wife, Margaret, became close friends of ours, a friendship that endured many years. Just a few years ago Gene died of cancer, but we still keep in touch with Margaret.

In the summer of 1958, the four of us boarded another airliner and headed west, back to Fort Benning. Several other officers from the 10th Division accompanied us. We had all been selected to spend a year at Benning attending the Infantry Officers Advanced Course. And yes, we were assigned "on base" housing.

During the three-year tour in Germany, racial prejudice had not come up once as a subject of discussion. As a result, Charlene and I had almost forgotten that some white Americans considered us inferior. Now that we were back in the good old USA, a stark wake-up call greeted us.

My U.S. driver's license had expired, so I drove to the city of Columbus, Georgia, to get it renewed. At the Department of Motor Vehicles were two lines, one for colored applicants and one for white ones. Three feet away, standing in the "white" line was someone with whom I knew I could share my frustration. She was the wife of one of the officers who lived and socialized with us in Germany. Her husband was a fellow classmate of mine.

"What do you think about this mess?" I asked, opening the conversation.

She ignored me, pretending we didn't know each other.

"What's wrong with you?" I asked, confused.

As far as she was concerned, I didn't exist.

Then came understanding . . . and with it, hurt. Evidently, she didn't want any of the white people standing in the line with her to know that she was the close friend of a Negro.

The next day her husband and I sat next to each other at coffee break. I told him what happened. "Do we continue to be friends, or would you and your wife prefer that we not speak?"

His face flushed. He stammered.

The following day he sought me out. "I'm sorry about what happened in town. I've had a long talk with my wife. She'll never act that way towards you and Charlene again." As couples, we continued to treat each other with civility, but the feeling of military comradeship we had previously shared was gone and would never be rekindled.

Fort Benning was followed by a six-week assignment to Camp Wolters, Texas, where the Army taught me to fly helicopters. Again, I was the only minority student.

Afterwards, my request not to be given a southern assignment was honored. We were posted to Fort Devens, Massachusetts.

9

Death in the Night

When I arrived at Fort Devens in the fall of 1959, I was assigned to the Second Infantry Brigade. Since the Brigade was not part of a division, it was reinforced with its own artillery, engineer, and signal units. The commander was a stocky man of medium height, Brigadier General Tom Yancey. Yancey was tough on himself, demanding of others, and thoroughly professional.

The Brigade's S-3 Operations Office was my new home. In any military unit, the S-3 office is in charge of planning, training, operations, and unit evaluation. My duties encompassed tactical training, planning, and military maneuvers. Under the tutelage of more experienced staff officers, I quickly learned how to write an acceptable staff paper and to successfully coordinate with prickly, egocentric commanders and staff officers in the subordinate units.

Often I escorted visitors from corps and army headquarters while they inspected the brigade. I learned to treat them deferentially, to deftly evade giving direct or complete answers to their questions, and to send them on their way with the feeling that all was well in the Second Brigade.

Each winter, the brigade formed a convoy of trucks, Jeeps, and pickups, which we drove to Fort Drum, New York, for cold weather training. Drum is one of the coldest spots on the North American continent. This particular winter, the brigade's training was directed primarily toward squads and platoons. Each squad had 6 to 12 soldiers, while each platoon had 30–40.

One cold, snowy day I escorted a colonel who had flown in from the Pentagon to inspect the brigade's tactical cold weather training. He was tall, lean, about six-three, and hard of stomach and mind. His dark, near-black hair was slicked back and parted on the left side.

He finished his inspection of our tactical training toward the end of the week and I brought him back to his quarters to clean up, pack his bags, and depart for Washington early the next morning. He would probably be writing his evaluation of the brigade's training that evening, so when he invited me to join him for dinner, my boss was pleased. He knew that I would put the proper "spin" on the colonel's visit.

Over dinner, we talked about how overseas duty compares with working and living in the United States. Then the conversation went to child rearing and the strain of moving families from post to post. Finally, as my boss knew he would, the colonel brought the discussion around to his inspection visit.

"This has been some of the best training I've observed since being assigned to the Pentagon," he offered. "You can be sure my trip report will be positive. Now . . . I've spent a lot of time talking to General Yancey about the use and employment of artillery in deep snow and cold weather. I'd be interested in hearing your personal take on the subject."

Smoothly I stayed on message, "Sir, our position is this . . . " Then, I outlined for him detailed considerations and recommendations on the employment of artillery under severe winter conditions. My boss and I had worked out my answers in advance, deciding what I should and should not say.

"Yes, Captain Curry," he parried. "I appreciate the Brigade's official position on the matter, but what does Captain Curry think about it?"

"Well, Sir," I said, "there are various options." I listed each of them and gave him the pros and cons for all.

"Captain," he asked pointedly, "do you or do you not have an opinion of your own?" He was sitting straight up in his chair, palms face down on the white cotton tablecloth. "If you do," he continued, "I'd like to hear it."

The truth was I didn't have an opinion of my own. The subject didn't interest me much and I had given it only cursory consideration. For the past year I had expertly learned how to take papers out of the "in box," figure out what my immediate supervisor or the commanding general wanted me to do with them, do it well, then toss them into the "out box."

Unconsciously, "process" had overtaken "content." As someone once said, process had become the enemy of progress. I had successfully become one of the best "processors" on the Brigade staff, to the delight of my bosses. As successful staff officers do, I had learned to read my superior officers' thoughts, to anticipate most of their questions, to make persuasive arguments, or present counterarguments. I had forgotten the old adage that, "Following the path of least resistance makes for crooked rivers and crooked men."

The visiting colonel stared at me for a long time and then, with a critical edge to his voice, said, "Captain Curry, I'm going to give you some advice. When you handle a staff action, first determine what you personally consider to be right or wrong about it."

"In all bureaucracies whatever you write or say will be filtered through two or three bosses between you and the final decision-maker, just as it should be. That's not bad. It's simply the nature of bureaucracy. It's also the nature of good staff work and a good organization."

I was getting restless, but tried not to show it.

"The filtering process is important, Jerry." For the first time, he called me by my first name. "Often it gets rid of soft or half-baked ideas or recommendations."

I nodded in agreement.

"When the boss turns to you and asks what you think of a particular subject, look him straight in the eye and tell him honestly and directly what you agree with or oppose." Instead of my putting the proper spin on his visit, the colonel was spinning me.

"Only by being honest with yourself, can you maintain balance and integrity. Remember, no one can take your integrity from you. You have to voluntarily surrender it.

"Only when you tell it like it really is can you be helpful to your commander. He doesn't need 'yes men' around him. He needs to be told the truth as you see it, even when your intermediate bosses don't agree with you."

I tried hard not to show how uncomfortable I was becoming, but I think he knew.

"Once General Yancey has made his decision, which may or may not agree with what you recommend, he expects you to carry it out in letter and spirit, even blindly if need be." His body language indicated that both dinner and the conversation were over.

We pushed back our chairs, stood and shook hands. I wished him a safe flight back to Washington. He wished me a successful army career. Because of him and others like him, it would be.

A week later, winter maneuvers at Camp Drum ended and the brigade retraced its way back over the frozen, icy roads to Fort Devens. We arrived without incident and that evening, over a candlelight dinner, I shared my encounter with the colonel with Charlene.

She summarized it this way, "Wrong habits can be changed. Wrong principles and character cannot."

Since then, when asked for an opinion, I've tried to call the shots as honestly as I see them. Sometimes it's ruined friendships. Occasionally, it's gotten me fired.

That winter Charlene was newly pregnant. We took it in stride. After all, we knew what having children was all about, didn't we?

From the east that May morning in 1959, a bleached-out color crept across the sky tentatively defining the horizon. By the time I found my slippers, pulled on a flannel bathrobe, shaved, and wandered into the kitchen to turn on the gas under the kettle, day was breaking over the maple trees in the backyard.

The sky began to take on color and the trees took on form. Individual leaves were not yet distinguishable, but I could make out the gray shape of the nearer fence posts as light reflected off them. I heard, more than saw, the morning birds serenade the neighborhood.

In the master bedroom, Charlene rested quietly and in the next room our two children slept soundly. She had experienced mild labor pains during the night, but seemed to be resting peacefully.

At the office, I was relieved to discover that my duties that day would be routine. I could hang loose, in case Charlene needed me. She did. The trip to the U.S. Army hospital at Shirley, Massachusetts, was speedy and uneventful. Having learned my lesson in Wuerzburg, I stayed close by, making only a quick trip to the town of Ayer to buy Charlene a dozen of her favorite red roses.

At the time, I didn't suspect how comforting they would be. For the most part the birth of children is miraculously routine, but complications can lurk in the dark recesses of the delivery room.

Soon a nurse sought me out and encouraged me to join Charlene in the recovery room. Gregory Jerome had yet to be cleaned up and laid in her arms. Though a bit groggy, Charlene smiled up at me. When I sat down next to her, her face relaxed and I took her cool right hand between two of mine and rubbed it gently.

"I didn't hear my baby cry," were her first words. "I pray everything is all right."

I heard shuffling footsteps behind me and turned to see the doctor enter the room. He was of medium build and height with a smooth, unwrinkled forehead and sallow complexion. *Probably Mediterranean extraction*, I thought.

His eyes met mine. A shadow crossed his face.

Anxiously, Charlene shifted her head toward him. Her eyes widened and she half sat up, "Is something wrong?" she asked.

Cautiously, the doctor answered, "It's my sad duty to inform you both that your son is not well."

I looked at the doctor.

"Medically, it's referred to as spina bifida. Generally speaking, your son's spine is deformed and spinal fluid is seeping through a hole at the bottom of his back." He passed a hairy hand over his forehead smoothing already taut skin.

"Oh, no!" we both cried, gripping each other's hands tightly.

"But it can be fixed, doctor—surgically I mean?" Charlene wanted to know.

"Sometimes it is surgically possibly to repair the problem," he answered guardedly, "but in this case, it might not be advisable."

"Why not?" I asked, looking at Charlene. Tears were streaming down her face and she was biting her lower lip.

Carefully he replied, "Sometimes surgery is partially successful, but in this case it won't be. Even if your son survives the procedure, he will be an invalid and die in childhood."

Abruptly, the doctor rose from the padded gray metal chair he had slumped into, as if trying to physically separate himself from the sentence his words had just pronounced over us.

"It's up to you," he said, pausing. "We'll do whatever you decide, operate or not operate." For a few seconds he watched our agony, then abruptly turned and left.

A few days later, I drove an empty-handed Charlene home from the hospital. Our son, Greg stayed behind. We both had deserts in our hearts. For Charlene, it was much more difficult. I could escape to my work, but with no new baby to nurse and cuddle, she felt barren and unfulfilled. For her the daytime hours spent alone in the house were awful, even with two other children to keep her company.

A week afterward, the hospital phoned to say that Gregory was ready for nursing home placement. Because we elected not to have surgery, they estimated that he would live between a few months and a few years. They counseled us not to bring Greg home to live with us. "It's best not to get too attached," one of the nurses advised.

But Charlene would have none of it. We took Greg home. Gently and tenderly, Charlene tried to nurse him around the clock. Fortunately, our sister-in-law, Olga, the wife of Charlene's brother, George, came to stay with us and help as best she could.

Every 45 minutes or so Greg's bandages had to be changed because of the continuous leakage of spinal fluid and the risk of infection.

Less than a month later, in June, when Greg was so weak that he could barely pull milk through a bottle nipple, we knew that the end was near. His breathing had become shallow and labored; his frail little body was dehydrated.

Sadly, one gray afternoon two weeks after Olga left, we took Greg back to the same hospital where he had been born. In Charlene's eyes, there was a weariness that I had never seen before.

The doctors and nurses were thoughtful, as helpful as anyone could be in such circumstances. They told us there was little hope. They were right.

Gregory Jerome died in the early hours of what to us was a particularly tragic night. And in the days ahead we often cried out of the bitterness of that moment. After a while, Charlene shared with me the aching emptiness of her heart, and how it matched the barrenness of the crib in the nursery, which adjoined our bedroom. It was then that we prayed for another child. Mercifully, God heard our prayer.

A year later, on April 14, 1960, in the same hospital, a perfectly formed little girl was born to Captain and Mrs. Curry. She had large, beautiful brown eyes, curly hair, and a wonderful, sunny disposition. We named her Toni Rene.

10

Korea

I took college classes at night for seven laborious years before I had enough credits to qualify for a bachelor's degree. I had been warned many times that when I applied to a college to be awarded a degree, all my credits earned at different universities around the world would be subjected to a rigorous culling out. So, over the years, I had taken core courses that would be acceptable at most universities. How to bring this smorgasbord of college credits to degree closure was the question.

By this point we were still at Fort Deven in Massachusetts. Fort Deven's Army Education Center counselor, whose name I've unfortunately forgotten, a gently rounded man of medium height with dark brown hair in permanent disarray, gladly offered to help me. His suggestion was that I first visit the local universities sited along the banks of the Charles River in Boston, which I did.

My first stop was Harvard University. As he poured tea from a Rosenthal teapot, the admissions officer summed up my situation this way: "You are a quality applicant and we would very much like to have you study with us. Of course, we do have a certain position to maintain." He smiled, "You do see the problem here, don't you? Our graduates are expected to have the university's 'stamp' on them, as it were. That can't be done in less than three years. You do understand?"

I understood; I even empathized, but that didn't solve my problem. Harvard had a tradition to uphold. I had a degree to complete. Farther down river, Boston University felt that it could place its "stamp" on me in two years. Other universities felt about the same. After years of working for the Army all day and going to school at night, I wasn't about to toss aside two or three years of hard earned credits simply to qualify for the right "stamp."

One day, the indefatigable education counselor phoned. "Jerry, this week I've been on the phone talking to other Army education counselors around the country." He paused, waiting for our thoughts to synchronize.

"Several of them out West recommend that you apply to the University of Nebraska in Omaha."

"Never heard of it," I said.

"Neither have I, but I checked it out. It's a small city university that maintains a good academic standing and is interested in talking to you."

"Way out in Nebraska? That means I'd have to leave a pregnant wife alone with two small children," I protested.

"When you're a hungry squirrel out of acorns, any nut will do. At least phone the admissions officer. I've got his name and number."

Over the phone, the University of Omaha's admissions officer made a strong pitch. That evening at dinner, Charlene and I discussed it. It would not be easy for her. In addition to expecting another child in April, she would once again have to be both father and mother. I would be home for Thanksgiving and the Christmas holidays, but would that be enough? Of course other military families living alongside us in base housing would try to take care of her, but that was not the same as having your own husband and the father of your children present.

With Charlene's blessing, I filled out an application, paid my out-of-state tuition and fees, and was accepted for the fall semester of 1959. The University of Nebraska/Omaha had agreed to waive the one-year residency requirement for a degree.

The Army kept its word and granted me a six-month leave of absence with pay. Charlene did her part and didn't complain even once during that cold New England fall and winter. And the university kept its part of the bargain and provided a high-quality education culminating in my being awarded a bachelor's degree.

This also meant that the military chaplain at the base chapel would have to find a new choir director to replace me. Char and I had sung in chapel choirs for years, but at Fort Devens I had agreed—for the first and only time—to be the choir director.

Directly across the Missouri River from Council Bluffs, Iowa, lies Omaha. Back then it was an overly large, delightful cow town with a huge stockyard at the south end. Dodge Avenue ran from east to west through the center of town. Omaha boasted the Joslyn Art Museum, plus the only symphony in America, the locals bragged, that consistently operated in the black.

Just before dusk, I drove into town. The sun slid down the horizon removing the blood-red reflections from west facing windowpanes. Suddenly, the light grew soft and quiet as it sometimes does just after sunset. A stillness hung in the air—suspended, motionless, and expectant.

This was to be my home for the next half year, and I framed the picture in my mind. Somehow I did not feel like a stranger. By the time I graduated, I had grown to love the city, the state, and its people, as well as the university.

In addition to attending classes, once a week I moonlighted as an announcer at a local radio station, KBON. The sports announcer was also the local jazz buff, who knew many local area musicians. Occasionally after the commercial establishments closed, the sidemen gravitated over to Don's house to jam.

Back then, in Omaha, if you were a jazz aficionado, there weren't a lot of places to hang out. Only one restaurant, *Orlando's*, consistently booked big-name entertainment. This, along with a fine menu, pulled in a good crowd on weekends.

Orlando's had booked the Oscar Peterson Trio for a week. By the weekend, the word was out that after Saturday's gig the Trio would be jamming at Don's. So Saturday evening, Don's place was crowded with local musicians long before Oscar arrived.

Hour after hour Ed Thigpen, the Trio's drummer drove the musicians tirelessly. Ray Brown on upright bass played until the tips of his fingers almost bled. Oscar did his thing at the piano and other musicians joined in as the spirit moved them. There was a dignity about Oscar's huge frame, as well as an air of quiet, inner beauty.

Every metropolitan area has its local version of what a successful jazz pianist should be. Omaha was no exception. The local was named Eddy. He played in a hotel basement cocktail lounge called the *Red Lion*. Trained as a classical pianist, Eddy was exceptionally talented and waiting to be discovered.

Propped with his back against a wall, his face full of wonder, he watched Oscar work. Occasionally, Oscar looked up and their eyes met. Finally Oscar motioned him over. Eddy edged in.

"It's your turn, man," Oscar mumbled. "Show us what you can do."

Oscar slid his considerable bulk to one side, the piano bench groaning under his weight. Eddy had been waiting for years for such a chance. He exhaled and went for it. Nimble, quick, and practiced, Eddy's fingers flicked all over the keyboard. Every note on the piano was fair game.

By most measurements, it was a virtuoso performance. With a flourish, his fingers tinkled through the last long, complicated run. The spontaneous applause must have been gratifying. Like a child who knows he has pleased his parents, with expectancy, Eddy turned to Oscar.

Oscar eased back toward the center of the bench, his head bobbing up and down. "Technically," he said, you're perfect . . . If you ever learn what to leave out, you'll be a real musician. Don't try to play it all, only what's necessary. No one can teach you that . . . you've got to feel it . . . know its right . . . inside."

Disappointment clouded Eddy's face, though Oscar had shared with him one of life's great truths. We can't live it all. Priorities have to be set. Success is often decided by what we choose not to do.

My life was influenced by Oscar's off-hand remark. Whether practicing the art of war, giving a political speech, painting a landscape, or singing an operatic aria, success is at times measured by what is left out. Clutter, excess, and overwork muddies a painting as surely as it does a line of reasoning.

One of the filler courses I took at the university was watercolor painting. Later in life I would switch to oils. Art had always occupied a special place in Charlene's and my life. Over the years, we dabbled in sketching and painting. Charlene had the most natural talent, but I worked harder at it.

Our time at Fort Devens ended when the Army posted me to the Presidio of Monterey in California to study the French language. Again, I was the only minority in the class. After successfully completing the course, the Army in all of its wisdom assigned me to Korea. In all my 34 years in the Army, I never did receive an assignment that required me to speak French—but it has proven quite helpful to my opera singing.

Unfortunately, the tour of duty in Korea was without dependents. This meant that Charlene and the three children would remain behind in California. We were not happy campers.

Historically, the nation of Korea was known as the "Land of the Morning Calm." Its culture is rich, its people inventive, industrious, and clever with their hands. For example, the world's first ironclad warships, called "Turtle Ships," were used by the Korean Admiral, Yi Sun-Sin, to drive off an invading Japanese fleet in 1592. This was 270 years before the Monitor and Merrimac fought to a draw off Hampton Roads, Virginia, on March 9, 1862.

In 1907 the Japanese forced the Korean King Kojong to abdicate his throne. He was replaced by Korean officials who collaborated with Japanese occupation authorities.

Systematically the Japanese set about eradicating Korean culture. They banned the study of Korean history and stopped Korean publications. School children were taught the Japanese language. Koreans were forced to assume Japanese names. The Japanese brought their religion, Shinto, to Korea. The Japanese cut down most of Korea's forests and shipped the timber to Japan. There was no reforestation program.

When the war ended, Koreans were stranded all over the Japanese Imperial Empire. Even today, some Koreans are said to still live as slave laborers in the foreign countries to which they had been forcibly shipped by the Japanese.

During the fifties and early sixties, few minority officers got desirable assignments—the kind that would lead to promotion. Minorities were routinely given dead-end jobs. Throughout the world, U.S. Army Headquarters Flight Detachments were, for the most part, *defacto*, all-white units even though official Army policy, at least on paper, pretended otherwise. The Korean Military Advisory Group (KMAG) Flight Detachment was no exception.

Upon my arrival in Seoul, I was told that I had been further reassigned to the city of Kwang-Ju located in the isolated southwest part of the country. I was to be an instructor and advisor to the South Korean Army Aviation School.

There was a slight problem. I had never been trained and certified as a primary flight instructor. Under the best of conditions, Army fixed-wing flight instruction was dangerous. The instructor sat in the back seat of the high-wing, single-engine, two passenger Cessna O-1 Birddog. The student sat in front.

There were no flight instruments in the rear. The trainee had an instrument panel in the front, but the instructor behind him couldn't see it. Quite literally, the instructor flew and taught the students to fly by the feel in the seat of his pants.

Some of the aviators assigned to the KMAG Headquarters Flight Detachment were certified as flight instructors and had years of teaching experience. Logically one of them should have been assigned to advise the Korean Army Aviation School. That was not to be.

In Seoul, a special one-week course of instruction was set up for me. At the end of the week, I was certified as a primary flight instructor. Fortunately, the officer assigned to teach me was diligent, hardworking, and determined to give me every benefit of his considerable teaching experience.

In that one week I did not become an accomplished flight instructor, but I did progress to the point where I could keep a student from getting the aircraft into a dangerous situation and killing both of us. "Tell me," I asked my instructor toward the end of the week, "wouldn't it be better to send a seasoned flight instructor like you to do this job?"

"Well, we have qualified instructors who could go, but the colonel says they're all needed here."

"You believe that?"

"It's best I don't comment."

"To your knowledge, has there ever been a Negro pilot assigned to KMAG's Headquarters Flight Detachment?"

"No."

"Just checking."

To distinguish one from another, KMAG Detachments were given different alphabetical designations. The Kwang-Ju detachment was designated Detachment K. It consisted of one airplane, one American crew chief, one Jeep with a Korean driver, and one American sergeant.

Fortunately, the Koreans did most of their own flight instructing. I only flew with trainees the Koreans culled from among their best students. They would "lose face," they thought, if a student crashed and killed the American advisor. "Impeccable," was how I characterized their logic.

In 1960 the Korean nation was struggling back from the devastation wrought by the North Korean invasion. Syngman Rhee had been Korea's wartime leader. Though he successfully brought the nation through the war, afterwards he became more of an authoritarian isolationist.

A student revolution broke out on April 19, 1960, in the southern city of Massan, touching off nationwide demonstrations. A week later, April 26, Rhee was forced to resign. He and his wife fled to Hawaii, where he died in 1965.

The new Prime Minister, Chang Myon, known to Americans as John Chang, unsuccessfully tried to run the new parliamentary-style government. He was not up to it. Politically, Korea splintered into competing factions vying for power. College students became politically alienated and destructive, and the military became very restless.

The result was that on May 16, 1961, Major General Park Chung Hee led a successful military coup, with generals and admirals from all branches of the armed services participating. Quickly they dissolved the National Assembly and declared martial law.

They designated the military government the Supreme Council for National Reconstruction, and then set out to change much of what ailed the nation. Surprisingly, they sometimes succeeded.

Perhaps more than any other American, General Guy S. Meloy deserves credit for Korea's early democratic miracle. As the senior military officer in Korea, he personally stood in the gap and protected the fledgling government from the vicissitudes of U.S. policy. Almost single-handedly, and at great personal risk, he helped diffuse and thwart impatient young Korean officers bent on toppling Park with a countercoup.

The Korean Army Aviation School had outgrown its facilities and needed to relocate. One of the possible sites was an existing airfield near the city of Taejon. An on-site visit and inspection was scheduled. Should Taejon be selected as the site, the existing airfield runway would have to be extended a few thousand feet across rice paddy farmland.

Taejon's city fathers, wearing their traditional long flowing black robes over white "pajamas" with black stovepipe hats atop their heads, came out to the airfield to meet with two of the ruling generals from General Park's Supreme Council.

Since I was the American Advisor to the school, KMAG Headquarters directed that I attend the meeting. So early one morning I flew up from Kwang-Ju, bringing with me Captain Choe, a South Korean Army officer who acted as my interpreter.

The city fathers began the parley by saying that they did not object to the aviation school being relocated to their area. But they very much objected to selling the national government the acres of farmland necessary to extend the runway.

After about half an hour of haggling, the senior Korean general signaled for silence. His teeth bit the tip of a cigarette. Miraculously, his lips didn't contact the paper nor did his teeth crush the end of the cigarette.

Must take a lot of practice, I thought.

As the general spoke, color drained from Captain Choe and the trembling faces of the city fathers. Choe's interpreting became halting. Halfway through the speech, Choe stopped interpreting altogether.

I didn't know his problem, but I knew the solution. "Captain Choe," I said, "your salary is paid by the U.S. Army, not the Korean government. If you want to get paid this month, you had better restart your interpreting."

Reluctantly, he stammered, "The general says that if the Supreme Council for National Reconstruction decides to relocate the Army Aviation School from Kwang-Ju to Taejon, they will do it. If the city fathers object, the Supreme Council will level the city and build the runway in the middle of what is now Taejon."

Fearfully the city fathers placed the palms of their hands together in front of their chests and began genuflecting. Then they graciously offered to provide as much land to the national government as was required, free of charge.

So much for Korean democracy, I thought.

In the end, for other reasons, the decision was made not to relocate the Korean Army Aviation School to Taejon, but to move it to the south central city of Chinju.

11

Pusan

One day in 1961, the American Red Cross notified me, through military channels that Charlene had been hospitalized with a bleeding ulcer. It had come on suddenly, probably caused by anxiety over the death of Gregory plus the strain put on her by our frequent separations.

Hurriedly she had parceled out our three children to military friends, and then admitted herself to the Fort Ord Military Hospital. Doctors recommended that either I be returned to the United States to care for Charlene and the children, or they be sent to Korea to join me.

The personnel officer in charge of the decision was an insensitive colonel with a history of proven errors of judgment. He opposed my family joining me in Korea, but thankfully Commanding General Sydney C. Wooten, overruled him.

A few weeks later I stood on a Pusan hillside near our new home, crumbling a dry clod of earth between my fingers as I watched the sunset. Far in the distance, mist formed at the bottom of the faded blue-gray-green mountains where the fingers of ridgelines overlapped in the broad Naktong River Valley. On the eastern side of the valley, dark beige earth freshly gouged out of a quarry caught and reflected back the fading light.

Closer in, but still at a distance, wedges of trees were barely distinguishable against the background of fading mountains. Nearer still lay rice paddy fields, splayed out like the leaves of giant water lilies, their boundaries outlined and accented by dikes. Here and there water buffalo hauled lumbering oxcarts along the narrow, sun-beaten paths that ran between the paddies.

On the close ridgelines I could differentiate maple trees from pine, and walnut from cypress. Now the sun dropped from sight. Deprived of its light, the distance lost its blueness and turned a flat slate gray then merged with the darkening sky as the fingers of mountains slowly were engulfed by the mist of night. Slowly the trees and tile roofs blurred into each other. Only the tops of the ridges that ran down into the valley retained a thin, translucent crust of light. Soon both earth and sky merged into one shade, one form.

To conserve farmland, farmers' houses squatted hard against each other in the small villages plopped down in the center of acres of rice paddies. In the transition area where farmland ended and the city of Pusan began, there were what looked like Mediterranean-style homes. These were interspersed with cement block buildings and corrugated tin warehouses, mixed in with small shops and businesses. Here and there a factory smoke-stack poked its stove-pipe neck up above the flatter and larger factory roofs.

In the fading light, the roofs ran together in a nondescript mass of tile and corrugated tin. The last shimmers of dying light obliquely glanced off the tops of the hot roofs, tricking the eye and giving an illusion of undulation.

The inhabitants lit candles and kerosene lanterns, just as I had as a child. Along the main streets of Pusan, the few buildings wired for electricity turned on their lights.

Perched grandly on a series of hills observing and presiding over all these mutations, was the U.S. Army's Hialeah Compound where Charlene and I and the children would live for the next two years. It was constructed on the site of an old Japanese thoroughbred racing track, hence the name, Hialeah, named after the famous race track in Dade County, Florida. Hialeah Compound, our new home, was surrounded by barbed wire, floodlights, and armed military guards. Some guards manned stationary posts; others walked their appointed rounds with police dogs held on short leashes.

Inside the military compound the western style homes sported cream-colored stucco walls, red tile roofs, hardwood floors, and small fireplaces, which contrasted sharply with the construction in the Korean parts of the city. One of our joys, as foreigners living in a foreign country, was gathering around the dining room table in front of a large floor-to-ceiling window eating, swapping stories, laughing, and pretending we still lived in America.

Early one evening during dinner when Charlene was pregnant with our fourth child, Natasha, the blackened sky was suddenly lit up by brilliantly colored machine gun tracer bullets. Down there in the city warring factions of Koreans fired back and forth at one another. Another attempted military counter-coup was in progress.

Looking out over the city's rooftops, the children were delighted with what they thought were fireworks. Our son Jerry jumped from his chair, ran to the window, and excitedly chanted, "Mommy, Mommy, look—the Fourth of July!"

Charlene looked to where he was pointing, frowned, and then admonished, "No, it's not fireworks. They're just changing governments. Now sit back down and eat your peas."

Of course in a larger sense the struggle below was over power and greed. What future course would Korea follow? Who would lead, and which Korean families would benefit financially?

From the U.S. perspective, we wondered if Korea could pull itself up out of the aftermath of war and push itself toward democratic political stability and economic prosperity. For Korea the years 1960 to 1963 were a time of playing, "You bet your nation!" reminiscent of the old Groucho Marx TV show, "You Bet Your Life." As a captain, I had only a worm's eye view of what was occurring. However, the nature of my job occasionally provided a privileged window through which to watch.

General Park and the coup leaders divided up the nation into geographical districts, each commanded by a Korean general or admiral who was also designated a civilian governor. Each exercised civilian and military judicial review authority. Trials were perfunctory, sometimes politically motivated, and the results were certain.

Trials were not the only way Korean military leaders disposed of troublemakers, or those who failed to support the military government's policies. On more than a few occasions, an American advisor arrived at work only to learn that the Korean counterpart he advised the day before had met with a "tragic accident" during the night, necessitating an immediate funeral and burial.

The Korean general who governed the Pusan Military District stood five-ten, weighed two hundred pounds and was by nature scholarly and reflective. He seemed more like a college professor than a major general. Working with Americans came easy to him. For the most part his high-wire act—balancing military dictatorship with civilian sensitivities and needs—worked.

Since the Koreans had no helicopters of their own and in many areas outside of Pusan proper there were no connecting roads, the general had to rely on me and my U.S. Army helicopter to get from place to place in his district. Month after month the two of us reconnoitered and explored the area from Pusan west to Masan, north to Taegu, and east to Ulsan. We also visited the islands close off the southeast coast.

"Land over there on that hillside," he might say, pointing. "Do you think this would be a good location for a new hospital or school?"

After landing, we would walk around looking the area over. He'd explain why he was interested in that particular location. Occasionally, we flew out to Ulsan to reconnoiter a possible site on which to build a national industrial complex. Ulsan was made up of rice paddies and farmland with no roads and no town. It was located 40 minutes flying time northeast of Pusan on the coast of the Sea of Japan.

It had a natural deepwater port, lots of land on which to build, and enough fresh water to support a major city and industrial complex. The local farmers did not welcome our visits. They surmised, correctly, that when the Seoul government paid attention to an area, it might result in a significant loss of rice paddy farmland.

As much as we Americans helped, most of the credit for the Korean miracle was due to the sacrifice, suffering, and hard work of the Korean people. At that time, Seoul was a wounded Phoenix. It had been burned and razed century after century by the Mongols, the Chinese, and the North Korean Army—twice during the last war. The chaos on Seoul's streets was endemic.

A mélange of oxcarts, ancient Japanese streetcars, heavy trucks, motor scooters, bicycles, pedestrians and busses pounded by hand out of metal from military 55-gallon gasoline drums—all intermixed and struggled for contrary passage. In opposition to each other, foot, motor, and oxcart traffic moved north, south, east, and west in the same lanes at the same time. The result was massive gridlock.

One day the Supreme Council announced that the confusion and chaos on Seoul's streets would end one week from Monday. On that day streetcars only would run on the tracks in the middle of the streets. Automobiles would be operated parallel to the streetcar tracks and move in the same direction as the streetcars. Oxcarts were banished to the far sides of the street near the curbs. Bicyclists were confined to the same lane as oxcarts, and pedestrians were directed to stay out of the street and walk alongside the open ditch sewers.

The Supreme Council's edict had a near zero chance of succeeding. No one, including previous Korean governments, Japanese invaders, nor American advisors had ever been able to tame Seoul's traffic snarl. Some things are bigger than all of us.

On the appointed day, shortly before daylight, Republic of Korea military trucks roared through the streets of downtown Seoul and screeched to a halt at major intersections. Rolls of concertina barbed wire were rolled out of the back of trucks and dumped onto the streets. Other trucks disgorged squads of Korean military police dressed in full battle gear.

Within minutes they erected circular barbed-wire enclosures near street intersections. Day broke and, as usual, Seoul's traffic ignored the new directive. But this was not to be a business-as-usual day.

Grim, humorless, no-nonsense military police grabbed each individual who broke the new traffic rules and herded him with clubs toward the barbed-wire enclosures. Once imprisoned, the offenders remained locked up in these temporary barbed-wire enclosures for 24 hours. Then they were released with an admonition not to trespass again. Chilled at night, baked relentlessly by sun during the day, babies and children, adults and the aged, oxen and carts, bicycles, motorbikes, automobiles, and trucks were arrested and impounded—without food, water or toilets.

Within a week, order and discipline were imposed on Seoul's streets and traffic. Streetcars ran in the middle of the street. Pedestrians walked on the dirt sidewalks, and all other traffic moved in its appointed lanes. As quickly as they had appeared a week before, the concertina wire and military police departed. It was the smallest of successes. A win, albeit a brutal one.

No detail seemed too small to escape the attention of the Supreme Council. For example, Koreans were paid by the government to make sun-cured, 12-by-12-by-2 inch concrete squares. Cottage industries sprung up everywhere, cranking out concrete squares. Rapidly the piles of blocks stored on street corners grew.

On an appointed day, all across South Korea, the blocks were miraculously fitted into place and sidewalks quickly spread up and down city streets. Open sewer ditches were also lined with these blocks—sides and bottom—then closed over. The cities began to gain a little control over raw sewage.

In Pusan, the Supreme Council also brought an end to a favorite Korean scam, fleecing money from road construction projects. Normally when the U.S. State Department, with U.S. taxpayers' money, signed a contract with a Korean construction firm to pave a fixed number of miles of highway or city streets, the firm was given a standard advance payment.

After paving a piece of roadway, the contractor more often than not declared that he was experiencing financial difficulty and asked for another advance payment, ostensibly to fix his financial problems and to enable him to complete the construction. Then he returned repeatedly for more money. Each time there was the traditional kickback paid under the table to the Korean government officials who enabled the scam. U.S. State Department personnel overseeing the project shrugged their shoulders, acknowledging that this was the way things had always been in Korea. It was part of the culture.

When contractors signed contracts with the new Supreme Council, they were in for a surprise. "If the paving is not completed on schedule as agreed upon," the Korean Army contracting officer impatiently explained, "all of your company's assets as well as your own personal property will be nationalized. In addition, the assets and property of all your relatives will be seized and any businesses or personal property they own will also become property of the federal government." Predictably projects, for the most part, were completed ahead of schedule and within budget.

For my family and me, our time in Korea was fast coming to a close. Yet there was one last bit of excitement waiting for me—in the clouds.

12

Mayday! Mayday!

The pre-flight inspection went fine but things didn't feel quite right. I was flying a single engine De Havilland *Beaver*; the military called it an L-20 or U-6. It was an all-metal, high-wing monoplane powered by a single Pratt and Whitney Wasp Junior engine, driving a Hamilton Standard constant-speed propeller. The Beaver is one of the most dependable airplanes in the world and is still a staple in Alaska's bush pilot fleet.

The weather in Seoul was lousy, chilling and wrenching. Flying conditions en route to Pusan were forecasted to be rainy and foggy, with continuous cloud cover up to 20,000 feet. All of the mountaintops were shrouded in clouds. At Pusan the weather was down to landing minimums and holding.

This meant the entire hour-and-a-half flight would be under instrument flight rules. We could fly in the clouds using instruments, but we had to see the runway to land. Upon arrival, should the weather deteriorate further, we would be unable to see the runway and would have to abort the instrument approach at Pusan and turn back to Taegu, our designated alternate airport, about 30 minutes north. I had wanted to make the flight earlier in the day, but my only passenger had been delayed until mid-afternoon.

He was a 40 year-old Army Signal Corps major whose hair had turned prematurely silver. I watched him shamble across the ramp toward the plane, chin down, thumbs hooked in his trouser pockets. He looked up at the sky questioningly. His voice was soft, and his words slowly fought their way through a southern drawl, "Those clouds sure don't look good to me. Maybe we ought to just stay here on the ground."

"It would have been better had we taken off a few hours ago, but we can still make it safely," I offered.

"Uh-huh," he noncommittally acknowledged, his eyes inspecting my face, probably searching for any indication of doubt.

Quickly, I briefed him on the aircraft route, time of flight, and emergency procedures. Then, I showed him the side door located just behind his seat and demonstrated how to jettison it with a small lever should he have to bail out. Of course, I reminded him to count to three before pulling the ripcord to open the parachute. This would insure that he was well clear of the airplane before it opened.

Since it was a single-engine plane and the flight would be in the clouds, regulations required that we both wear parachutes. I set him in the copilot's seat and helped him into his parachute.

"I don't enjoy flying all that much," he offered, giving me a look of concern. "If this military business I've got to take care of down south was not so important, I'd just stay in Seoul."

"Don't worry," I reassured him. "Other than a little forecasted turbulence en route, the flight should be uneventful. But as a precaution, in the unlikely event we do have to bail out, bend over and pull this plunger." I took his hand and placed it on the plunger. "That unlocks your seat from the floor. Push the seat to the rear, jettison the door and bail out. I'll follow right behind you."

"I understand," he said, looking worried. "You don't think we're going to have to do this, do you?"

"Certainly not, just following regulations."

The old reliable nine-cylinder, air-cooled engine purred encouragingly to life. As required by the checklist, prior to taking the runway, I made a fullpower engine static check. Something about the sound of the engine troubled me, but all the gauges indicated in the green, and investigate as I might, I couldn't detect even the slightest malfunction.

Just to be sure, I also listened with my feet, feeling for even the most insignificant vibration. Then I listened with one hand on the throttle lever and the other on the wheel. With all my senses I listened, searching—there was nothing amiss.

The tower directed us to taxi onto the active runway. I rechecked that the flaps were in takeoff position and double-checked the tuning of the navigational radio aids. We had lots of fuel on board and I was starting to feel good about the flight.

"Army 32838," Departure Control said, "you're cleared for takeoff."

"Roger," I replied. "Understand cleared for takeoff."

The engine roared up smoothly and powerfully as I advanced the throttle. Not having cargo or other passengers to weigh it down, the U-6 lifted off the runway effortlessly.

Climbing through five hundred feet, I manually pumped up the flaps from takeoff to climb position, retarded the throttle, reduced the propeller, and gently turned south.

We leveled off at 10,000 feet. I checked the gauges and instruments, cleaned up the checklist and positioned everything for normal cruise. An hour later, we uneventfully crossed the Taegu non-directional radio beacon and turned south toward Pusan.

Ten minutes later, Taegu Control directed, "Army 32838, you're cleared to descend to minimum en route altitude."

"Roger Taegu, Army 838 beginning descent," I radioed back.

Minimum en route altitude was as low as Control could authorize us to fly and still provide safe ground clearance. If we dropped below that level, we could crash into the side of a cloud-shrouded mountain. Intermittent rain pelted the windshield. We hadn't seen the ground since takeoff. The engine continued running smoothly. We still had lots of fuel, and in 20 minutes we'd be safely on the ground.

Almost imperceptibly, the engine shuddered. Unconcerned, I scanned the instrument panel but detected nothing. Everything was operating within normal safe limits. The engine shuddered again . . . still imperceptible to my passenger, but clearly something was amiss. Now every nerve strained to detect some instrument variation, some fault, some sound vibrating through the engine or airframe.

We flew on for another five minutes with no reoccurrence. Then came another shudder, this time stronger. Ignition was okay, cylinder head temperature was operating within normal limits, oil pressure was up, fuel pressure was low but within limits, and air speed was okay.

"Not to worry," I told myself. Then came a violent shudder. This time my passenger noticed it and turned his head to stare at me.

I smiled back at him with what I hoped was my most reassuring smile. Cross-checking the instrument panel, I noticed that the fuel pressure was dropping. Just then the red "fuel low-pressure warning light" blinked on, and I instinctively mashed the radio mike button.

"Taegu Control, this is Army 838, over?"

"Army 838, this is Taegu, go ahead," the voice crackled back through the radio static.

"Experiencing engine trouble and am declaring an emergency at this time."

"What are your intentions, 838?"

"We're halfway between Pusan and Taegu. Pusan airfield does not have crash rescue equipment. Request permission to execute a 180 degree turn on the airway and return to Taegu for an immediate instrument approach."

"Roger, 838. You are cleared from your present position direct to Taegu. Upon arrival you are cleared for an immediate Automatic Direction Finder (ADF) approach. Crash and Rescue equipment will be standing by."

My passenger turned a sickly gray. The cords in his neck stood out like celery stalks. The color of my face couldn't have been at the warm end of an artist's palette either.

With every turn of the propeller, the engine shuddered. Fuel pressure continued to drop. In seconds my mind raced through and analyzed the possible list of emergencies that might apply.

"Probably the fuel pump," I concluded, but there was no way to be certain. Suddenly the engine quit altogether and the propeller started wind milling. The sound of my heart beating and the wind whistling past the airplane were the only sounds in the cockpit.

Airspeed dropped off sharply and we started slowly falling out of the sky. We were still in the clouds and it was likely that we would run out of altitude and crash into the side of a mountain without even seeing it. Standard operating procedure in such a situation was to immediately bail out.

"Mayday! Taegu, Mayday!" I radioed, trying to keep my voice calm. "This is Army 838, engine failure. I repeat, engine failure . . . we're bailing out."

Turning to the major, I said, "This is it! Bend over, pull the plunger on the floor at the bottom of your seat, push your seat back, jettison the side door and jump. Now get moving!"

He tried, but his body jerked spastically and he lost control of his arms and legs. If by a miracle he got his hands on the seat disconnect plunger, he'd never be able to pull it.

I knew the feeling well. The difference between us was that I'd lived through so many close calls over the years that I'd learned how to pretend I wasn't scared and how to make my body obey, even when it didn't want to respond. The major didn't have my advantage.

He was incapable of bailing out and we were out of time and altitude. No choice remained so I hurriedly initiated engine restart procedures, even though we were now 1,500 feet below minimum safe altitude.

Fortunately, high-wing utility airplanes like the U-6 have an excellent glide ratio. If we only clipped a mountain side, we still just might walk away from the crash. Of course, if we ploughed directly into the side of one . . .

Sticking out of the instrument panel near my right foot was a six-inch lever referred to in the aircraft operator's manual as a wobble pump. The book said that in the event of engine-driven fuel pump failure, if the pilot took hold of the wobble pump and vigorously moved it up and down in its race, maintaining fuel pressure at five per square inch, the engine would keep running. I went through restart procedures and began pumping.

To my surprise, the engine coughed and in fits and starts sputtered back into life. The big propeller turned faster and faster, biting the air as the engine took hold. We were passing through 2,000 feet below minimum safe altitude. Either we had come down into a valley or this was heaven. Either condition was perfectly acceptable.

But the operator's manual didn't cover all aspects of the problem. Holding onto the wheel with my left hand, I had to twist to the right and bend down to grab the wobble pump. Now instead of looking out through the windshield, my face was staring directly into the instrument panel. As long as we were flying in the clouds, it was manageable, since I couldn't see anything outside anyway. But executing an instrument approach and then landing while bent over was going to be interesting.

Slowly we climbed. I prayed hard that the valley didn't make any sharp turns. A thousand feet more and we'd be back up to minimum en route altitude.

"How're you doing, major?" I asked.

Color was returning to his face, and he managed to weakly mutter something unintelligible.

"Look," I said, "in that satchel on the floor between the seats is a leather-covered, loose-leaf binder. You saw me use it during takeoff. Remember?"

He nodded, "Yes."

"Pull out the book and open it up."

With effort, he located it and balanced it on one knee.

"Now," I calmly said with great effort, "you see those tabs lettered A through Z?" Inside I felt like Jello. "If you turn to Tab T and flip through the pages, you'll find a page entitled Taegu Instrument Approach Chart." Continuing to pump, I directed, "Take the approach chart out of the book and hold it up in front of my face. Taegu doesn't have radar so they can't talk us down."

"I understand," he said, his voice calm though his hands continued to shake. Too quickly he snapped open the loose-leaf binder and the approach charts exploded out of the book.

"Stop," I screamed, as he bent over to grab them.

"You just told me you needed them to land!" he angrily shouted back, fear and frustration getting the better of him.

"I do need them," I shouted. "But if you get those pages out of alphabetical order, it will take forever to find the Taegu chart. I can't keep this wobble pump going that long. So when you reach down there, try to get a hand on each end of the charts and compress the pages together," I begged. "Try to bring the whole pile up in one bunch."

He nodded, bent over, followed my instructions, and there, still in its proper sequence, he found the Taegu chart. I could have kissed him.

He held the chart against the instrument panel in front of my eyes while I memorized the magnetic headings, altitudes, and time and distance instructions. When we arrived over the Taegu radio beacon, I turned the aircraft outbound to begin the instrument approach.

As we descended from altitude, it required less pumping to keep the engine running. By the time we broke out of the clouds on short final approach, I was able to let go of the wobble pump and make a normal landing.

At Taegu, the local flight detachment commander was Captain Jim McWhorter, a dear friend of Charlene's and mine. His mechanics immediately took charge of the airplane and over night repaired the engine-driven fuel pump. Jim and his delightful wife, Jane, put me up, fed me, entertained me, drove me to the airport the next morning, and saw me off to Pusan.

As for my passenger, he caught a Jeep ride to the local Taegu train station and took a Korean train to Pusan. He also rode back to Seoul by train. I didn't blame him.

At home, I found Charlene and the children anxiously awaiting my arrival. "I think I've had enough excitement for one overseas tour," I told them.

They agreed. And as if we'd planned it, new orders came in the mail the next day. They said we were going home, back to the United States, assigned to the Fourth Infantry Division at Fort Lewis, in Washington State.

13

Task Force Smith

We arrived in the Pacific Northwest, a land of lush green forests and breathtaking mountain vistas, in mid-summer of 1963. Some Washingtonians complain that the state is too damp, overcast, and rainy. Clearly, they have not endured dreary central European winters.

West of Spokane the arid, sun-baked, desert-like land undulates up the eastern slope of the Cascades. Knifing through the Cascade Mountain Range are narrow cuts with names like Snoqualmie, Swauk, Cayuse, and Chinook Passes. Presiding grandly above them all is the quiescent snow-capped volcano, Mount Rainier, elevation 14,410 feet.

Locals say that when you get up in the morning, if you can clearly see majestic Rainier, then carry your raincoat. If the volcano is shrouded in clouds or obscured by fog and mist, wear your raincoat because it will be raining by the time you get where you're going.

To the northwest of Rainier lies Puget Sound, a deep, long, violent gash in the earth. Far to the west of the Sound, on an almost inhospitable seashore, lives the Pacific Rain Forest.

Defining the southern border with Oregon is the mighty Columbia River. It drops down out of Canada to Pasco, loops south past

The Dalles, slams into Portland, then careens northwest, disgorging its torrents into the Pacific Ocean at Cape Disappointment.

Soon after our arrival, the colonel commanding the infantry battle group to which I was assigned called me into his office and said, "I've been ordered by the division to send one officer to Fort Bragg to attend the Special Forces Operations Officer's Course. You're new and haven't gotten into the swing of things yet, so your absence will hurt the unit least. You leave next week. Any questions?"

"Yes, Sir. I just arrived from Korea. Couldn't you send someone else and let me get my family settled?"

"The military comes first, you know," he said smiling benignly.

I saluted, faced about and left. Since I would be gone for two months and since our parents hadn't seen Natasha, our daughter born in Korea, Charlene and I opened and closed our new house at Fort Lewis at the same time. Taking the children with us, we flew east to McKeesport, Pennsylvania.

We didn't want to burden either family too much, so we split up. Charlene and our two youngest children stayed with her parents, the Coopers. Our two oldest, Jerry and Charlein, stayed with my parents in Liberty.

Saying goodbye to them, I flew on to Fort Bragg, North Carolina. There, Special Forces billeted me along with the other student officers in old WWII quarters constructed atop piles of burned out sand called Smoke Bomb Hill.

Special Forces schooling went well. Things did not go well in McKeesport. Charlene's ulcer, which we thought had healed, violently erupted. Blood spurted profusely from both ends of her body.

With sirens screaming, an ambulance rushed her across town to McKeesport Hospital. The same doctor who officiated at my birth and with whom I share middle names, Dr. Matthew Ralph Hadley, took charge of Charlene's emergency. He was now McKeesport Hospital's chief of staff.

A third of her stomach was removed, which took care of the large duodenal ulcer. In the operating room there was a mix-up in medicines and her heart stopped but was restarted. In recovery, a malfunction occurred in the machine siphoning fluid out of her stomach. Char's mother was sitting beside her, saw her stop breathing and called for help.

Next, Char had an unusually severe reaction to penicillin. Many times before she'd been given the drug with no ill effects, but this time her system rejected it. And because her bed was located too near a drafty window, she caught a very bad cold.

Several times the Army let me fly to McKeesport to visit her in the hospital. Even though her frail body was racked by excruciating pain, and in spite of the needles in her arms and tubes in her stomach and nose, each time she managed to say, "Thank you for coming."

"You know I couldn't stay away," I replied, kissing her forehead.

She was unable to talk without great discomfort. But our silence held great meaning for us. I will never forget that first visit. When I left, the picture of her pain-tormented eyes went with me.

I was so thankful that dear Charlene was going to recover. It had been such a shock to learn that her life had been in danger, after thinking that the problems with her ulcer were behind us. I sat at her bedside, thanking God for sparing her life and praying for her recovery.

A few hours later, I had to return to Special Forces training. I felt awful. I wished there had been a way to stay with her, but I had not been given a choice. I had to be grateful that the Army had let me come see her at all.

A week later I was able to visit her again.

A month later, Special Forces training came to an end. In McKeesport I rendezvoused with the children and a mending Charlene. The children remained with our parents until Christmas break, while Char and I flew back to Fort Lewis hoping that without the responsibility of caring for children, she'd recover more quickly.

Before leaving Fort Bragg, I attended a profoundly disquieting classified lecture followed by a question-and-answer session. This one lecture made the trip to Fort Bragg worthwhile. The lecture was given by an elderly, silver-haired Polish patriot of World War II fame. He was of medium height and stood ramrod erect in the center of the stage, instead of behind the podium as was customary.

Prior to WWII, Russia had signed an agreement with Hitler jointly dismembering Poland. This man had fought against the invading Russians. Captured by them and imprisoned, he escaped and eventually made his way via the North Sea to England.

Then Hitler did to Russia what they had both done to Poland. Breaking the peace treaty he had signed with Stalin, Hitler unleashed his armed forces in a lightning thrust toward Moscow.

Our lecturer, then living in England, volunteered to parachute back into his native Poland and help the Polish resistance fight a guerilla war against the Germans. For a while he succeeded in interdicting German units and supply convoy, but eventually the Nazis captured him and marked him for execution. Miraculously, he again escaped, made his way out of Europe and back to England.

This day his lecture was on the subject of how to successfully organize and fight guerilla wars. During the question-and-answer period, one of my classmates, referring to President Kennedy's recent intervention in Vietnam, asked, "How do you save a nation from communist enslavement when the inhabitants refuse to fight for their own freedom?"

"You don't," he said. "You let them be enslaved!" Scornfully he added, "If a people are unwilling to fight to secure democracy for themselves, you have two choices. You can occupy them and take over their government and armed forces, including promotion authority. This assumes that you also run their communication systems, transportation, and public schools.

"If your nation is willing to make such an extreme economic investment, commitment, and sacrifice for 20 or 30 years, perhaps

you can successfully educate, train, motivate, and raise up a generation of young people who will embrace your values and be willing
to fight and die to preserve their own freedom.

"But perhaps not. Personally, I think there is only a small chance
of success," he shrugged. "The other alternative is to write them off
as a free nation."

Many times over the years, particularly during my two tours in
Vietnam, I thought back on his remarkable, frightening answer. At
the time his comments seemed unduly cynical and harsh. Later I
concluded that he had been right. You can't do for other nations
and people what they won't do for themselves.

Back at Fort Lewis, I dedicated myself to nursing Char back
to good health. At the same time, a defining event rescued my
military career from mediocrity and elevated it to star status. That
event can be summarized in two words: Jack Doody.

Lieutenant Colonel Jack Doody commanded the First Battalion, 22d Infantry Regiment. The battalion was nicknamed "The
Regulars." Jack was a West Point graduate, Class of 1949, one of
the finest officers and gentlemen I have known. Jack stood an erect
six-one, weighed 180 pounds and was ruggedly handsome. He was
one of my few Army mentors. Fortunately, he came along when I
needed him most, though I didn't know it at the time.

Being a minority and having started out in the Army as an enlisted man, I lacked the bureaucratic knowledge and finesse necessary
to successfully negotiate my way through the Army Officer Corps'
corporate maze. Jack spent hours straightening out my thinking.

His focus was on competence, performance, and contribution,
not race. And he asked that I be assigned to his battalion in the
coveted operations officer position.

Jack believed that he owed it to the country and the U.S. Army
to help me realize my full potential. Patiently he explained which
military jobs led to dead-end assignments and which ones could
lead to success and advancement. In short, Jack taught me how to

successfully and effectively work the Army's bureaucratic assignment and promotion system.

Early each morning he walked through my operations office. As is customary in the military when the commanding officer enters a room, everyone stands to attention.

"Have you any instructions, Sir?" I asked.

He always answered, "No," then passed through the room and left by the far door.

I was perplexed and so one day I said, "Sir, every morning you walk in. I snap to attention and ask what you want. You say, 'Nothing,' and you leave. Am I missing something?"

I had been newly promoted. "Major Curry," he said, "the nature of your job dictates that you run my battalion. That's what operations officers do," he smiled, "but I never want you to forget who's boss!"

I never did. Jack didn't know it, but he was one of my heroes. Over the years, I've often looked back on our relationship with great fondness. Jack, secure in himself and his own abilities, surrounded himself with the strongest officers possible and gave them maximum latitude to succeed. In return, we were intensely loyal to him and tried hard to support him in every way.

One day the First Battalion, 22nd Infantry was alerted to pack up and deploy to the Mediterranean on a classified combat mission. The orders came while the battalion was on maneuvers at the Yakima Training Area.

While the battalion logistics officer gathered the officers and men together to convoy them back to Fort Lewis, Jack and I hurried back early in an army sedan. As usual that winter, the Cascade mountain passes were snow-covered and icy.

The moon was full and high in the dark sky and the usually twisting wind that howled through the passes was calm. Still, driving was treacherous and slow. It was many hours before we arrived at Fort Lewis.

As I drove, Jack told me that he and his wife, Jean, had been stationed in Japan when the Korean War broke out at 3:30 A.M. the morning of June 25, 1950. Communist North Korean military forces had crossed the 38th parallel, the internationally agreed upon border with South Korea.

The United Nations Security Council, with a pouting Soviet delegate boycotting its sessions, asked member nations to furnish military assistance to South Korea. Fifteen nations did: Australia, Belgium, Great Britain, Canada, Colombia, Ethiopia, France, Greece, Luxembourg, The Netherlands, New Zealand, the Philippines, Thailand, Turkey, and South Africa.

First Lieutenant Jack Doody was a platoon leader in the 21st Infantry Regiment, 24th Infantry Division, stationed in Japan. On paper, Jack commanded a platoon of infantrymen, but in reality, the unit was made up of athletes who played baseball, football, and basketball for the military.

In those days, it was tradition for regional military commanders to take their best athletes, officers, and enlisted men, and assign them to a single military unit. This enabled Japan to play Okinawa in football, or Hawaii to play the Philippines in baseball, or West Berlin to play Stuttgart in basketball.

When President Truman decided to commit U.S. ground troops in Korea, Pentagon staff officers logically chose to send to Korea military units in the Pacific that were closest to being manned at full strength. Why send a battalion that was half manned to war when the records showed that there was a battalion stationed in Japan that was at full personnel strength? No one asked if the battalion was full of soldiers or professional athletes.

So B and C Companies of the First Battalion of the 21st Infantry Regiment, which was nicknamed the Gimlets, reinforced by artillery, signal, and engineers were alerted for combat duty. The group was named Task Force Smith for its commander, West Pointer (1939) Colonel Charles B. (Brad) Smith. Its orders were to enter the Korean Peninsula at Pusan in the south, move north, make contact with the North Korean invaders and stop or defeat them in place.

Upon arrival at Pusan, Colonel Smith commandeered a Korean train, loaded his troops, weapons, ammunition, food, and medical supplies aboard and directed the engineer to head north toward Seoul at the best possible speed.

Twenty miles south of Seoul is the small village of Suwon. Between it and Osan, another village a bit farther south, is a low hill. Standing on the hill, Brad Smith could see a gentle valley of rice paddies. He was determined to carry out his orders, "Meet and defeat the North Koreans."

Lieutenant Doody was assigned to protect the north-north-west sector of the circular defensive perimeter. Brad Smith's headquarters were in the center. At 7:30 A.M. on the morning of July 5th, Jack and his men heard the clack-clack-clank of tank track pads laying down on hard-packed earth. Shortly afterward, North Korean tanks lumbered into sight heading directly for Jack's position.

Clay Blair in his excellent book, *The Forgotten War*, says that early on the morning of July 5, Task Force Smith was approached by 33 tanks of the 105th North Korean Armored Division (NKPA). "The NKPA was confident that the bad weather protected it from air attack but unaware that American infantry lay in wait."

While Jack and his men waited for the approaching tanks, they put the 75mm Recoilless Rifles and 2.36-inch Rocket Launchers to their shoulders. But the logisticians in Japan had sent them off to war with a mixture of training and target practice ammunition. Only six rounds were combat-ready and armor-piercing, high explosive anti-tank (HEAT). The staff officers in Japan had gambled that this was to be only a training exercise.

"The North Korean tanks rolled over our position without even slowing down," Jack said. "We were so impotent and frustrated, that we fired the inert rounds at the tanks just to see the sparks fly." By early afternoon the North Korean armor and infantry had passed far to the south, leaving Task Force Smith surrounded by North Korean soldiers and stranded on top of Suwon Hill.

"Jack," Brad Smith said, "our position is untenable, hopeless."

"Abandon the hill and have your men break down into groups of twos and fours," Jack replied, grimly shaking his head. "Try to work your way south through enemy lines . . . and good luck."

"So we paired up and struck out in small groups," Jack told me. "Fortunately, my group was able to make it through the enemy lines under cover of darkness. About half of the others made it out. Those who did not were never seen again, not even after the end of the war when prisoners of war were exchanged."

Jack's tale became part of my mental checklist, which proved helpful in the early spring of 1965, when a telegram arrived from the Department of the Army at the Pentagon. It said, "Major Jerry Ralph Curry will form the 220th Aviation Airplane Reconnaissance Company at Fort Lewis, Washington. Once formed, trained and equipped, the unit will deploy under his command to South East Asia."

The Vietnam War had begun. For me, it didn't make sense tactically or strategically for the United States to commit sizeable combat formations to the Vietnamese Peninsula unless we intended to cut off the head and source of the terrorist insurgency—in other words, not unless we intended to invade North Vietnam and defeat it. I felt that we should have learned from the Korean War that an enemy cannot be allowed a safe haven from which to grow, train and export terrorism, rape, murder, and war.

But following and implementing orders that I didn't agree with was often par for the military course. I had done it all my military life. Soldiers don't make or critique national policy. Ours is the profession of arms, of defending the nation and its interests, of defeating our nation's enemies on the field of battle.

14

Bound for Vietnam

The 220th Aviation Company was organized on April 15, 1965, at Fort Lewis, Washington. We processed personnel for overseas deployment; updated, polished and reinforced their military skills; and made everyone go through rigorous physical conditioning. By Herculean efforts, we requisitioned all of our equipment—other than aircraft—then issued, packed, and delivered everything to the dock in Tacoma, Washington, for ocean transport to Vietnam on June 10, 1965.

"Don't burden your soldiers with weapons and ammunition," instructions from the headquarters U.S. Military Assistance Command, Vietnam welcoming packet read. "You won't need weapons until long after your arrival in Vietnam." Obviously these instructions had been written long before U.S. combat troops were committed.

I remembered Jack Doody and Task Force Smith. "Ignore those instructions," I directed. "Weapons and ammunition will accompany the troops on their planes."

Command Sergeant Major Carol Simpson added, "War is full of surprises. We wouldn't be the first unit to get diverted to another destination." Simpson was a wiry, cigar-chomping, natural-born leader of men. Nothing or no one unnerved him.

In response to a question asked by one of my junior officers, I added this admonition, "Don't obey orders blindly. When instructions fail to make sense, modify them. The bottom line is saving lives. That's what officers are supposed to do. Protect the lives of your men and win battles."

Chief Warrant Officer Don Behny nodded his head in agreement. Don was hard and lean, just over six feet tall with a great sense of humor that often resulted in his chuckling more at himself than others. He exuded focused determination and raw competence. In a fight with the enemy you always wanted someone like Don covering your back. Also assigned to the company was Sergeant Pablo Sandoval, a magnificent chief cook and master scrounger.

Once again there was a flurry of activity in the Curry household. Providentially, Charlene was granted permission to remain in government quarters at Fort Lewis while I was away in Vietnam. This meant the children would not have to change schools or make new friends, and Charlene would have the comfort and support of the other military families we'd gotten to know so well during the past two years.

Army doctrine teaches that the second in command, the executive officer, goes ahead of the main body of troops with a small detachment to prepare for the unit's arrival. It seemed to me that major decisions would have to be made by the advanced party as soon as it arrived in Vietnam, and those kinds of decisions should fall on the shoulders of the commander, not the second in command.

So on June 19, 1965, I led a party of seven officers and nine enlisted men to Vietnam to advance the 220th's arrival. My executive officer, Captain Bill Schmale, brought over the main body later. Bill was an intense, tough officer, who knew how to lead men and get the job done right and on time. I had no qualms about his being able to complete the loading, close out the unit's stay at Fort Lewis, and move it to Vietnam.

The day we departed was one of those rare Seattle-Tacoma summer days when the sun shone brightly and the sky was pure blue. So unaccustomed were we to brilliant sunlight that we had to squint when saying our tearful goodbyes. Then my men and I swung aboard the chartered commercial bus that took us to nearby McChord Air Force Base.

Out over the Pacific Ocean halfway to Honolulu, the Air Force crew chief motioned me to follow him to the back of the cargo plane. He stood five-nine, had red hair parted down the middle, and talked with a twinkle in his eye.

"Major," he whispered conspiratorially, "when this airplane gets to Hawaii, it's going to break down. It'll take me three days to fix it. So you and your men just might want to relax and enjoy your-selves for awhile." He smiled. "You see, my girlfriend lives on Oahu. Haven't seen her in some time. We got a lot of catching up to do."

The crew chief kept his word. Shortly after we landed in Hawaii, word came over the public address system in the military passen-gers' lounge that our airplane had developed mechanical trouble and that the flight would be delayed for four hours. We were di-rected to report back at that time for further instructions.

Three and a half hours later, the same metallic, disembodied voice informed us that the airplane could not be repaired and that a part was being flown in from California. We would have to re-main in Hawaii overnight and report back in the morning.

The next day, we were informed that the wrong part had arrived from the States and a new one would have to be ordered. Our in-structions were to report back the following day. We did, and were told that the plane would not be ready to depart until the third day. It was great to have a short time in Hawaii. All of us enjoyed it im-mensely, but when time came to leave, we were more than ready.

Upon arrival in Saigon, we learned that the 220th's location had changed from a safe area in the south to a front line location with the Third U.S. Marine Division in the far north.

Yes, we needed weapons and ammunition immediately upon arrival. "Jack Doody, you were right," I said.

The advanced party completed its preparations in Saigon on the 30th of June. The mechanics had had to assemble five of the unit's aircraft, which had arrived by ship. We left a work party behind to assemble the other 27 aircrafts, while we flew ourselves north to the 220th's new home.

Our airplanes were the always-dependable Cessna L-19s—small metal two-seaters with high wings, powered by a single six-cylinder, air-cooled engine. As the engines droned on, pulling us toward the northeast, the tropical sun pierced the cockpit's Plexiglas, burning our exposed arms and necks. Behind me, Don Behny sat proudly upright, his forehead wet with perspiration and sweat bumps popping out on his forearms.

Slowly, the sun arched across the sky, following its ancient path. At the city of Phan Thiet we reached the brilliant white sand beaches of the South China Sea and turned north. Later, we overflew Phan Rang and Nha Trang. Then came Tuy Hoa, followed by Qui Nhon, where we stopped to stretch, refuel our mounts, and eat.

Now the coastline slanted to the north-north-west, the final leg of the flight. In a way it was like a horse turning toward the barn at the end of a long day's ride. It was only our imaginations, but the aircraft engines seemed to pick up the beat, and the whizzing metal propellers appeared to turn a little faster.

After Qui Nhon came Quang Ngai in Binh Dinh Province, that bitterly cruel center of communist-terrorist activity. Suddenly, the huge U. S. Marine complex at Danang came into view. We flew over it and kept flying, now tracking northwest.

Soon we were bumping over the Hai Von Pass followed by a descent into the Hue basin, the new home of the 220th Aviation Company.

15

Hue-Phu Bai

Our new home at Hue-Phu Bai had a small, asphalt-paved single runway airport and was located about 60 miles north of the city of Danang. It was named after the old Imperial City of Hue, which was fourteen kilometers northwest on the Perfume River.

Stepping down from the Cessna's cockpit, I was greeted by Lieutenant Colonel "Rough House" Taylor, commander of the Third Battalion, Fourth Marines. He was five-ten, sandy-haired, the oldest U.S. Marine battalion commander in Vietnam and one of the best. Taylor was a no-nonsense officer whose waist was as broad and hard as his shoulders.

The sun was setting and stored heat vibrated up from the hot asphalt. As I looked up at his rugged, weathered face and we shook hands, his eyes reflected the setting sun's reddening rays.

"Welcome to Phu Bai," he grunted. Gesturing over his right shoulder, he added, "The front lines are about a hundred yards in that direction. Dig your foxholes from that clump of trees around to the dry stream bed over there." Squinting into the sun, he gestured with a big knuckled forefinger. "My rules of engagement are simple; anything that moves outside the barbed wire after dark gets shot. Questions?"

"No, Sir."

"Then I suggest your men stay put once the sun goes down. When you get settled, come see me. There's a lot to discuss."

He sat down in the passenger's seat of a Kaiser-built aluminum Jeep. The engine roared to life, the gears clashed, meshed, and it loped off across the rolling sand hills and scrub grass.

My executive officer, Bill Schmale, and the main body of the 220th arrived in Vietnam at 02:30 in the morning on the 4th of July. All two hundred of them touched down at the Marine Air Base in Danang in three large C-130 U.S. Air Force transports. After refueling and a rest stop, they continued north to join us at Phu Bai.

All hands were immediately put to work expanding the camp and building fortifications. Under the direction of Command Sergeant Major Simpson, the enlisted men filled sandbags, built bunkers, and reinforced foxholes. There was little time for socializing.

My operations officer, the irrepressible and solid Dick Quigley, had the officers don thick leather engineer gloves, pound metal stakes into the ground, and string triple concertina barbed wire fences around our perimeter. Dick had served a previous tour in Vietnam and from experience knew exactly what to do. He was the one who gave the 220th its radio call sign name, "Cat Killers." Since the official Army name for the aircraft we flew was "BirdDog," Dick reasoned that birddogs, or hound dogs, loved to chase cats.

The first operational surveillance mission was flown the next day. Aircraft averaged 120 hours of flight time a month for the first six months of flight operations, far more than any other similar aviation reconnaissance unit in Vietnam. This was directly attributable to Chief Behny, our aircraft maintenance foreman, Bob Covino, my signal officer, and the leadership of Captain Jay Weight, our outstanding supply and maintenance officer. They did such a good job maintaining the aircraft that we were able to fly more than any other group.

But there is more to winning wars than men and equipment. There are many small actions that influence the outcome. Each one in and of itself is insignificant, but in aggregate they subtly influence the texture and tone of all that happens.

Mr. Ngo, the Vietnamese civilian airfield manager, was a case in point. He looked more like a mystic than a Vietnamese bureaucrat. His overly long legs made him tall for a Vietnamese. But something had gone wrong in the construction of his body. It was as if he were two bodies in one. The bottom half was long and the top half was short. He seemed to have been cut in half at the waist and mismatched in reassembly.

His dwarfed upper torso caused his long arms to dangle down so far that the tips of his fingers almost touched his knees. When he walked, his stooped shoulders hunched forward. When he talked, his lips peeled back revealing gold-capped, protruding teeth.

His office was located halfway up the old beige stucco airfield control tower built many years ago by French military forces. It provided an excellent view of the entire airfield.

Chief Behny and I went to visit Mr. Ngo to discuss some negotiations that had been dragging on for weeks. The 220th sorely needed more aircraft parking space. Our airplanes were jammed so close together that the explosion of a single VC mortar round would damage or destroy several aircraft at one time.

Mr. Ngo graciously brewed us tea. "I prefer coffee," he said, "but it is much too expensive."

I made a mental note of his request. We sat and drank and talked about the monsoon weather which contributed to the area's 121 inch average annual rainfall. Then we discussed our children. He told us how lovely Vietnam had been before the wars, when Saigon had been known as the Paris of the Orient.

At last, when he could no longer postpone the purpose of our meeting, he fetched a blueprint out of a rickety wooden wall cabinet. On it were the location of utility lines, the limited airport parking ramp, and some other technical information.

Smiling obliquely, he said, "Mr. Behny, the area you have requested as a parking area for your airplanes is quite difficult." Again he smiled. I thought I heard contempt in his voice. He obviously believed that we could do him no harm.

"As you can see here on the paper and can observe through the window, there is a house located in the middle of the area where you want to park your airplanes. It is occupied by a number of families," he gestured out the window. "It is Vietnamese government property and cannot be used by U.S. forces."

I nodded noncommittally, "Yes, but we both know it's dilapidated. A strong wind would blow it down."

He ignored my reply. "Of course I will forward your request to the Saigon government," he assured us in a sweet reasonable tone of voice. "Certainly you understand that it will take a year or two for Saigon to answer."

Now I emulated the smile I had seen the Korean generals use when addressing the city fathers standing on the runway at Taejon Airfield.

"Tomorrow morning at sunrise," I said very softly, "the U.S. Marine bulldozers will arrive to prepare the area for an asphalt parking ramp. The house you see out there in the middle of that area will be leveled, along with anything or anyone in it."

I followed this statement of fact with a slight bow. Paling, Mr. Ngo bowed to me in return.

Chief Behny and I departed. That night, we heard noises emanating from the house—the noises of people moving around and calling back and forth to one another.

I don't know where the people and their belongings went, but in the morning there was not much left at the site. At first light, two Marine bulldozers clanked into position. Quickly, the Marines leveled the empty relic and began constructing the badly needed parking ramp. As soon as it was completed, Chief Behny moved the aircraft onto it.

Three months later, I received a request from Mr. Ngo asking me to come for another visit. Don and I participated in the now familiar ritual of bowing and drinking tea. Finally, pleasantries over, Ngo took a new blueprint out of the old rickety cabinet and proudly unrolled it on top of his desk. "Major Curry, this came today from Saigon."

On the blueprint of the airfield were hatched lines with a statement saying that the 220th's aircraft parking area, which we had already confiscated, was now designated as U.S. Government property.

Bowing, I said, "Mr. Ngo, it is always a pleasure to do business with you. Rest assured that my government deeply appreciates your efforts on its behalf."

When we got back to the company, I had Sergeant Sandoval take Mr. Ngo two five-pound cans of coffee. He was very grateful.

The 220th had two primary missions. First was daily intelligence reconnaissance over South Vietnam's I Corps area. Some areas were important enough to merit daily overflights. Others were covered once or twice a week, and a few received only monthly coverage.

Eventually, we ended up with map overlays of the entire corps area. Our American pilots flying with South Vietnamese officers in the rear seat as observers quickly learned what was normal in the area and where there had been change, even subtle. All changes, such as the construction of a new footbridge across a jungle river, were posted to the master map daily.

Soon VC terrorists were referring to our BirdDog aircraft as the "old women, who told everything they knew," which was exactly what we were doing.

The 220th's other mission was to provide direct support for the Third U.S. Marine Division. The Marines didn't have their own observation aircraft, so the Army provided them airplane reconnaissance. Marine officers rode in the rear seat of the BirdDogs and handled communications with Marine units during fighter-bomber or naval gunfire missions.

16

Combat Flying

Unlike jet fighter-bombers, the planes that our pilots flew had no armor plate. Not even the seats were protected. The fuel tanks were neither self-sealing nor fire retardant. Bullets sliced through the one-sixteenth-of-an-inch aluminum skin like tissue paper. Yet to mark targets the pilots had to fly at unusually low altitudes, constantly exposed to enemy rifle and machine gun fire. Fortunately, as the war progressed, these safety deficiencies were corrected.

One of our first combat actions took place east of Dong Ha, a district headquarters located just south of the Vietnamese Demilitarized Zone (DMZ) in no-man's-land, a denuded transition area between South and North Vietnam.

Standard operating procedure was to deploy two aircraft at a time. The low plane, flying about a thousand feet above the ground, was directly involved in the military action that was taking place on the ground. The men on board were the eyes and ears of the ground commander. They could alert the commander to what was happening on the ground and reconnoiter areas difficult to reach on foot. They would check out possible enemy unit locations; look for signs of ambush, roadblocks or other enemy activity; adjust artillery and naval gunfire; and act as the liaison between widely deployed units.

The high-flying plane monitored the general development of the battle, while keeping the low plane in sight at all times. If the low plane was shot down, the high plane took over the mission.

I Corps was broken down into geographical tracts. The tracts were further subdivided into zones, and map overlays were developed for each zone. On these overlays we annotated every scrap of intelligence information that we could find. All kinds of demographic data were listed, such as population density and road traffic. Identifiable jungle trails were sketched in as were the location of rope bridges built over swiftly flowing streams and small rivers.

Any changes in the area, no matter how slight, were recorded and later collated for intelligence evaluation. Anyone planning a combat operation in the corps area, U.S. Marine or Vietnamese, first checked with the intelligence center at the 220th.

Some enemy activity required an immediate response from artillery, naval gunfire or fighter-bombers. A Cat Killer flying with a U.S. Marine observer in the back seat who located an enemy unit kept it under surveillance until the jets arrived. Then he marked the target with rockets.

The jets watched the impact and explosion of the marking rockets, rolled in for a pass, and blew the VC unit away. At least that was the plan. Once the target was destroyed, the jets flew back to their air bases to rearm and refuel, while their lucky pilots headed for the Officer's Club.

Cat Killers enjoyed no such luxury. When the jets went home, we stayed to search for new targets. Once a new target was identified, we again radioed for the fighter-bombers to fly out and attack them. The cycle repeated itself until the aircraft ran low on fuel. Only then did the crew return to home base. Three-hour missions were not unusual.

It was a dangerous, demanding job that jangled nerves and drained the flight crews of energy, stamina, and good judgment. There were mental and emotional limits as to how many such missions pilots and observers could fly in a week, or month. One day near Dong Ha, while I was flying low and my wing man was flying high, covering me, he suddenly radioed, "My aircraft's been hit . . . the Vietnamese observer is dead."

The observer was a bilingual Vietnamese officer riding in the back seat. His job was to communicate with Vietnamese military units on the ground.

"You mean he's been wounded?" I queried.

"No, Sir. He's dead. Dong Ha's only a few minutes away. It's got a short, dirt airstrip. Let's rendezvous there."

"Roger that. I'll meet you on the ground and I'll radio ahead and have someone meet us."

By the time I shut off the engine and climbed down from the cockpit, my wingman had already dismounted and was waiting for me.

Vietnamese are slightly built. They have little bone or muscle mass to absorb the impact of or to deflect bullets and shrapnel. A single machine-gun bullet had struck the officer's left arm halfway between the shoulder and elbow. It drilled a tunnel straight across the chest cavity, ripping apart the heart and other vital organs, and then exited through the right arm. The chest split open like a ripe melon, and bits of bone and tissue splattered against the back of the pilot's seat and all over the observer's compartment.

About then, a U.S. Signal Corps major and sergeant arrived in a military pickup truck. We grimly greeted each other. The other Cat Killer took the dead officer's feet and I grabbed his shoulders and we laid him in the back of the pickup. Then I took a clipboard and scraped the gore from the back of the pilot's seat and passenger compartment. Using a handkerchief and water from my canteen, I cleaned up more of it, but the smell of the blood and gore would not go away until the compartment was hosed down with water and disinfectant. Right then we didn't have time for those amenities.

The signal corps major spread a rubberized poncho over the back seat, heaved his considerable bulk in on top of it, and strapped himself into the seat. "I'm ready if you are," he said, "and I speak Vietnamese."

* * *

Just north of Danang is a rugged, mountainous ridgeline through which the French had blasted a railroad tunnel around the turn of the century. One day, as I flew from Phu Bai south to Quang Ngai, I heard one of my pilots call the South Vietnamese Operations and Intelligence Center located at Danang.

"Center, this is Cat Killer One-Three," he radioed.

"Roger, One-Three, this is Center, Go."

"There is a South Vietnamese train four miles north of the Danang tunnel. It's under fire, being attacked by VC. Scramble your Emergency Reaction Force and get them up here on the double."

"Roger, stand by . . . "

About two minutes passed during which I wrongly assumed that the Reaction Force was being alerted and dispatched.

"Cat Killer One-Three, this is Center. I have some information for you."

"Roger Center, ready to copy."

"Transportation Operations informs me that there is no train scheduled to be in that vicinity at this time, over."

There was a long pause followed by a dry chuckle. "Roger, Center, the train that is not scheduled to be here at this time is located four miles north of the Danang tunnel and is getting the daylights shot out of it. If you don't want it blown away, you'd better get some help up here quick."

This time the operations center ignored the printed train schedule and dispatched the standby reaction force of fighter-bombers, helicopters, and infantrymen. They drove off the VC attackers, inflicting heavy casualties on them. The train, its cargo, and passengers were rescued.

A few weeks later, I flew a borrowed UH-1 Bell helicopter from Qui Nhon to Saigon. UH-1s were used to ferry loads of 8 to 10 troops or carry supplies. The troops called them "Slicks" because they were unarmed except for a pair of door gunners, making the sides smooth compared to helicopter gunships, which had many weapons protruding in all directions.

The scheduled refueling stop was a field location south of Tuy Hoa. My brother, David, was stationed somewhere in the general area working as a paramedic with the 101st Airborne Division. I hoped to locate him and visit for a spell before continuing on to Saigon. According to army practice, siblings are not supposed to be in the same combat zone. The Army doesn't want a family to lose several children out of the same family, as happened during WWII, but both of us had signed waivers so we could be in the same war zone at the same time.

Why his division had selected this site, south of Tuy Hoa, for a heliport was less than obvious. As each helicopter landed, the downwash from the main rotor blades stirred up so much powdered red dust and sand that the pilot momentarily lost visual contact with the ground.

The only safe way to land was to flare the helicopter as little as possible when slowing down, and then quickly drive the skids deep into the dust. At least that was the theory. If I did everything perfectly, the helicopter skids would grip the ground before you became disoriented in the blowing red powder and crashed.

On short final approach, I noticed a soldier sitting on the stump of a palm tree not far from the place where I was about to land. He wore a bulletproof flak jacket, his M-16 rifle leaned against his left leg, and he was eating from a can of C rations with a white plastic spoon.

A steel helmet was jammed on the back of his head. Judging from the thick layer of dust clinging to him and his clothes, he had been sitting on that stump for an awfully long time. Perspiration had carved muddy lines down his dirt-caked face.

Breaking off the landing approach, I flew low over the area to give him time to move. Then climbing back up to altitude, I herded the Slick around in a lazy circle, and re-initiated the approach. The soldier didn't move.

As I landed, the Slick's rotor blades whipped up so much dust and dirt that it momentarily blocked out the sun. After engine shutdown, my crew and I waited until the rotors stopped turning. Then we were able to open the doors with a minimum of dust blowing in. Quickly we jumped down, and slammed the doors.

The soldier was still sitting on the palm tree stump, his right hand clamped over the mouth of a can of C rations, trying to keep the dust and dirt out. I trudged toward him through the red powder.

"How long have you been sitting here?" I asked.

He squinted up at me and, forming the words in his mouth before speaking, answered, "All day."

"Why don't you move when a helicopter lands?" I asked. "You enjoy getting dusted off?"

"No, Sir," he replied, smiling broadly. "Today is my last day in 'Nam.' My first sergeant told me to come down here to the helipad and wait. He said that sometime today a helicopter would fly in here bound for Saigon. I'm not going to leave this helipad until I get on that bird. My first sergeant told me that a 'copter' was coming and he never lies!" he added with conviction.

Slowly struggling to his feet, he awkwardly saluted and asked, "Sir, are you that helicopter?"

"No," I replied. "But in a couple of hours I'm flying on to Saigon. If you're still here when I get back, I'd be glad to give you a lift." He was and I did.

Sometimes when things seem confused, I think of that soldier covered with dust and grime sitting there on that stump. It helps me keep my perspective. Sometimes even when we stick to what seems right, we still end up with a mess on our hands.

For example, all units of the 220th Aviation Company flew daily combat missions. But one platoon in particular attracted more enemy ground fire than any other unit. Their aircraft came back from missions full of bullet holes. Worse, they burned out engines at an alarming rate. Even their propellers were nicked and gouged by enemy bullets.

As I look back on it, I realize that the reason they got shot up so badly and so often was that their area of operations was the most hostile. But at the time, my concern was that maintenance couldn't keep up with repairs.

Chief Behny's sheet metal repair specialists were working around the clock patching bullet holes and repairing combat damage. Keeping the planes flying put a strain on the aviation mechanics and the supply system.

So one day I called the offending unit commander in for a "straightening out," as my father would say. The captain was an exceptionally solid, competent aviator who was overly proud of his southern heritage.

To his surprise, instead of getting a commendation from me, he got a severe dressing down. "When you get back to your unit," I told him, "assemble your pilots and tell them that I'm tired of patching up their airplanes. Tell them they'll have to do a better job of avoiding enemy ground fire. Maintenance is running out of repair parts and sheet metal."

Properly admonished, he climbed back into his BirdDog, started up the engine, and roared down the runway, the propeller blade slicing its way through the thick, damp, hot tropical air.

An hour later, the field telephone rang in my tent.

"Sir," the captain said, "I've got a problem and I need help." His words were slurred.

"Yes?" I answered annoyed.

"I got back to the platoon, just as one of my pilots was landing. He had 23 bullet holes in his aircraft. Both gas tanks were punctured and gas was leaking from the aircraft's wings. In addition, the cockpit Plexiglas was shot out.

"Well, your words were fresh in my mind, so without thinking, I lit in to him. And I finished it off by telling him that if he ever did that again, he was grounded."

"Well, did he get the message?" I asked.

"He punched me square in the mouth."

"I'll have court martial papers drawn up right away!" I said.

"No, Sir, I don't blame him. His life is far more important than any old airplane. I should have been glad he came back alive, not bawled him out for getting the plane shot up."

Humbled, I asked, "How can I help?"

"Well, I've got a swollen lip, I can hardly talk, my ego's bruised, and I've been embarrassed in front of my men," he said, clearing his throat. "Help me find a way out of this mess as graciously as possible."

"OK," I said. "Have him pack his belongings, throw them in the back of a plane, and have him fly himself up here. I'll take care of it from there."

"Thank you, Sir, and we will try to be more careful." He rang off.

Well, smarty, I told myself, *you've really gummed this one up.*

I had Captain Quigley ready a courier flight to Qui Nhon while I phoned the battalion commander, Major Joe Rogers. "Joe," I said, "I need a special favor. I haven't time to explain all the details, but I have an officer who needs to go on R & R, today! Do you have any quotas available?"

"There's an Air Force flight out of Cam Ranh Bay for Hong Kong leaving tonight."

"Fine, I'm sending him down to you right away. Put him on that flight even if you have to do it under armed guard."

"It's that serious?"

"It's that serious."

"OK, I'll make it happen."

Ten days later, when the lieutenant returned from Hong Kong, he was a few thousand dollars poorer, but had a smile on his face that would brighten up the dense jungle at midnight.

"Well," I inquired, "what do you think I should do with you?"

"Sir, any punishment I get I deserve. I'm really sorry I punched the captain." His smile faded.

"So am I. First thing I want you to do is to apologize to him, publicly."

"Yes, Sir."

"Second, you're transferred to another unit."

"But I want to go back to my old unit," he complained.

With a wave of the hand I dismissed his protest, "Third, I'm putting a letter of reprimand in your file. If you stay out of trouble, it'll be torn up when you leave Vietnam. But if you so much as look cross-eyed at a senior officer, I'll court martial you on the spot. Understand?"

"Yes, Sir," he said, "and, Sir, thank you."

"Thank your captain," I said. "It was his idea."

Nearly a year had passed and my tour of combat duty with the 220th Aviation Company was coming to a close. So it was no surprise when one hot South East Asia day, orders arrived in the mail pouch. I was directed to report to Fort Leavenworth, Kansas, to attend the U.S. Army's CGSC.

17

Something Called Failure

For an Army officer to have a successful military career, he must go by way of the Command and General Staff College (CGSC) at Fort Leavenworth, Kansas. About 50 percent of Army officers are selected to attend the school. Those who do not make the cut face truncated careers followed by forced early retirement. Those who successfully complete it get assignments of increased responsibility, hopefully leading to promotion and distinguished careers.

On the first day of school, we students were told that it was critical to rank high in the class at graduation. Supposedly, class standing signaled to the Pentagon a student's potential for higher rank, for additional military schooling, and more prestigious assignments. At least that is what they told us.

Of course this was patently untrue. Advancement in the military, as in most institutions, depended on who your parents were, your source of commission, the type of jobs you had held, how well you performed them, as well as how well your bosses liked you and how well you played the Army's game.

If you were a West Point graduate you began at the top of the pecking order. The officers who had graduated from military academies such as the Virginia Military Institute or the Citadel formed the next level down. Next ranked graduates of ROTC programs followed by Officers Candidate School (OCS) graduates like myself, who started at the bottom of the picking order. This is probably as it should be, for if West Point officers didn't possess more potential than OCS graduates, then the nation's funding of military academies such as West Point was money poorly spent.

Before leaving Vietnam, I promised myself that when I returned home I'd put Char and the children first. In Vietnam I had put my country and the Army first, but this year, I felt, belonged to my family. Contrary to what the Army demanded, my studies at the Command and General Staff College were second on my list of priorities.

One day a note arrived from our son Jerry's fourth grade teacher. It said, "An urgent conference is needed as soon as possible. Please phone the school to set up an appointment."

Charlene and I called Jerry in from playing and asked him to explain the note. He said he could not. As far as he was concerned, school was going great and he liked his teacher just fine. Charlene scheduled a conference for the following week.

"Your son is not applying himself in school. He is hyperactive and often disrupts the class," said his teacher, an alert, serious-minded, and dedicated woman. "Something drastic has to be done, and quickly," she said. She stood five-five and had a soft, round face framed by straight, dark auburn hair. Carefully she chose her words, "Not only does he disrupt the class, he diverts the other children's attention and keeps them from learning."

We were meeting that evening with the teacher, the school psychologist, and the principal. The school psychologist suggested, "Perhaps the best course of action is to ignore him. This may be nothing more than an attention-getting device on his part. Once he sees that he's having no affect, he'll probably settle down."

Jerry's teacher exploded, "Ignore him? You've got to be kidding! No one ignores Jerry. When class begins, either I get immediate control of him or he takes over the class. I'd love to see you try to teach my class and ignore Jerry. He'd eat you for lunch."

"Enough!" said the burly principal. "The Currys weren't invited here to listen to our disagreements."

Turning to us, he said, "Major and Mrs. Curry, before you arrived, we decided to ask whether or not you'd agree to have your son psychologically evaluated, because until we know whether he's mentally capable of taking instruction and performing better than he does, we won't have a starting point."

"Certainly," Charlene agreed for both of us. "The sooner the better."

They recommended a private psychologist we would have to retain at our own expense. He turned out to be competent, pleasant, and easy to work with.

Through a lengthy series of tests, he established that Jerry was above average in intelligence. This gave us a badly needed frame of reference. In addition, we had him evaluated by a military psychiatrist. After another series of tests, he too concluded that there was nothing medically or mentally wrong with Jerry. This should have made us feel better. It didn't.

Both medical professionals had strongly hinted that the problem was us, the parents, not Jerry. The implication was that Char and I had failed in our parenting.

We reported the test results to Jerry's school and another conference was scheduled. Once again, the homeroom teacher took on the school psychologist, and the principal took on both of them. Soon the conference degenerated into confusion and name-calling. But in the end, the principal pulled it together.

"As you can see, it's a little unclear as to how we should proceed," he said. "But I think we are in agreement that Jerry does need help with his homework assignments. If he starts being successful there, perhaps it will encourage him in his class performance."

So that is how I became Jerry's private tutor. In the process, I discovered some complications. Jerry had loved his first grade teacher in Liberty, Pennsylvania, where he had started school. He had done well in that school. Then halfway through the year, after Charlene recovered from her ulcer surgery, we uprooted him and took him from Pennsylvania back to Washington State.

He successfully completed the remainder of first grade in Washington, but often complained that he missed his teacher back in Liberty. Second and third grades went reasonably well, but then I returned from Vietnam and uprooted Jerry again, when we brought him to Leavenworth.

Subconsciously Jerry concluded that schoolteachers and schools must not be important. If they were, they wouldn't be interrupted so often by moves from one city to another.

He compensated for these interruptions by attaching himself to a little friend, Tinky, a paper worm. A preschool teacher in Pusan, Korea, had taught Jerry how to fold strips of paper together in spring-like fashion, so they formed a long worm.

Each day Jerry carried Tinky to school in his book bag. He sat in the back of the room, opened his schoolbook, and propped it up on the desk in front of him. Then he would hunker down in his seat and pull out Tinky.

Tinky and Jerry, through the fantasy of an over active imagination, wound their way down little roads, or whatever else was in the picture book, deep into enchanted forests, much like Alice stepping through the looking glass. Once safely inside his fantasy world, Jerry and Tinky laughed, played and had a great time together. Neither Charlene nor I, nor his teacher knew what was going on behind that book.

Naively, I blocked out Jerry's homework assignments for a week at a time. Then I dictated them into a tape recorder, explaining to Jerry how to complete each one. At night when he finished working on his personally tailored, self-paced tape recording, he and I sat down at the kitchen table and measured the progress he had made that evening in math, English, spelling, reading, or writing.

Naturally, while Jerry was in his bedroom with the tape recorder running and the earphones on, he was playing with Tinky. So, for two or three hours each night, I "tutored" Jerry with dismal results, which caused all sorts of family conflict and frustration.

It got so bad that Charlene refused to remain in the apartment during tutoring sessions. She would go out to visit friends as soon as we started. I had to phone her and let her know when we were finished so she could return.

Only after the sessions with Jerry were over could I do my own CGSC homework. This year of spending dedicated, quality time with Charlene and the children, other than Jerry, was not working out as I had planned.

All year Jerry's school communicated with us by written notes and phone calls. A little progress would be made one week, followed by no progress the following week. Toward the end of the academic year, all of us involved in Jerry's education agreed to meet for a final conference to evaluate him academically.

His homeroom teacher began the meeting by saying that, "We are all pleased with Jerry's progress this past year."

"Yes," the psychologist chimed in, "he got off to a somewhat rocky start, but has finished quite well."

"Perhaps the key question is whether Jerry passed the fourth grade," Charlene said, trying to bring the conversation back to some semblance of reality.

I nodded.

Too quickly and a little defensively, his teacher replied, "Oh, clearly he should be passed on to the fifth grade."

"Yes," the psychologist added, "you should be very pleased. Obviously Jerry is achieving according to his ability."

I looked at Charlene who signaled harmony with what she knew I was about to say. "Mrs. Curry and I don't agree with you," I began. "We too have worked hard with Jerry all year and we are convinced that he's learned very little."

This statement got the psychologist's attention, "It is important that Jerry progress through school with his peer group," he said. "He's quite large for his age, you know. And if he were kept back, next year he would look quite out of place physically. It could seriously damage his self-esteem."

The subliminal message was that Char and I were being warned off. If we knew what was good for us, we'd submit to expert opinion.

"Well," I replied, "we respect your professional opinions. But as a father who has tutored his son all year, I can positively say that Jerry has failed the fourth grade, and Charlene and I feel strongly that he should repeat it."

The meeting degenerated into more argument than discussion and soon became an "us" against "them" confrontation. They wanted to pass Jerry on to the fifth grade. We wanted him retained in the fourth grade.

However, the principal appeared to be wavering. Finally, he said, "Most parents try to convince us that their children should be passed. This is the first time in my career as an educator that I've encountered parents who wanted their child failed. Tell me, what is it you hope to teach your son by failing him?"

"Doctor," I said, "I want to teach my son that there is something in life called *failure*. And I want him to learn it in the fourth grade. I don't want him to learn it when he's 30 years old.

"In the world we live in, no employer cares whether or not an employee has achieved to the best of their ability. The question is, did or did they not get the assigned job done right and on time. Achieving according to one's abilities is irrelevant!"

Charlene laid a calming hand on my arm.

The principal nodded, "I think I understand. Would you please excuse us while we have a private conference?"

"Certainly," we said, standing up to leave the room.

After a few minutes, the principal came out in to the hall, found us, and beckoned us back inside.

Thoughtfully he said, "Jerry will be retained in the fourth grade as you both requested. His school records will reflect that decision . . . and, good luck."

When we got back home, Jerry cheerfully asked, "How did the conference go?"

"Splendidly," I responded. "You did not pass."

He was stunned. So we sat with him and patiently explained as best we could.

Soon afterward, I finished the Army's CGSC and for the third time was posted to Germany. I was assigned duties in the Office of the Deputy Chief of Staff for Operations at Headquarters U.S. Army Europe in Heidelberg.

We moved to Germany and in early September I came home from work and found Jerry waiting for me. Neatly stacked on the kitchen table were his school books

"Dad," he said enthusiastically, "it's time for us to do my homework."

I thought for a minute, then sat down beside him and put my arm around his shoulders. "Son, together you and I attended fourth grade last year. But there is a difference. I passed and you didn't. "While you may not have learned much, I do know you did learn how to study. So I am confident that you can complete the fourth grade without my help. In fact, I insist on it."

Hopefully, that day Jerry began to understand that ultimately success or failure in life depended on him, not others. Somehow he managed to struggle through that school year on his own. His grades were not great, but they were not failing either.

In the fifth grade he did a little better. By the time he reached the eighth grade he was a slightly below average student. He finished high school in the middle of his class and went on to college, dropping out in his junior year. Ten years later Jerry returned to school and graduated from Virginia Commonwealth University.

What wasn't known then was that his problem was much more complicated than the psychologist, psychiatrist, his teachers, or even Charlene and I knew. Years later as an adult, he was diagnosed with a severe form of attention deficit disorder (ADD), among other medical problems, all of which responded well to treatment.

If there is a hero in this story, it is my son, Jerry. He is the one who persevered and succeeded despite the ignorance of his parents, doctors, and educators.

18

Racism Rears its Ugly Head

The last time we Currys flew to Europe it was on a propeller-driven airplane that refueled in Iceland and Shannon, Ireland, before continuing on to Frankfurt. This time we flew nonstop from New York to Frankfurt on a commercial jet. It was wonderful. We didn't miss the vibrating throbs of the old reciprocating engines a bit, nor the hours of watching black oil leaks slowly discolor the wings.

In my briefcase, tucked away beneath the seat, was a letter from the Pentagon. I'd been told to hand carry it to West Germany and to personally deliver it to the Personnel Office at U.S. Army Headquarters in Heidelberg.

The letter said, "Recommend that Lieutenant Colonel Jerry Curry be given command of an infantry battalion during his three-year tour of duty in West Germany."

Only half of the officers who graduated from the CGSC got these kinds of letters. It meant that I had successfully climbed over another hurdle in the Army's culling-out process—*or did it?*

In Heidelberg, I was assigned as a staff officer in the Office of the Deputy Chief of Staff for Operations. The office set Army aviation policy in Europe, did aviation war planning and approved construction of aviation facilities. It also coordinated and negotiated aviation and air space matters and agreements with the West German government's equivalent of the FAA.

After a month or so on the job, I carried the "Command Letter," as it was called, across the street to the Office of Personnel. There I was directed to a pudgy, truculent lieutenant colonel with a pockmarked face.

"You'll spend 18 months working here in Heidelberg," he lied, "and then another 18 months commanding a mechanized infantry battalion somewhere in Germany. Come back in a year or so and we'll talk about details."

Six months later, while visiting one of the Army's subordinate headquarters, VII Corps in Stuttgart, Germany, I dropped by the office of Big John McCleod who worked in the Corps Personnel Office.

"Jerry!" Big John exploded as I walked into his office. "Great to see you again!"

I was the only African American aviator on the Army Headquarters Aviation staff, and he was the only one on the VII Corps Aviation staff. John shot out a huge right hand that swallowed mine. How he shoehorned all that bulk into an airplane cockpit was a mystery to me.

"I've been hoping you would come down to our lowly headquarters for a visit," he said laughing. "I've been holding a classified, internal Corps memorandum to show you."

Digging into one of his desk drawers like a squirrel hunting for a lost acorn, he quickly recovered the memorandum and slid it to me across the desktop.

"Unknown to you, Jerry, one of your white classmates at Fort Leavenworth wrote his friend in the VII Corps aviation office, said some great things about you, and recommended that you be assigned to this headquarters. The Corps aviation officer requested that our personnel office review your file and make a recommendation as to whether or not you were good enough to be assigned to us."

I nodded.

"What you have in front of you is the personnel analysis that was done on you. Notice that the conclusion is that you are not qualified for the Corps staff because you have no experience with ground troops. Also notice that a white officer has been recommended for the job in your place because he has extensive ground troop experience."

The analysis was confusing, so John explained it.

"One of my jobs is to review the personnel files of all aviators being considered for assignment to VII Corps headquarters. But I was bypassed on this. This analysis was done secretly without my knowledge. It wasn't until a month after you were disapproved that I found out about the memo, quite by accident. Notice that it's stamped 'confidential.'"

I flipped back to the front page. Yes, it was classified confidential. Analyses like these were routine and seldom classified.

"So, Jerry, I confronted the officer who wrote the memo. He was stunned that I had seen it. 'This memo is a blatant lie,' I told him, 'Curry's record is full of ground assignments. He commanded an infantry company in Schweinfurt. He was in S-3 Operations at Fort Devens. With the Fourth Division he was on both the battalion and division staffs. He's been an acting infantry battalion commander. Don't tell me you're such a poor reader that you missed all of that in his records?'"

"'And what about this other officer who you say has so much troop experience? He doesn't have a single non-flying assignment, yet you recommended him over Curry who has tons of non-flying experience.'"

"What did he say?" I asked.

"Jerry, I caught him in a bald-faced lie and he knew it. Worse, the Corps aviation officer is no dummy. When he read the memo and looked at the personnel files, he too knew it was a lie. But he went along with it anyway."

"John, if I wasn't considered good enough to be assigned to VII Corps, so how did I get assigned to Army Headquarters?"

"I was so furious that I pulled a few strings of my own. Your boss, the Army aviation officer in Heidelberg, is a personal friend of mine. I used to work for him, and I saved his ass on a few occasions. He owes me.

"The first chance I got I flew to Heidelberg and showed him the memo and cashed in a few blue chips. He requested that you be assigned to his office at Army Headquarters."

"I'm in your debt forever, Big John. But what's really going on here? Why does anyone care if I get assigned to VII Corps headquarters?"

"Simple, you're a threat to the white officers because you can successfully compete with them. As you approach the top of the military pyramid, the good jobs become fewer and fewer and the competition for them becomes fiercer. So if they can secretly knock African Americans like you out of contention, they reduce the size of their own competition."

"I see. So from now on it's dog eat dog?"

"It always was. You just didn't recognize it."

"John, are you telling me that for the rest of my military career there will be hidden nuances, secret and dishonest memos, code words, and all sorts of plots hatched against me because of my race?"

"You can count on it, Jerry. This time they got caught. But you can be sure that these sorts of things go on routinely, and African Americans like you and me may never know why we got beat out of a choice assignment, until it's too late to do anything about it. The good news is that not all white officers are like this."

Back at Heidelberg, I toiled diligently for several more months then reported back to the personnel officer I had seen previously, and again handed him a copy of my Command Letter.

"There are six months left to serve on my 18 month tour here in Heidelberg," I said. "When my time on staff is up, which battalion do I get?"

"Sorry," he said, "I've been meaning to phone you for some time. Due to circumstances beyond my control, battalion commands have been filled up for the next two years. Unfortunately, you won't be staying in Germany that long. Perhaps when you return to the United States someone can find a battalion back there for you to command." He didn't look up at me.

With difficulty, I kept my temper under control. I knew he was lying. Bile bubbled up into my mouth, burning my throat. I appealed to his supervisor to no avail. With civility scarcely concealing contempt, they both lied, "Things change. Sorry we didn't notify you earlier, but we are quite busy you know. Hope you understand."

Because of my previous conversation with Big John McCleod I did understand, only too well. White officers who had arrived in Europe long after me had been deliberately advanced on the command list ahead of me.

Ella Wheeler Wilcox, the famous American poet once said that nothing is finally settled until it's settled right. These two personnel officers who were playing me for a fool didn't suspect that the matter was far from settled.

Serendipitously, I was ordered back to the Pentagon to participate in a two-week special study group updating the Army's European war plans. The trip could not have been more fortuitous.

In advance, I wrote to the Infantry Officer Assignments Branch in Washington requesting an appointment. After the study group completed its work in the Pentagon, I headed for their office.

The assignment's officer, a tall, lean, articulate lieutenant colonel, tried the predictable bureaucratic stall on me, but I wasn't in the mood.

"Either you level with me, or you're going to witness a performance no one in this building will ever forget," I half-shouted. "People will come out of their offices and stand in the halls just to see what's going on." One officer had already done so.

"You'd do that, wouldn't you?" he said grimly.

"Try me," I replied.

"OK," he nodded, "Come with me."

I followed him to a back office where he turned me over to Lieutenant Colonel Tom Tait, a pleasant, business-like officer of medium build with lots of red hair parted down the middle. My American Indian ancestors would have loved to have lifted a scalp from him to display as a trophy. I even gave a little thought to it myself.

"Cut to the quick and show him how you really do your job," the assignments officer directed, then frowned and left.

Tait nodded, "OK, my job is to select officers for special assignments." With that preamble completed, he dug my personnel file out of a metal filing cabinet drawer and rapidly thumbed through it.

He began with the day I enlisted in the Army as a private in March of 1951. In five minutes, he'd skimmed completely through my life. Just watching the rapidity of it all caused my palms to sweat.

Looking up at me, Tait asked, "In 1963 your career changed. Until then your efficiency reports were average. Suddenly in '63 they shot up to the top of the chart and have stayed there. What happened?"

I swallowed hard, thought for a few minutes, and then slowly put things together. In 1963 I had gone to work for Jack Doody. Jack had given me the highly desirable battalion operations job. Later, after I was promoted to major, he elevated me to battalion executive officer, his second in command. The next summer, Jack was placed on temporary duty as commander of an ROTC summer camp. Before leaving, he had persuaded the division commander to make me the acting battalion commander.

When the time came for me to be reassigned from his battalion, Jack saw to it that I got a career enhancing assignment in the Fourth Infantry Division's G-3 office. Because he was a winner, Jack wrote winner efficiency reports on his hard-working subordinates.

Tait listened to my story without comment, and then leafed back a few pages as though refreshing his memory on specific entries. Finally he tossed the folder aside, leaned back in his chair and folded his hands behind his head.

"Jerry, who should I select to attend the prestigious War College?" he rhetorically asked. "An officer like you who had only average ratings his first 10 years of military service, or someone who has had outstanding ratings since the day they graduated from West Point?"

It was a classic Catch-22. I was reaping the bitter fruits of institutional discrimination. Though Tait might be willing to help me break out of the institutional containment field, his actions were constrained by hard facts.

"Is there any hope?" I asked.

"Let me think . . . Yes," he finally replied. "But it's slim. You have serious problems to overcome.

"First, you are a minority. Don't ever underestimate the weight of that accident of birth. It will always color your Army career, no pun intended."

I smiled grimly, "No offense taken."

"Second, you're an ex-enlisted man. We in Army personnel don't think your 'kind' have much potential, at least when compared to a military academy or ROTC graduate.

"Third, you received your college degree by going to night school. Personally I'm quite impressed. But the Army personnel system doesn't look upon that as a very legitimate way to get a college education."

"Other than that, Mrs. Lincoln, how did you like the play?" I quipped.

He smiled, "You're learning. Perhaps I've overdramatized it. But I don't want you walking out of here thinking that if you just work hard, everything's going to be OK. It's not."

"You've got my undivided attention," I said. "Now, what do you recommend, if anything?"

Slowly, deliberately, Tait laid out the options. "In my opinion, and I want to stress that this is only my opinion and not that of the Department of the Army; even if you execute what

I suggest perfectly, it may not work." He got up from his chair and sat on the corner of the desk. "I may be wrong, but I think there are two things you have to do simultaneously if you want to compete with your peers.

"When you were going to night school at your own expense earning an under-graduate degree, your peers were going to graduate school getting masters or doctorates at government expense. While you weren't looking, the goal line moved." He frowned, "You sure you want to hear the rest of this?"

Numbly, I nodded.

"In my opinion you need a master's degree. We won't send you to graduate school because you're too old. It's too late in your career for the Army to get any use out of an advanced degree. So you have to go to night school and get one on your own."

"I'm tired of working for the Army all day, going to college at night, and spending my weekends writing papers and studying," I complained.

"You asked for my opinion and I gave it. What you decide to do with it is your choice. I'm not paid to be in the sympathy business. As for your more immediate problem, at best, there is less than a slim chance that you can pull it off. I'm talking about your getting command of a battalion.

"When you get back to Germany, the first thing you need to do is locate a division commander who is willing to ask for you by name. Even if you can find one, and even if he asks for you, Army Headquarters in Heidelberg will disapprove the request. Why? Because the personnel types in Heidelberg are taking care of their own. They want their friends to command battalions, not outsiders like you.

"And I can tell you without equivocation that you aren't one of their friends. But if you can get a general who is commanding a division in Europe to request that you be given a battalion in his division to command, and then you can figure out a way to get the request referred to this office, we'll approve it."

For the first time, the assignment's officer who had returned and stood silent and immobile had something to add.

"For the 'in' guys, the 'water walkers' as we call them, they don't have to go through all this. We just phone Heidelberg and tell them that Lieutenant Colonel so-and-so must command during his three-year tour in Germany. That's all there is to it."

"Let me be sure I understand what you're telling me," I said. "If I don't know a major general who is currently commanding a division in Europe well enough to get him to stick his neck out and request that I command one of his battalions, then I don't get a command?"

"That's right," Tait confirmed, standing up and offering his hand, "and for all practical purposes your military career will end."

I departed for Reagan National Airport hurt and angry. During the flight home, I rehashed that debilitating conversation again and again. The words of Nietzsche, not one of my favorites, kept coming to me, "When you look long into an abyss, the abyss looks into you."

I only knew one division commander, Major General George P. Seneff. He commanded the Third Infantry Division headquartered in Wuertzburg, Germany. During the Vietnam War, the 220th Aviation Company, Cat Killers, had been assigned to him toward the end of my tour. Seneff's personal combat exploits were the things of which legends were made. He had formed and commanded the Army's First Aviation Brigade, a celebrated and historic unit. I later had the honor of designing the shoulder patch and unit crests for the Brigade which were officially adopted by the Army and are still in use today.

Once back in Heidelberg, I phoned him, even though I felt uneasy about it. My years in the military had taught me that lieutenant colonels didn't call generals and ask for personal favors.

To my amazement, Seneff came on the phone. He listened carefully, and then directed me to put my request for battalion command in writing.

Meanwhile, Colonel John B. Stockton, an acquaintance for whom I had once worked and who was now retired from the Army and living in Europe, interceded with Seneff on my behalf. Stockton had served as Seneff's Deputy Commander of the First Aviation Brigade in Vietnam.

J.B., as he was called, was a colorful, forceful officer who was later portrayed as the helicopter air cavalry commander in the film *Apocalypse Now*. His Vietnam War exploits were tamed down for the movie.

No matter what General Seneff or I did, the Army Personnel Office in Heidelberg kept turning down the request. Finally, in disgust, Seneff sent his division chief of staff, Colonel Woody Shemwell, to Heidelberg to have it out with the personnel types face to face.

"Colonel," the diminutive Woody began, "it's time to fish or cut bait." The tip of his right finger stabbed the personnel officer's chest.

"Curry says the Department of the Army in the Pentagon approves his being assigned to Seneff's division to command a battalion. Your office keeps saying that's not so. One of you is not telling the truth."

"Sir, I'm sure that this is all just a little misunderstanding," the personnel officer explained.

Woody frowned. "The general's tired of playing this game, Colonel. He's got more important things to do with his time. So pick up the phone and dial Washington. Get the guy on the line who has final authority to say yes or no. I'm going to listen on the extension."

Dutifully the personnel officer placed the phone call and as soon as it went through, Colonel Shemwell took charge. "I'm General Seneff's chief of staff," he said to the people back in Washington. "The boss wants Lieutenant Colonel Curry approved to command the Second Battalion, 30th Infantry. Now, for the record, is or is not Curry cleared to command a battalion in General Seneff's division?"

"Yes, Department of the Army approves Curry for that battalion command assignment," the voice confirmed.

The now red-faced personnel officer eased the phone back onto its cradle.

"Do you have any questions Colonel?" Shemwell asked.

"No, Sir," the personnel officer stuttered.

"Then make it happen!" Shemwell ordered as he stomped out of the office and the personnel building.

That should have ended it, but it didn't. He and his fellow personnel officers tried every cheap trick and end-run they could devise to prevent my taking command. At every twist and turn Shemwell helped me beat them off. This continued up until the week before I reported to Seneff's division.

The day finally arrived when I took command of the Second Battalion, 30th Infantry Battalion. Phase One of the Tait plan was completed. Phase Two took a little longer. It meant that once again I had to attend college at night. This time it was at Boston University's overseas campus in Heidelberg.

It was not easy. Toward the end, I almost gave up. Twice a week, I had to drive two-and-a-half hours from Schweinfurt, where my battalion was located, to Heidelberg. In Heidelberg I went to school for three hours, then drove two-and-a-half back to Schweinfurt. Then I caught a few hours of sleep before standing reveille with the battalion. After two long years, the hours and lack of sleep began to get to me.

When I weakened, I thought of that dust-covered soldier sitting on the stump of a palm tree in Vietnam waiting for the helicopter to fly him to Saigon. Then I dug down a little deeper inside and continued the march.

Two exhausting years later, I completed a Master's Degree in International Relations. Graduation ceremonies were held in the King's Hall of Heidelberg Castle.

When I was driving back and forth between the Boston University campus in Heidelberg and my home base in Schweinfurt, I thought of many things. Race riots were not one of them. But sometimes events leap into the saddle all by themselves and ride away with us, and they have a nasty habit of choosing their own time.

19

Civil Wrongs

In 1964 President Lyndon Johnson forced a landmark Civil Rights bill through Congress. For my family and me, it meant that we could travel anywhere in the United States and be legally guaranteed the same public accommodations in hotels and restaurants that white families routinely enjoyed.

President Kennedy had given lip service to America's monumental civil rights struggle for justice and equal treatment, but President Johnson got the job done and signed it into law. Not since slavery was abolished has America undergone such a far-reaching cultural realignment as that precipitated by the multifaceted civil rights movement of the 1950s and 1960s.

It was comprised of many movements and many types of people all rolled into one. For example, there were black elites like Nobel Prize winner Dr. Ralph Bunch and General Fred Davison, the second black Army colonel in the history of America to reach the rank of brigadier general.

These black elites quietly, and with great dignity and difficulty, fought their way up through the Byzantine levels of governmental and military bureaucracy. Their noiseless achievements and contributions were reinforced by the civil rights movement's central message that all racial segregation is wrong, no matter how reasonably or cleverly packaged.

Great Americans like U.S. Supreme Court Justice Thurgood Marshall, then an attorney for the NAACP, painstakingly laid the solid legal foundation necessary for success in the difficult and dangerous fight for civil rights. This was crucial because, although the struggle primarily concerned black Americans, deliverance for all minorities would come through the NAACP's judicial success.

In Oliver Brown vs. the Board of Education of Topeka, Kansas, the Supreme Court of the United States ruled that the popular practice of "Separate but Equal" had no place in America's educational system. This forced Congress and the Executive Branch to move toward securing equal treatment for all Americans, regardless of race.

As in every mass movement, this one needed a spokesman, a unique voice to call the nation to arms, to fire America's imagination and spirit. History seems to indicate that whoever blows the trumpet pays an extreme price. Jefferson was right; the roots of America's tree of liberty are watered by the blood of its patriots.

Dr. Martin Luther King, Jr. became that leader, a voice in the wilderness crying out against injustice, bigotry, and prejudice. It was he who led the assault to pound down the doors of exclusion, flattening them into tables of inclusion. He made the ultimate sacrifice for justice.

Another group that helped America make this quantum leap was less politically correct. They were the African Americans whose motto was "Burn Baby Burn." Black militants like Rap Brown and Stokeley Carmichael, and radical fringe groups like the Black Panthers let white America know that if they didn't move quickly to end racial discrimination, it would be terminated by force. Their violent threats scared white people and played singularly well against Dr. King's reasoned nonviolence and the NAACP's studied determination to pursue peaceful legal remedies.

On television, the nation and the world watched American cities like Chicago, Detroit, and Los Angeles seethe and burn until they resembled war zones. Only a nation of fools could refuse the modest requests being made by the mainstream civil rights movements. The alternative was terror, arson, and anarchy. The nation and the world waited.

For Americans like us, living overseas, civil rights seemed to be the only subject foreigners wanted to discuss. The Europeans were scared. Each country had its own peculiar "minority" problems which no country had successfully resolved. European governments were looking to the United States to fashion a workable solution.

The U.S. military forces in Europe were certainly not immune to racial tension. There were black militants and professional race-baiting agitators within the U.S. military forces in Europe. Some had been drafted; others had enlisted in the armed forces for a host of unsavory reasons. Some had participated in race riots and the burning of neighborhoods in the United States. One I came to know well had been trained by the Black Panthers and allowed by the courts to enlist in the Army in lieu of a jail sentence.

They passed on their hatred, militancy, and rebellion to soldiers and military dependents. When soldiers influenced by these groups committed crimes, as they inevitably did, left-wing American Civil Liberties Union (ACLU) lawyers came from the United States and defended them. The ACLU types used the trials to advance their own political agendas.

In 1969, James H. Polk, the commanding general of all U.S. Army Forces in Europe, sensed that there was a racial storm brewing among our military forces. He directed 13 battalion commanders to come to his headquarters in Heidelberg, to explore ways to improve race relations.

At that time there were seven black lieutenant colonels commanding battalions in Germany. We were joined by six others who represented the hundreds of white battalion commanders.

For three days we discussed and assessed the racial climate and conflicts that appeared to be on the horizon. There were serious tensions between black and white soldiers. If swift actions weren't taken to ease the pressures, we all feared an explosion.

Jointly we drew up what we felt were a few common sense recommendations as to how the Army might mitigate the coming racial firestorm in Europe. Fundamentally we believed that the Army's best bet was to visibly increase black leadership at all levels of command. So our unanimous recommendation was that, on a crash basis, the U.S. Army significantly increase the numbers of black battalion and brigade commanders in Europe.

In the nearly two hundred year history of the American Army, there had never been a black division commander—anywhere. We wrote up our recommendations and signed them, feeling we had done the best we could. But adding a black division commander to the command structure in Europe was apparently out of the question.

The last evening of my stay in Heidelberg, I was invited to a cocktail party with a dozen or so fellow black officers who lived in Heidelberg and worked at Army headquarters. As the evening progressed, the conversation worked itself around to battalion command assignments. Many of the officers had received Command Letters similar to mine and each was waiting for his turn to command.

I told them my story, adding this gratuitous advice, "If you think the people in the personnel office are going to give you a fair shake, you probably believe in the tooth fairy. If you don't fight for battalion command, you're not going to get one."

One of them opined, "Jerry, you're paranoid. What happened to you was an aberration. It isn't going to happen to all of us."

"It's possible to be paranoid and still be right," I countered.

They would have none of it. Years later I learned that of the six lieutenant colonels with Command Letters that I had talked to that evening, only one went on to command a battalion. And that came about only after he threatened to file an official complaint with the Inspector General.

A few days after the meeting concluded, General Polk was briefed on the results of the meeting by Lieutenant Colonel Don Shaw, the headquarter's staff officer who had chaired it. Don, a delightful anglophile with a neat, dark-red, waxed cavalry officer handlebar mustache, until recently had been a fellow battalion commander with me in Schweinfurt.

Soon after briefing General Polk, he phoned, "Sorry, old man," Don began, "the commander-in-chief evinces little interest in the report and the recommendations on how to prevent racial conflict in the U.S. Army in Europe."

"You mean the meeting was a sham," I countered.

Don cleared his throat, "If you ask me, the report will probably be buried deep in some filing cabinet, never to see the light of day."

During the conference it never occurred to me that U.S. Army Europe was just going through the motions, just using us to pretend something real was being done to improve race relations between our soldiers, their families, and the German communities. To this day I'm convinced that my fellow battalion commanders who attended the conference with me, black and white, believed in what we were doing.

Several months later, when the race riots broke out, the number of black battalion commanders in U.S. Army Europe had decreased from seven to six. Perhaps if our recommendations had been implemented and the number of black commanders been increased, the racial crisis would not have been so severe.

20

Civil Rights

My battalion, the second of the 30th Infantry, was conducting field training in a forest near Schweinfurt. Black night had gently drawn down its curtain as the companies maneuvered to gain tactical advantage over each other.

"Is this Colonel Curry?" the voice on the radio urgently queried.

"Roger," I replied. For security purposes in Soviet-dominated Europe, it was forbidden to say a commander's name in the clear over a tactical radio.

"Sir, this is the brigade duty officer. Colonel Wickham says that you are to turn your battalion over to your executive officer, Major Jon Mills. You, alone, are to return back to headquarters immediately. Your battalion is to remain in the field overnight and return tomorrow."

"This is crazy. Are you certain the brigade commander is ordering me to return without my battalion?"

"Sir, I know it's unusual, but that's what the colonel told me to tell you. And he asks you to hurry!"

"I'm on the way," I assured him, motioning for Major Mills, who had been listening in.

The Jeep ride back to Ledward Barracks took less than an hour. The closer I got to the city, the more troubled and perplexed I became. As we neared the Kaserne, I radioed ahead for more information.

"Sorry, Sir," the duty officer replied. "My instructions are not to discuss the matter over the radio."

My driver swung the Jeep to the right through the Kaserne gate. The parade ground in front of Brigade Headquarters was awash with hundreds of restless, milling soldiers. The Jeep's headlights showed the crowd to be African American. A Military Police Officer stepped out of the shadows into the street and motioned us to the curb.

"Sir, better leave your vehicle here where we can protect it," he said saluting. "Colonel Wickham is waiting for you inside Brigade Headquarters."

As I pushed my way through the milling mass of hostile soldiers, I thought back to other times when I had waded through similar crowds. The first time had been with my father outside a United Steel Worker Union Hall during a strike vote. Emotions flared, tempers were high, and anyone resisting union orders got his head busted.

Then there had been the time in Korea when I got caught in a mob of thousands of antigovernment demonstrators in the southwestern city of Kwang-Ju. The crowd pressed against me so tightly that I was swept up off my feet, and my head and shoulders popped up above the swirling sea of humanity like toothpaste squirting from a tube. The same law of physics that pushed me up pushed down small Korean women and children. They died where they fell, squashed under thousands of stomping, grinding feet.

Fortunately, a Korean Army officer spotted me being carried along by the crowd. He formed a platoon of Korean military police into a flying wedge. Ruthlessly wielding oversized nightsticks, they beat their way through the seething mass of demonstrators. Skulls cracked with sickening "thunks." Relentlessly the MPs bore down on my position, extricated me, and on their shoulders whisked me off to safety.

As I mounted the granite steps of Brigade Headquarters, I took a last look back at the churning mob swirling around the parade ground, just to fix the sight in my memory. Then I pushed through the huge, heavy wooden doors. *The crowd might yet be persuadable*, I thought, but I also knew that soon events themselves would mount the wild horse.

Colonel John Wickham, the brigade commander was an intelligent, smallish West Point graduate, as well as a first-rate officer and gentleman who later became Army Chief of Staff.

John was sitting in his large, high-ceilinged German military office behind a huge oak desk looking puzzled and feeling humiliated. Anguish and strain were hard upon his face. He had sustained defeat without combat.

"I just don't understand," he muttered more to the office walls than to me. "I've tried to reason with them, but they ignore me. They refuse to disperse. They don't respond to threats or orders. Nothing I do or say seems to affect them. It's almost like I don't exist."

"What do they want?" I asked.

"That's the frustrating part. They don't seem to know. Some of your fellow battalion commanders have tried talking to them through bull horns and so have the military police." Lines of worry and weariness showed around his eyes. "If we don't get control soon, I'll have to use force . . . and who knows where that will lead?"

"Mind if I try?" I asked.

"No, that's why I called you in from the field. But I must confess that I've just about given up hope of a peaceful resolution."

I saluted, dropped my side arm and steel helmet on a chair, and stepped to the door. Along the far boundary of the parade ground and standing in the cobblestone street were the military police. Like Colonel Wickham and me, they also were nervous and unsure. They had steeled themselves for the inevitable clash if orders came to clear the area and restore order.

To exist, an army must maintain military discipline. Military Police know from training and bitter experience that they are the final instruments which maintain that discipline. So if the orders came, they were prepared to execute them no matter what, even though they recognized the faces of many of their friends in the unruly mass. They stood their ground, but their feelings reached out to touch the hostility of their fellow soldiers.

It was dark and since I wasn't wearing a helmet, the soldiers couldn't make out my lieutenant colonel rank until I was within touching distance. By the time they recognized me, I had moved beyond them, and so I arrived at the center of the crowd unimpeded.

Standing there on the hood of a Jeep was a black soldier loudly shouting inanities. He was entertaining the crowd, much as a clown does at a circus. Quickly I climbed up on top of the Jeep and stood beside him. When he tried to speak, I spoke louder. If he shouted, I shouted louder. What I was saying was gibberish, but that didn't matter. My father had been a leader in the labor union. He had taught me that mobs listen with their emotions, not their minds. They respond to passion, not reason. It was a crapshoot, but I decided to make the most of it.

After a few minutes, the soldier became so frustrated that he jumped down and pushed his way through the crowd. I had the mob's attention, but I knew it wouldn't last for long. So I shouted that if they would select a few men to represent them, I guaranteed that Colonel Wickham would immediately meet with them and honestly respond to their complaints and grievances.

After a few threats and a lot of haranguing on my part, a dozen of them followed me up the cold stone steps of the headquarters building. Simultaneously, the MPs slowly and carefully moved in and dispersed the crowd.

Colonel Wickham talked with the soldiers' representatives most of the night. In the end, complaints seemed to center around two points: it took longer for minorities in the brigade to get promoted than it did for white soldiers; and white soldiers received less severe sentences for committing the same offenses as minorities. Investigation later proved both allegations were essentially correct.

Wickham and his boss, Brigadier General Charles Simmons, took direct, positive action. This led to active cooperation from officers and enlisted men of all races, as well as their families. Legitimate grievances were addressed and, for the most part, satisfactorily resolved.

After a few more months of tense racial unrest and confrontations, things started settling down. Local German officials and businessmen cooperated. At first they didn't want to help, but General Simmons pointed out that if the soldiers got out of control, they just might decide to burn down the city. From then on he had the Germans' rapt attention and willing cooperation. One result was that the Germans abolished racial segregation in their restaurants and clubs.

Toward the end of that warm summer, the American military community leased a large German beer tent which seated a couple of hundred people, and set it up in the middle of a grassy area between two enlisted barracks. Soldiers came to the "Fest" in droves, bringing their wives, children, and German girlfriends. Everyone was ready to party, and soft drinks and beer flowed. Mountains of German *wurst* were consumed while a lively German "oomph-pa" band played German folk music and drinking songs.

We were having such a wonderful time that we forgot about the professional racial agitators who were malevolently circulated among us. It was a huge mistake for those of us in leadership.

Seated around long picnic tables, our soldiers, black and white and every color in between, had a grand time eating and drinking together and just being good Americans. We felt that the racial tensions and unrest of the past several months were finally behind us.

Suddenly a short, black soldier ran from the far end of the tent toward the band platform screaming obscenities. He bullied his way across the dance floor, knocking one couple completely off their feet. Leaping onto the platform, he jerked the microphone out of the hands of the German singer and screamed, "Did you hear what that white S.O.B. just called me?"

Everyone looked up. Dramatically, he gestured toward a timid-looking white soldier who was quietly seated at a table near the band platform. Lunging from the stage, he took three quick steps and smashed his fist into the unsuspecting white soldier's mouth, splitting his lip. Blood splattered all over the tablecloth and floor.

Stunned and hurt, the white soldier tumbled off the bench onto the floor. White soldiers at his table leaped to his defense. Black soldiers jumped to the defense of the agitator. The tent exploded in curses and swinging fists. It took half an hour for the military police to bring the melee under control. But the riot that day was only a Pyrrhic victory for evil. To everyone's credit, tempers cooled quickly. Intuitively, the soldiers rightly guessed that they had been shamelessly manipulated. Racial warfare in Schweinfurt was over. This deliberately concocted disturbance signaled the final catharsis.

For me the events in that beer tent raised broader questions, ones that tennis great Arthur Ashe seemed to understand intuitively as he wrote in his exceptional book, *Days of Grace*:

> We were once a people of dignity and morality; we wanted the world to be fair to us, and we tried, on the whole, to be fair to the world. He said that for some Black Americans, revenge and getting even had replaced morality and justice.

* * *

One day the phone in my office rang and a voice said, "This is the Army personnel office in the Pentagon. When you leave Germany, you'll be assigned to command another battalion in Korea, on the DMZ."

"Do I have any other options?" I asked.

"Yes, you can go back to Vietnam, but I must warn you that we can't guarantee you battalion command over there. You could end up as an advisor to some small Vietnamese unit out in the jungle."

"I'll take my chances," I said. "Assign me back to Vietnam. If I have to be separated from my family for a whole year, at least let it be for a good cause. Besides, it's the only war we've got."

My decision was based on the old military tradition of, "Go to the sound of the guns." Going to peacetime Korea would be like asking a first string NFL player to suit up and sit on the bench all season.

One glorious day soon after the phone call, five hundred officers and men from the Second Battalion, 30th Infantry lined up in formation for a final command inspection. It was the warm, kind summer of 1970.

How tall, proud, and erect the men looked with their sergeants and officers standing in front of each platoon and company. The creases in their khaki uniform trousers were razor sharp, haircuts neat, the brass on their collars and belt buckles polished and gleaming bright. Even the carefully manicured grass of the parade ground seemed to be standing unusually tall and green that day.

As I halted in front of each soldier, they snatched their rifles up from beside their right legs, spun them through a series of snappy movements, and presented them to me for inspection. Each weapon was meticulously cleaned, carefully oiled, and so shiny that the sun glinted along their blue metal barrels.

As I paused in front of a particularly outstanding soldier who was wearing an unusually sharp uniform and presented to me an immaculate rifle, I casually asked, "Soldier, how long have you been a member of this battalion?"

"Sir," he snapped in a clipped military voice, "I have been assigned to this battalion for two years and I am proud of it."

With pleasure I took his rifle, inspected it, and returned it to him. "Do you know who I am?" I asked, almost as an afterthought. Since the question was rhetorical, I moved to inspect the next soldier in line.

As I stepped past him, the soldier confidently shouted after me, "Sir, I don't know who you are. But you are not my battalion commander!"

His belated answer caused me to chuckle. He had worked for me personally for two years and still did not know me! I had been his commander for a year and a half. A neatly framed picture of me hung on the bulletin board of every company and platoon in the battalion, as required by Army policy.

Not only that, but I had been prominently featured in the newspapers as a "hero" who had helped diffuse race riots during a very tence time for the U.S. Army in Europe, yet he still did not know me by sight. I realized that there were some soldiers we commanders were never going to reach, no matter how hard we tried.

21

The 41st ARVN Regiment

In June 1970, on a day blanketed by stratus clouds, Charlene and I, and our four children flew from Frankfurt to New Jersey on a military charter aircraft. We landed, took a sweltering ride across town in two station wagons loaded with 26 pieces of luggage, and arrived at the Port of Bayonne. There, we picked up the family Volkswagen van and Charlene's Fiat Spyder convertible, which I had given her the year before as a birthday present.

Our two-car convoy crept west along the Pennsylvania Turnpike towards McKeesport. Charlene hadn't slept much on the plane, so every few miles she started to nod off. The children made a game of watching until her eyelids drooped, then gleefully pouncing on her.

On a scale of one to ten, our visit to McKeesport after three years of living in Germany was a 15. During the stay my mother, a Presbyterian minister by the name of Jack Kennedy, and a friend named Fred Shawl prayed with us to be filled with the Holy Spirit. That prayer profoundly affected the rest of our lives.

Before the prayer we thought we were Christians; after the prayer we knew we were. There was a new, deep certainty within us. Then all too quickly it was time to move on.

After loading the cars with luggage, and saying tearful goodbyes, we once again drove west. Columbus, Ohio was closely followed by

Indianapolis, and soon St. Louis was behind us. The monotonous landscape of Western Kansas hurried us on toward Colorado.

The air conditioners in our VW Bus and Fiat Spyder, built to operate in cool European climates, were overwhelmed by the heat of the American Plains. Charlene grew faint; the children became hot, weary, and irritable. Late one hot, rain-squally afternoon, with multicolored storm clouds sweeping up past 20,000 feet, we crested the eastern approach to the Rocky Mountains and descended the long, undulating slopes that abruptly end at Colorado Springs—our final destination.

Across Monument Creek to the west towered the eastern flank of the Rockies. Suddenly, a red sun broke through ragged holes in lightning-filled storm clouds and bounced shafts of light off the eastern slopes of Cheyenne Mountain, the rugged guardian of the city's westward passage. The sun's rays gloriously stretched from sky to earth, as though spun from spools of angel hair.

The magnificent western landscape paintings of Wilson Hurley, that we had so long enjoyed in magazines, instantly sprang to life before us, and from that magical moment on, we knew we would always love Colorado.

In no time at all we rented a house in a subdivision called Skyway and quickly arranged for our household goods to be delivered. Fortunately, they had already arrived from Germany. At the local animal shelter, we bought 13-year-old Jerry a long-promised puppy. He was all paws and nose, and insisted on licking everyone's face. Jerry named him Leo.

With the house hastily settled and the children enrolled in school, I once again prepared to go off to war. Tearfully we said goodbye, hugged, kissed, and cried. I promised to write often. It was a difficult parting. We both felt that this tour in Vietnam would be harder and more dangerous than the previous one. We were right.

When I arrived in Vietnam and reported to U.S. Army Headquarters in Saigon, those processing me knowingly shook their heads.

My assignment was to a South Vietnamese fire base in the Binh Dinh Province. For decades, this province had been well known for Viet Cong (VC) and North Vietnamese Army (NVA) activity.

Saigon's population had swelled during the war to over two million. It was South Vietnam's chief port, major industrial center, and capital city. Overall, the population of South Vietnam was about 16 million. Most of them lived in the fertile Mekong River Delta within a 50-mile radius of Saigon.

A few days after my arrival and four hundred air miles later, I helicoptered into Landing Zone Crystal. From the air, the landing zone looked about the size of a water lily pad. This was to be my home for the next year. The U.S. Army helicopter pilot who flew me in didn't believe that I was going to stay. He knew the place for what it was, a flyspeck of an outpost plopped down square in the middle of a sea of VC.

A tall, wiry warrant officer about 30 years old, he sported a shock of unruly red hair atop a hard boned face. "Colonel," he spat a stream of tobacco juice out the rolled-down Plexiglas window past me, "I'll keep the helicopter sitting right here on the pad with the rotor blades turning for 10 minutes—in case you get smart and decide to fly out of this death trap."

He bottomed the collective pitch, rolled off the throttle a tad, and cinched up the lock collar. That would keep the helicopter rotor blades turning, hands off, without speeding up or slowing down. He obviously thought I'd lost my mind and made no effort to hide it. As I threw my gear from the helicopter into the swirling red dust stirred up by the helicopter's rotor blades, he shouted after me, "Colonel, I wouldn't stay here for a million dollars in gold!"

That suggestion has real merit, I thought.

Landing Zone Crystal was the command post of the South Vietnamese Army's 41st ARVN Regiment. ARVN stood for Army of Viet Nam and was the acronym we used for the South Vietnamese Army. The regiment was commanded by Colonel Vy. He was five-four or so in combat boots and perfectly proportioned. Despite his tiny size—he weighed only about 130 pounds—he was a brave and honorable officer. He had been a paratrooper in the French Colonial Army. Between 1946 and 1954, the French forces had fought and lost the Indochinese War. Over 35,000 Frenchmen were killed in that war, and another 48,000 were wounded.

A gentle and thoughtful man, Vy had a scholar's face, quiet dignity, and great inner strength. Only his dark brown, almost black eyes bore evidence of having witnessed too much pain, suffering, and death.

In 1954, the French withdrew their military forces from Vietnam. Over the next year, the South Vietnamese military had fought on against the North Vietnamese, who continuously broke the terms of the previously agreed armistice with France and South Vietnam by infiltrating regular army forces into South Vietnam. In 1955, the South Vietnamese requested and received noncombatant U.S. advisors. In 1961, President Kennedy escalated the war by authorizing U.S. Army combat arms advisors.

In April 1954, as a sergeant in the French Colonial Army, Colonel Vy had volunteered to parachute into the living hell of the French Dien Bien Phu fortress. Dien Bien Phu was an avoidable disaster that, by accident, became the decisive battle of the Indochinese War.

General Henri Navarre personally selected the location that was to become France's humiliation. An isolated, forsaken outpost in western North Vietnam near the Laotian border, Dien Bien Phu had no tactical or strategic significance. It simply existed.

General Navarre, for reasons he was never able to satisfactorily explain, selected the location, garrisoned it, and dared the North Vietnamese Army, the Viet Minh, to come fight. They did. Forty thousand of them. Following his instructions, the French forces had dug in their positions on a narrow, elliptical plain at an elevation of only 1200 feet. The communist Viet Minh occupied the surrounding mountain peaks. This forced the French artillery to fire almost straight up, while the Viet Minh artillery could fire nearly straight down. Obviously, the Viet Minh won.

Of the defending French forces, 25 percent were French Regular Army troops, another 25 percent were French Foreign Legion, 20 percent were French African troops and 30 percent were South Vietnamese regulars, which included Sergeant Vy's parachute battalion.

The end of the tragic, gallant, magnificent Dien Bien Phu affair is best told by the French historian, Dr. Bernard Fall: "As the night fell over Dien Bien Phu that Friday evening, May 7, 1954, the men of the Third Battalion of the 13th Foreign Legion Half-Brigade could see the waves of the enemy infantry surge toward them." The battalion prepared to meet the enemy by providing as best they could for their wounded and destroying all unneeded supplies and weapons. Finally, Colonel Lalande had his soldiers fix their bayonets to their rifles and led them in one final charge against the enemy, "Six hundred French forces against 40,000 Viet Minh."

Following this debacle, the spirit and political will of France was broken. They were no longer willing to fight the war through to a successful conclusion. When the war ended, Sergeant Vy was repatriated back to South Vietnam.

After a few disappointing weeks as Colonel Vy's intrepid American advisor, I took him aside and respectfully pointed out some of the regiment's tactical shortcomings.

"Colonel," I began, "for an old combat veteran like you it must be painfully obvious that your troops desperately need more training." Meekly he nodded, yes.

"Colonel Vy, your troops are a tactical disaster. The first time they get involved in a major fight with the enemy, they'll probably be massacred."

"It is most unfortunate that you feel that way, Colonel Curry," he replied. "Perhaps you could help me develop some kind of tactical training program for the regiment?"

"Certainly," I said, "if that's what you'd like me to do."

Immediately I set about designing a vigorous combat training program aimed at the lowest unit level, the squad. I was pleasantly surprised at how rapidly and positively the ARVN soldiers responded. Squad operations and ambushes, set to kill VC guerrillas, resulted in consistent successes. So after only a few weeks, the regiment was able to raise its training to the platoon level.

Eagerly, I stepped up the difficulty of the training. Soon we were conducting company- and battalion-sized operations. The 41st ARVN's military professionalism in combat operations couldn't have been better. They were successful in driving many VC units out of the area.

The graduation ceremony from this six-month intensive combat retraining was a full-scale regimental sweep of an endemically troubled area adjacent the South China Sea. For this, Colonel Vy used a classic "hammer and anvil" tactic.

"The ocean will serve as the immovable object," Vy explained. "We will strike hard, with the battalions conducting simultaneous sweeps through the jungle that borders the coast."

"Like beaters on a tiger hunt," I observed.

He smiled broadly, "Yes, and the VC will be flushed from their hiding places. My infantry battalions will hunt them down or drive them into the sea. Standing off the beach will be South Vietnamese naval patrol craft. Orbiting overhead will be U.S. Army reconnaissance aircraft."

The tricky part of the operation was knowing exactly where to insert the infantry battalions. Only then could they successfully execute their sweeps to drive the enemy toward the South China Sea. To help us, the U.S. Army Chemical Corps loaned us a team of "people sniffers."

"Here's how it works," the slight, wiry, sunburned technician explained. "You hang these big, black metal boxes out the door of your helicopter. Then you get a pilot foolhardy enough to fly his chopper low, skimming along just above the treetops," he smiled mischievously. "Chemicals are used to compare and contrast the air that flows through the boxes. People's bodies give off distinct chemical odors that are clearly detectable. So if the box gets a nose full of people smells, it tells us where they are. My part is easy, colonel, providing we don't get shot down. The hard part is yours, killing the VC after we locate them."

"You and your 'sniffers' ever make mistakes?" I asked.

"Sure, but not often. Every once in a while, a herd of water buffalo confuses things, but I can sort that out quickly."

We shook hands, "OK, Sergeant, you got yourself a deal!"

Like me, Vy had never seen a "sniffer" operate before. But unlike me, he was highly skeptical. We found the Chemical Corps sergeant to be right, and that day the 41st ARVN broke the back of VC operating in that part of the coastal region of Binh Dinh Province.

The VC that the ARVN didn't kill outright, they drove out onto the white sand beaches. This gave the VC the choice of surrendering, or getting slaughtered by helicopter gunships. But it wasn't all one-sided; it never is. The 41st ARVN also suffered casualties.

At the conclusion of the fight, the helicopter deposited Vy and me atop one of the small hills that mutely overlooked the broad ocean beaches. On foot, we threaded our way down the gentle sandy slopes picking a path that avoided the numerous clusters of cactus plants.

North of us lay a horseshoe-shaped natural harbor, that was home to a South Vietnamese fishing village. Bare-bottomed children in faded, colored shirts skipped along beside us. Vy and I stepped around the old women and preteen girls who squatted on their heels providing day care for the village's children.

At the mouth of the harbor, as the sun drew down below the palm trees, fishermen sculled their boats toward shore. Gracefully, their bodies rocked back and forth, propelling the fishing craft homeward. Like magicians they timed their approach so perfectly that the boat bottoms caught the last large breakers just as they approached land, propelling them far up the beach.

Still higher up on the beach squatted small clusters of fishermen. Using their toes as well as their hands, they stretched out their tired old fishnets for examination, and mended them by hand with spools of cord.

As was the custom, a smiling parade of village elders led by the village chief, came to greet us. *Strange*, I thought. Less than half an hour ago VC were being killed on this same beach. Yet, the villagers laughed and went about their affairs as if nothing had happened. I didn't dwell on the fact that they would just as happily have welcomed the VC had we lost.

The village chief had a chin that jutted forward like that of a Punch and Judy puppet. Midway along the bottom of his left jaw, down low toward his overly long neck, was a purple-black mole the size of a thimble. Several strands of hair, each about five inches long, sprouted from the mole. No two hairs grew in the same direction. Drawing back his lips over protruding teeth, he invited us to join him for dinner. We did. It was a delicious meal of rice and fresh fish.

Afterward, when we were alone, Vy asked, "When are you being transferred to corps headquarters?" Even though his regiment's victory was cause for celebration, he sounded sad. Perhaps he was thinking of the casualties we had suffered. Warmly I reassured him, "I'm not being transferred."

"Oh, yes," he replied knowingly. "All senior U.S. regimental advisors get transferred after six months. Soon it will be time for you to go. We will throw you a big party."

"That is very kind," I replied. "But I have asked not to be transferred. I will spend the entire year with you and the regiment."

Dusk chased after the sun leaving darkness behind to cover us until morning. Now night stars popped out of the thick velvet sky. We burrowed into the sand and slept, soldiers keeping guard.

After this victory, 41st ARVN combat operations continued in high gear. Continuously, the regiment located and destroyed well-entrenched VC units. *Perhaps Binh Dinh Province will be pacified after all*, I mused.

Often during those weeks, Vy returned to the subject of my departure. He seemed obsessed with it. Finally one evening at supper, he desperately blurted out, "Colonel Curry, you must not stay here as my advisor."

"Don't look so grim, colonel," I said. "I am staying. You can count on it. The last few months your regiment has killed more VC, captured more enemy weapons, and won more battles than any other ARVN regiment in the corps. I really mean it when I say that I am proud to serve with you."

Sadly, he replied, "Thank you, my friend. I appreciate your sincerity. But I must beg you to leave as quickly as possible. If you do not," his head dropped, "I shall be relieved of my command."

Seeing the shock on my face, he hastily added, "You have proven to be more like a brother than an advisor." Tears formed in the corners of his eyes. "And because of that, I owe you a full explanation, but you must swear to secrecy!"

I agreed and, as Alice in Wonderland would have said, "Curiouser and curiouser." "We Vietnamese military commanders work on a cycle," he explained. "When a new U.S. advisor arrives, I instruct the regiment to pretend that it doesn't know how to conduct combat operations. The advisor always prescribes extensive retraining, just as you did when you arrived."

He caught up my hand in one of his. It was surprising how soft it was to the touch. For an Asian, male hand-holding is a sign of bonding, but for an American like me, it was unnerving.

"Are you saying that all the U.S. advisors who leave Vietnamese units after six or seven months, and who think that they have accomplished so much, have in reality been manipulated?"

"Yes," he slowly explained. "So long as elementary training and squad-level combat operations are taking place, the regiment suffers few casualties. When combat actions are stepped up, more of my soldiers are killed or wounded." His dark brown eyes pleaded for understanding.

"By staying here past the usual six months tour of duty, you have kept the regiment's combat operations at the highest level we have ever experienced. Daily, we fight the VC and mostly we win. But the regiment's cumulative casualties are the highest the division has ever sustained."

A tear trickled down one cheek. "To my superiors, keeping casualties low is more important than killing VC. If I do not immediately reduce the numbers of our casualties, I will be relieved of my command."

I shook my head in disbelief.

"Do you see my dilemma?" he begged. "Will you help me?"

"Let me be sure I understand. The United States of America is risking the lives of its sons and daughters and spending exorbitant amounts of U.S. taxpayers' money, to help South Vietnam win your war as quickly as possible, so you can preserve your nation's freedom. But your commanders' objective is to minimize Vietnamese military casualties?"

"Precisely."

"When I volunteered to extend my stay here from six months to a full year, and to continue risking my life as your advisor, I thought I was helping you."

"Yes," he nodded.

"Instead, I am about to get you relieved of your command?"

Again, he nodded, "Unfortunately, that is the Vietnamese way. I hope you understand."

"If I agree to your request, the VC in this province will never be defeated?"

"That is right."

"The war will go on and on with no end in sight."

"Yes."

"You understand that this undermines the whole purpose of my country's sending military forces here to help your country?"

"That may be true," he confessed dropping his eyes.

"This is too much for one day," I said confused. "Let's talk about it tomorrow." That night I slept little and prayed a lot. My inner conflict beggared description. All night my mind vacillated back and forth like a teeter-totter.

Early the next morning, I met with my friend and agreed not to insist on continuous large-scale combat operations, and at a minimum he promised to keep his unit's combat actions at a level high enough to exceed that of all the other ARVN regiments in the corps.

We both kept our word. That is, until fighting erupted around FB-6.

1966 | *Aviation Company in formation at their home base at Hue Phu Bai near the North/South Vietnam Demilitarized Zone*

1971 | *Jerry pausing at a jungle stream*

1971 | Jerry on a quiet day at Landing Zone Crystal

1972 | The Curry Family at the U.S. Army Command and General Staff College at Fort Leavenworth, Kansas

1972 | *The Curry family at the Hall of Heroes in the Pentagon*

Jerry's "Combat Bible" that saved his life—the piece of shrapnel still imbedded inside its worn pages.

1972 | *Aerial view of FB-6. Artillery has stripped the area of vegetation*

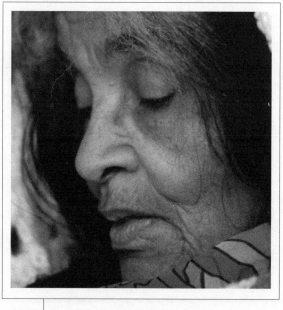

1977 | *Jerry Curry's paternal grandmother, Rose Anna Campbell*

1980 | *Jerry standing beside his "Cobra" helicopter gunship*

1981 | *Jerry as Press Secretary to Secretary of Defense Caspar Weinberger*

1981 | *Jerry with friend Clint Eastwood*

1981 | *Jerry as Commander of troops celebrating General George Washington's victory at Yorktown, Virginia*

1981 | *Jerry Curry standing with President Reagan*

1981 | *Jerry meeting with President Reagan in the Oval Office*

1982 | Jerry standing with Queen Beatrix and her
       husband, Klaus

1982 | Ray Costanza, Director of Arlington National
       Cemetary, standing with President Reagan,
       Jerry Curry, Charlene and daughter, Natasha.

1984 | *Jerry picking grapes in the fields of Germany*

1984 | *Jerry standing with Kenneth Kaunda, President of Zambia*

1982 | *Jerry with President Diouf of Senegal.*

1984 | *Jerry and his wife, Charlene*

1988 | *Jerry in the Oval Office with President Reagan holding his "Curry for Congress" sticker*

1989 | *Jerry in the Oval Office with President George Bush Sr.*

2003 | Children, grandchildren, spouses, and extended family at Jerry and Charlene's 50th Wedding Anniversary—photo taken by Henry Schulz

2004 | Jerry and Charlene's home, "Chateau Antioch"

22

An Khe Pass

Every few years, the North Vietnamese dictator, Ho Chi Minh, sent a North Vietnamese Army (NVA) division south to invade South Vietnam. The U.S. Congress would not let the U.S. troops or the ARVNs attack the NVA while they moved through the adjacent countries of Laos and Cambodia, even though the NVA were violating the neutrality of these two countries. It did not make sense, but to those of us on the frontlines, decisions made thousands of miles away from the fighting often did not make sense.

From inside Laos and Cambodia, the NVA positioned themselves to attack South Vietnam and kill ARVN and U.S. soldiers, as well as South Vietnamese civilians.

The North Vietnamese Army took full advantage of their congressionally-mandated safe passage. In 1971, a NVA division slashed its way south across the highland plateau into the soft underbelly of South Vietnam's Kontum Province. Along the way, it pillaged, looted, and burned to the ground every village of "little people" that resisted their demands.

The "little people" were the Montagnards, as the French called them—brown-skinned aborigines who hunted with bows and arrows and threw spears. They were called the "little people" because both men and women stood about four feet tall. The men wore loin cloths while the women wore wrap-around skirts, naked from the waist up. Children wore nothing. They practiced slash and burn farming. Until the war, they had lived in splendid isolation, far from the Vietnamese population centers.

Young male Montagnards that the NVA chanced across were captured and pressed into service as slave laborers. They were treated as human pack animals, forced to carry rockets, mortar rounds, ammunition, and military equipment on their backs, sometimes over distances approaching a thousand miles.

These NVA invaders were not the VC guerilla fighters, known for wearing the baggy black "pajama-like" Ào Ba Ba. Unlike the guerilla fighters, the NVA didn't hide among the civilian populace by day and attack local government or military installations at night. These were regular military forces, part of a 12,000-man, regular army division. They wore uniforms and helmets, and were supported by mortars and heavy rockets.

Generally the ARVN, advised by Americans and supported by U.S. units, successfully repulsed these incursions; but not before the NVA exacted a heavy toll in misery, torture, and death from the civilian population.

First blood this year was drawn by a battalion of the 42nd ARVN Regiment, which blundered into the path of the 66th NVA Infantry Regiment as it spilled across the South Vietnamese border near the Ben Het Special Forces Camp. The ARVN battalion collapsed and was annihilated. There were no escapees, no wounded left alive, nor any prisoners taken.

A few days later, a second battalion of the 42nd ARVN also encountered the 66th NVA Regiment further east. This time a few of the ARVN soldiers escaped and made it back to friendly lines. From them we learned that the NVA was hoping to capture a high ridgeline on which were situated two South Vietnamese outposts named FB-5 and FB-6. The U.S. Armed Forces newspaper, *Pacific Stars & Stripes*, reported it this way:

Fighting has centered at Fire Base 6 since early March when, according to responsible sources, a battalion of the South Vietnamese 42nd Regiment was 'destroyed,' and a second battalion was 80 percent wiped out.

American helicopter pilots attempting to rescue the survivors told a story similar to that of the pilots flying support in Laos—South Vietnamese soldiers clinging to the skids, overloading, having to be pushed off so the choppers could rise. The commander of one of the decimated battalions was ordered off a helicopter at gunpoint. A small OH 6 Scout chopper was so burdened with desperate soldiers that it crashed into a tree while trying to take off, killing one man.[1]

With two of its four battalions destroyed, the 42nd ARVN was desperately in need of reinforcements. The 44th ARVN Regiment was operating 75 miles to the south. They were alerted and rushed north to help the 42nd blunt the NVA invasion. Events did not bode well for the 44th.

Our regiment, the 41st, was ordered to move into the area. We headed out. Colonel Vy's Jeep led the convoy, mine followed directly behind his, and hurriedly the rest of the regiment, two thousand men in all, were strung out behind us, moving south down Old Mandarin Route One.

Our convoy included Jeeps, 2½ and 5 ton trucks carrying soldiers, ammunition, mortars, and other weapons, along with food and equipment. Wrecker trucks were spaced throughout the convoy in case a vehicle broke down and needed towing. Gasoline tanker trucks also accompanied the convoy should any vehicles need refueling.

Twenty miles south of Landing Zone Crystal, the convoy swung west onto Route 19, just north of the village of An Nhon. Climbing the Annamitique Mountain foothills, we cautiously picked our way through the rugged and dangerous An Khe pass. Alongside the road lay the still smoldering remains of a burned-out ARVN convoy that had been ambushed by the VC about an hour before our arrival. Remnants of French convoys ambushed many years ago by the Viet Minh, rusted where they had been destroyed, strewn along the downhill side of the dirt and gravel road like metal sculptures in the courtyard of a modern art museum.

Slowly, the convoy snaked through the pass, clinging first to the road on one side of a mountain, then slithering over to secure a grip on the other side.

I thought of *Groupement Mobile Number 100*, a French convoy that, in the spring of 1954, had attempted to force the same pass on a similar relief mission. The ubiquitous 108th North Viet Minh Regiment ambushed and slaughtered them. There were no survivors.

The French had buried their dead high above the pass standing upright in their coffins. For eternity, they would stand in their coffins looking down on the place where their defeat had betrayed the honor and glory of France.

Once we were through the An Khe Pass, the road dropped down a thousand feet to the central plateau. In wide arcs it looped past the clusters of huts that made up An Khe village and then writhed westward. Not far away was a huge American base camp, our last place of refuge, should we need it.

Ten miles west of An Khe and the U.S. Base of refuge, Route 19 emptied onto a small plain. There, the thick, six-feet-high, yellowish green elephant grass that edged the road provided excellent cover—a great place for a VC ambush.

Without incident, we pushed farther west across the plateau and the road once again started climbing. Throwing up a blanket of sunburned dust behind us, our vehicles threaded their way through the Mang Yang Pass, 55 miles east of the city of Pleiku.

Spilling up and over into the 18,000 square mile Central Highland Plateau, which was boxed about by the inhospitable Chaine

Annamitique Mountains, our convoy swung north up Route 14. A few hours later, we passed through the small town of Kontum, then continued on toward the fever infested jungles and rain forests of Dak To Province.

> Kontum was the province of the Special Forces camps . . . which came under siege in years past, and of the bloody battle of Dak To, where on Hill 875 in November 1967 about 100 Americans were killed in five days. This year, Kontum is Fire Base 6: a dusty mountaintop outpost which helps guard the populated areas against infiltrating enemy troops.[1]

We had entered the mountanous land of the little people, the Montagnards, and just before dark, our convoy closed at Tanh Canh, an old French military camp. U.S. engineers had added such amenities as running water and latrines, making it barely habitable.

In the sector of the camp assigned to the 41st, a large corrugated tin building stood out among a sprawling nest of smaller buildings. The tin siding extended about a meter above the ground. From there to the rusting, corrugated tin roof, the upper walls were made of screen wire tacked to aged wooden two-by-four frames.

Occasionally, a bayonet, slotted on the end of a rifle barrel slung over the shoulder of some weary South Vietnamese soldier, had sliced through the screen wire when he had turned too abruptly and his rifle had brushed the wire. Jagged holes, ripped by whizzing fragments of shrapnel made similar statements. Here and there were unmistakable bullet holes.

In Vietnam's central highlands, the summer monsoons arrive at the beginning of April and hang around until early September. At times, the torrential rains cut horizontal visibility to a few hundred feet, sometimes less.

Continuous sheets of water, whipped and blown by the tropical depression, lashed out at buildings, crops, and every exposed creature. Little moved during the storms. At times, it was difficult to be heard above the wind's howl, even when shouting.

In places where the monsoon rains had washed away the humus and eroded the silica, the remaining alumina and iron oxide soil of the Vietnamese uplands hardened like cement. In other places it is coarse, dark brownish-red, subsistence-farming soil, but in the highlands, it was mostly grainy and good for nothing.

Where the feet of natives, the boots of soldiers, or the hooves of animals had worn paths, the earth was milled down to a fine brownish-red power a half-inch thick. During the monsoon season, when the rains came, the dust turned to mud as the rains flooded the land.

It was the end of March—suffocating and relentlessly hot. Though the rains fell daily, they were now only sprinkles or brief sudden downpours that stopped as suddenly as they started.

At Tanh Canh, I checked in with the U.S. Advisors to the 42nd and 44th ARVN Regiments. They briefed me on how the battle was progressing. Our side wasn't doing well.

As often happens in war, it was a case of hurry up and wait. That wasn't all bad. It gave Vy's regiment an opportunity to clean weapons, redistribute ammunition and supplies, and to get ready to be deployed.

Four days later, we got our first combat mission assignment. We were directed to send one entire battalion, more than four hundred men, out to reconnoiter the area south of Tanh Canh—an area of suspected enemy activity.

The U.S. advisor to the ARVN battalion was Larry McNamara, an incredibly brave and resourceful officer with a wide-across-the-cheekbone face. Larry's laughing blue eyes and infectious Irish grin belied his indomitable will and determination.

Larry stood five-feet-ten and weighed a solid 180 pounds. There was something about the way he squared his shoulders when he walked that told you that he didn't know how to quit, and wasn't about to lose. To Larry, surrendering or being captured alive weren't options. If the NVA gave him an opportunity to surrender, we both knew he would decline, and it would not be done gracefully.

As senior U.S. advisor to the 41st ARVN Regiment, one of my duties was to keep American advisors like Larry alive. His well-being had been entrusted to my care by the U.S. Army, and, like all senior U.S. advisors, I took that responsibility very seriously.

Most U.S. battalion advisors like Larry slept on the ground—or in the foxholes—with the ARVN soldiers. They ate rice three meals a day with their ARVN troops, and only supplemented that simple fare with American food rations flown in by U.S. helicopters when they were back at base camp.

Advisors to South Vietnamese infantry battalions lived precariously. By twos, sometimes alone, they risked their lives and sometimes died, while futilely trying to leaven the ARVN with the will to fight and win.

As infantrymen at Fort Benning, Georgia, we were taught, "Your mission is to close with the enemy and kill, capture, or destroy him." To the average ARVN military man, that kind of philosophy was unthinkable.

Most ARVN soldiers and their officers had no intention of fighting for their homeland or their way of life, let alone for the abstract concept of freedom. But paradoxically, this was not true of ARVN elite units such as the Rangers or Airborne. For the most part, they were highly motivated and effective fighting units.

In 1975, the South Vietnamese would lose the war, their country, and their freedom, primarily because they refused to fight to win. Freedom has no grandchildren. Each generation must be willing to sacrifice, fight, and if need be, die, for their own freedom.

Like me, Larry was a father. We had talked about home, and shared family pictures and memories. I felt personally close to him, as I did to all the officers and men on my team. We were more like a family than a collection of military professionals.

We U.S. Advisors were not to complain or to allow ourselves to sink into sloughs of self-pity or self-righteousness. Our duty was to serve our country in this dangerous and miserable assignment.

Larry's ARVN battalion left on reconnaissance early the next morning. Wrongly, our intelligence sources predicted little chance of enemy contact. Starting around noontime, Larry's battalion became engaged in a series of deadly firefights with the NVA.

Sometimes, when circumstances forced an ARVN battalion to fight an NVA unit, the ARVN officers suddenly became sick, got lost, mysteriously disappeared, or in some other way managed to separate themselves from the killing fields. In the process, they ripped the insignia of rank from their fatigue shirt collars and threw them away. If captured by the enemy, they tried to pass themselves off as enlisted men.

It was routine for captured ARVN officers to be tortured, interrogated, and shot by the NVA. Theirs was not an easy lot; nor was that of their U.S. advisors.

Right now, Captain Larry McNamara was three miles out in the jungle clinging to the top of Hill 867, along with a pitiful remnant of ARVN soldiers and a few, brave ARVN lieutenants and sergeants. The senior ARVN officers had fled. Grossly outnumbered, Larry and his men were surrounded, and the NVA were tightening the noose.

23

A Wall of Artillery Fire

It was the end of the day. The bloated bodies of the dead Vietnamese soldiers baked under the cruel equatorial sun. They littered the jungle hillside surrounding Captain Larry McNamara's position like rotting clumps of jellyfish cast up on a hot sandy beach. Larry and his American sergeant and about 40 ARVN soldiers were surrounded and trapped.

Miles away, at the command post, the radio barked to life. Captain McNamara's muffled but recognizable voice cut through the heavy static. "Can't hold on much longer," he said, his voice urgent, but controlled. "They're killing us with 82 mm mortars and B-40 rocket-propelled grenades!"

Reaching out, I grabbed the radio telephone handset and mashed down hard on the push-to-talk switch. "Larry," I said, in what I hoped was my calmest, most professional, most reassuring voice, "just hold on . . . We need a little more time to get you out of there."

With a heavy heart, I laid the handset on the wooden campaign table and averted my eyes so that no one, especially not the sergeant, could tell that I had no idea how to extricate Larry, and the ARVN soldiers he was advising, from the clutches of the encircling NVA.

Across the post, a large tactical map was smoothed out on top of two campaign tables placed end-to-end. The ARVN artillery officers had stuck a red-capped pin at the spot where they guessed Larry and the ARVN soldiers might be trapped, but they were only speculating. The fighting had been so intense that Larry hadn't been able to verify his coordinates. Earlier, I had tried to get a fix from him, but had failed. All of us were desperately searching for solutions.

"We've lost them," Colonel Vy sadly concluded. Suddenly, it was dark.

Sick at heart, I stepped out of the rusty, corrugated tin command post building into the open air. Glancing up at the radio antennas silhouetted against the moonlit sky, I leaned back against the rough bark of a palmetto tree.

The moon was full. I could see most of the way across the clearing, but I knew that deep in the jungle, where Larry and his men were fighting for their lives, precious little moonlight would filter through to their jungle graveyard.

If their position was overrun by the NVA, Larry would be captured, and if he was still living, he might disappear forever. All soldiers going off to war were told to settle their affairs first, because there was no promise of return.

I had done the same thing before leaving Charlene and the children in Colorado Springs. I had told her that should I disappear in combat and not be repatriated when the war was over, she should assume I was dead, and she and the family should go on with their lives. No matter how much she loved me, I didn't want her to wait around for 20 years clinging to the ethereal possibility that I might still be alive.

Near the command post, dug into the clay-like earth, was a sleeping bunker I had borrowed from another U.S. advisor who was currently on R & R in Bangkok. I stepped inside to pray.

I ducked under the dusty burlap curtain that separated the office-sitting room from the sleeping area and knelt on the concrete bunker floor and prayed that somehow God would give me wisdom. I asked Him to show me a way to save Larry and his men. How long I knelt there I don't know, but at last I felt that everything was going to work out, and I thought I knew how.

Calm now, I stood up, secured my pistol belt and purposefully strode from the bunker. As I stepped into the command post, the anxious officers and sergeants looked at my face. When they saw that it was no longer troubled, they relaxed a bit, but only for a moment. Over the radio we could hear the unmistakable hammering of heavy machine gun fire, the chattering of AK-47 assault rifles, and the deadly whump thud sound of incoming mortar shells.

Scattered across a several mile area were six U.S. and ARVN artillery battalions. I gathered the ARVN officers and U.S. advisors around me and pointed to the red pin stuck in the map.

"Let's plot a horseshoe-shaped, one hundred meter thick wall of artillery fire around Captain McNamara and your men, Colonel Vy. Then we'll fire a time-on target."

A time-on target meant that we would fire each artillery tube at a precisely calculated moment, so that each round would explode at the same time, causing the ground to roll and shake as brilliant flashes of light fractured the darkness. The concussion alone, from the exploding artillery shells, would shatter the eardrums of the dazed and confused enemy survivors. Those who were not killed outright, would be left bleeding from their ears and noses. My hope was that in the resulting chaos, Larry and his men could fight their way out the open end of the horseshoe.

Of course, this would only work if we knew precisely where everyone was. In this case, we knew the precise location of the six friendly artillery units, but we could only guess at Larry's position, and we had no idea where the enemy units were located, so the artillery would be firing near blind.

"The chance of our artillery missing the enemy and landing directly on top of our own forces is about 80 percent," one of the

ARVN officers said. He was the artillery fire support coordinator so he spoke loudly. I knew he had one goal: to have witnesses if we failed—witnesses who would testify that he had warned Colonel Vy and me.

Picking up the cue without thinking, Colonel Vy echoed, "Yes, it's very risky."

"Risky or not, there's no other option," I countered. "It's a choice we have to make. If we do nothing, they'll be overrun and killed."

This was nothing but theater. I was talking for the benefit of the others in the command post, not Colonel Vy. Vy wasn't afraid to make the right decision no matter how risky, provided I found a way to cover him if things went wrong.

The tension in the command post was explosive. All eyes were on Colonel Vy. Larry and his U.S. sergeant were my responsibility, but the forty ARVN soldiers clinging to Larry belonged to Colonel Vy. As my orders stated, in such cases only the ARVN commander had the authority to make the final decision.

Like magpies, the ARVN artillery officers kept chirping to each other and shaking their heads. They were going through the time honored ARVN ritual of accepting no blame for an action that might have disastrous consequences. They wanted to clearly and publicly make the case that if the artillery shells killed our troops, they were not to blame.

Wearily, Colonel Vy passed a cold hand across his forehead, smoothing out wrinkles and, perhaps, fears. A final time he looked to me for support in making a decision we both knew was the only hope. I nodded.

Raising my voice for effect, I spoke loudly, "Let the record reflect that I advised Colonel Vy to fire the artillery. If anyone is killed, it is my responsibility and mine alone."

These were big words; the reality was something else. If this didn't work out as planned and we killed Larry and his ARVN soldiers, there would be an official inquiry. It would be clear that

I had knowingly overstepped my authority and my military career would be terminated under the klieg lights of the evening news.

During the Vietnam War, the news media imputed all sorts of evil motives to U.S. military actions, at times manufacturing motives that those of us fighting the war couldn't have imagined had we tried.

If things went wrong, I would not be given the benefit of the doubt. The news media would accuse me—either deliberately or through negligence—of causing American deaths by "friendly fire."

Colonel Vy knew that what I was saying was purely for the consumption of his officers. A professional military commander like Vy would never transfer responsibility for a decision to his advisor.

Furrowing his brow, Vy nodded absently as if to himself, and then in a formal voice declared, "Thank you, Colonel Curry. Your advice and assumption of responsibility is noted for the record." This was pure Hollywood.

Turning to his officers, he snapped, "Do whatever Colonel Curry tells you!"

Then drawing himself up to his full military height, he squared his shoulders, and without looking back, marched out of the command post into the jungle night.

24

The Star from the East

With the responsibility-and-blame question temporarily set aside, the ARVN artillery officers quickly plotted the horse-shoe-shaped artillery fire.

Over the radio, I urged Larry to be patient. "We're working on it, we'll get you out. I promise."

"You gave me that crap a half hour ago, Colonel," he threw back at me. "We can't hold on . . . it's now or never!"

At last each of the fire direction center had the information they needed and were ready. Each individual artillery piece was loaded. U.S. and ARVN soldiers were standing by their cannons, clutching lanyards in their hands.

Sergeants stared at stopwatches, waiting to shout, "Fire number one! Fire number six! Fire number three!" At each command, a soldier pulled on the lanyard. The timing was exact down to the last second.

Now came the tricky part. Larry had to know where to lead his men once the firing started. If I gave him instructions over the radio, the NVA would also hear and react. When our guys tried to fight their way out of the encirclement, they would be butchered.

I couldn't encode the information either, because Larry would be shot the second he snapped on his flashlight to copy down the code and decipher it. No matter how careful he tried to be, the enemy was close enough to spot him. Darkness was one of Larry's few friends.

Again, I picked up the radio handset. Larry's voice was faint, the machine gun and mortar fire louder. Briefly, I explained the plan, then I asked, "Do you remember the Bible story about the birth of Jesus?"

"Of course I do!" he snapped. "Men out here are dying, and you're telling me Bible stories like some religious nut!"

Ignoring him, I continued, "Do you remember the star when Jesus was born?"

Pausing for a second, he responded with a little understanding, "Yeah, I remember."

"Do you recall the direction the star came from?" I continued.

"Yeah . . . you bet," he confirmed, the timbre of his voice lightening.

"That's the side of the horseshoe that's open," I shouted, over the sound of exploding mortar shells. "Fight your way out in that direction!"

"Give me five minutes," he hoarsely croaked.

After what seemed like an interminable wait, Larry's voice came in clearly, over the radio static, "We're all set!"

Turning to the ARVN artillery officer, I ordered, "Fire!"

He echoed the command over his radio to the waiting artillery battalions, "Fire!"

Thunder boomed out across the jungle battlefield as a myriad of artillery tubes belched fire and death into the night. In the distance, the sky glowed pink, yellow, and white as tons of explosives cruelly churned the earth. Cold sweat trickled down the inside of my camouflage fatigue collar.

As abruptly as the barrage started, it stopped. The sound hung in the air, impotently, now that the explosions were spent.

Then came the hard part . . . waiting. In war there is much waiting, particularly when the outcome of a battle is in doubt. On a roll of success, you can feel the momentum in your body; and at times even taste it in the air. Somehow you know deep within that victory is certain, but this was not one of those times.

Larry and his ARVN soldiers still had to painstakingly pick their way through the jungle blackness to safety. They could be ambushed at any moment. Until they escaped from enemy controlled territory, they had to maintain radio silence to avoid giving away their position.

Returning to the bunker, I tried to sleep, but couldn't. I made my way back to the palmetto tree. Over at the command post, soldiers and advisors drifted in and out, drinking coffee, smoking cigarettes, and asking the radio operators over and over, "Any word?"

For seemingly the thousandth time, I looked up anxiously at the sky. Faintly, the east paled.

Where is Larry? I asked myself once more. *Is he dead, or captured and wounded, or lying out there on some vermin-infested hillside?*

I felt helpless. Finally, stiffly, I stood and brushed the dirt and bugs from my jungle fatigues. I belted on my .45 and Randal killing knife, and walked through the calm of dawn.

Quickly, the sun stepped over the horizon and brought with it instant heat. Waiting for me were Colonel Vy and my driver, Sergeant Lee. Sinking down in the right front passenger's seat, I waved my hand for the chase vehicles to follow and nodded to Lee. This time Vy's Jeep swung in behind mine as we lurched forward, sucking along behind us a cloud of red dust, in spite of the dew that lay thick on the ground.

Sergeant Lee, my ARVN driver, had never quite mastered a manual gearshift, let alone learned how to properly steer a Jeep. Predictably, he jerked us all over the road. I rationalized that his lack of driving skill probably made the Jeep a poor sniper's target.

The truth was that he was a very likeable fellow with a nice family, and I didn't have the heart to fire him. I had met both his wife and his two children. He had a fine boy and a lovely doe-eyed girl.

Lee was a gentle, quiet mannered man, slender as most Vietnamese are, about five three and weighed perhaps a hundred pounds. His teeth protruded and both his lower and upper lips were elongated from stretching to cover them.

I rested my right foot on the lip of the door well, periodically, flexing my back and leg muscles so that if I had to move quickly, I'd be ready. My right arm dangled comfortably at my side. The flap of my .45 holster was unbuttoned and my fingers rested near it. By choice I didn't carry an M 16 like most advisors. From experience I knew that when the dying starts, there were always lots of extra weapons lying around.

As we rode along, I swept my eyes in an arc that extended out about 45 degrees to either side of the road; I was searching for telltale signs of NVA. The hedgerows, irrigation ditches, rice paddy dikes, and clumps of trees, out to about 150 meters, were my primary concern.

I carefully watched the location and movement of the women and a few men and buffalo boys who worked the flooded rice paddies. If an ambush was planned or if there were snipers in the trees, the workers always knew their location and weren't about to get caught in a cross fire between the NVA and us.

In the jungle, staying alive came with practice; you have to live long enough to develop safe habits. It took self-discipline, such as the ability to freeze in place and remain perfectly still. Also you developed a sort of sixth sense about the approach of danger. Those of us who survived learned to detect sounds others did not hear, like the difference between the movement of a man, the wind, and a small animal.

American footfalls were heavier, purposeful, and made one sound. Vietnamese being lighter in weight with a smaller foot surface and a different stride, made an entirely different noise.

Passing through a small village, our Jeeps lurched to a stop near a rope bridge strung across a sluggish, mud-colored river. There near a laurel tree, the village chief and the local Buddhist priest slouched in rickety, wooden chairs gossiping as though no war existed. Resting on the small, varnished, plywood table between them was a discolored China teapot. Celluloid tape held its cracked spout together. Ignoring them, our security forces fanned out quickly, taking up protective positions.

The priest's shaved head sloped up and to the rear from bushy, black eyebrows. He was wearing a brown cotton robe, slit up both sides to the waist. Its top was slipped over his left shoulder and tied under his right armpit. Beneath the robe, he wore white silk Ào Ba Ba pajamas and bare slippered feet.

His round, yellowish tan face displayed only a hint of a chin. His wide mouth was made up of detached, fleshy lips that seemed to move and talk by themselves, while his head and face remained immobile. Stubby, soft fingers, obviously unaccustomed to manual labor, ended in dirty, inch long fingernails.

Passing time, I commented to Colonel Vy about the inhumanities the Vietnamese people had suffered throughout their history, first under China, then during World War II under the brutality of the Japanese, and finally after 1946, during the constant war with the Communist North.

Vy replied, "There is a longer view. A race of people called the Chams were the original inhabitants of the Vietnamese Peninsula. They were a cruel, pagan people, who practiced cannibalism, human sacrifice, and necromancy. Yet, they managed to establish an unusually advanced civilization.

"When we Vietnamese migrated to the peninsula, we unleashed a storm of genocide against them that nearly exterminated their race. Supposedly, before the last high priest of the Chams was murdered by us, he cursed the Vietnamese people, prophesying that we would never inhabit the peninsula in peace."

"Sir," my radioman interrupted. "It's the captain!"

"Where are you?" I shouted into the radio telephone handset.

Larry's voice burst through strong and jubilant. "Almost to the river!"

For what seemed like hours but was probably only minutes, Colonel Vy and I stood at the near side of the swaying rope suspension bridge that connected the two banks of the river, watching and waiting.

Suddenly with a shout, Larry sprang from the green forest wall at the far end of the rope bridge. An Irish grin distorted his perspiring, mud-smeared face. He waved joyfully.

Exhausted, but happy, ARVN survivors plodded wearily across the swaying rope footbridge following close behind him.

At the time, I didn't suspect that this was only the beginning of Larry's troubles.

25

FB-6

War is horribly destructive of nations, people, communities, and families. My heart ached for the gentle Montagnard people of the highlands, who longed to live in peace in their thatched huts and great tribal lodges perched atop scaffoldings of thick, yellow bamboo poles.

What compensation did they get for their destroyed crops, dead goats, stolen chickens, and priceless water buffaloes—for them the equivalent of John Deere tractors? Who would replace their kidnapped sons enslaved and murdered by the North Vietnamese? Who would help them rebuild, physically and spiritually? Certainly not the North or South Vietnamese governments. The North and South Vietnamese despised these "little people." They ridiculed them, cheated them when they could, and when they resisted, the Vietnamese robbed or killed them.

But this day, it was the spiny mountain ridge, not the Montagnards, that occupied my thoughts—a bony line of mountains that ran 20 miles northwest from Tanh Canh to the Ben Het Special Forces Camp, situated on the Laotian border.

Atop the ridgeline were several knobby, boil-like protuberances that reminded me of corns growing on top of an abused toe. Unattended, they had a nasty habit of festering at a most inopportune time.

Two of the more prominent "corns" were tactically significant. The eastern one was named FB-5, the western one FB-6. In the center of each fire base, the ARVN had dug in 105-millimeter howitzers that commanded the valley and Route 512, which ran from the juncture of Route 14 at Tanh Canh, northwest along the valley to Ben Het. Whoever occupied these positions oversaw the villages of Tanh Canh, Dak To, and Ben Het, and would be able to dominate any fighting taking place in the valley below.

If the NVA captured the two fire bases, it would be the massacre at Dien Bien Phu all over again. Their artillery would fire straight down on the ARVN, who in turn would be shooting straight up at the NVA—again.

If Ben Het, Dak To, and Tanh Canh also fell into enemy hands, it would be like rolling a bowling ball south down Route 14. Kontum would tumble, quickly followed by Pleiku, and the entire central highland plateau.

This is what actually happened four years later, in 1975 when NVA regular forces supported by tanks and artillery, successfully invaded and overran South Vietnam. At that point, they put into action a plan they had first used in the spring of 1971. The battle for FB-5 and FB-6 was a dress rehearsal for the final invasion of South Vietnam four years later.

In 1971, we stopped the NVA because the American advisors in Vietnam were still there to pull the rabbit out of the hat for them. In 1975, the ARVN were on their own. Their performance in 1971 was a shadow, a precursor of what would happen in 1975.

The fight for freedom, the fight to protect the South Vietnamese homeland and way of life would fail. That day, the foreground may have been only a charcoal sketch, but the background was finished, painted in minute detail.

From a military point of view, there was a fundamental flaw in the decision to establish and garrison the two fire bases. They were located too far apart. Neither could support the other if they came under enemy attack. Each had to beat off the NVA by itself. Its neighbor could be of no help.

Remnants of an ARVN Regiment, never a particularly aggressive nor effective fighting unit, garrisoned FB-5 and FB-6 with approximately a battalion of troops on each—but these were troops who lacked the will to fight and win. Their U.S. advisors did their best, but it wasn't good enough.

In the last week of March 1971, the 95th NVA Sapper Regiment encircled FB-6. Sappers were soldiers who were specially trained to breach barbed wire and fortifications of all types. At the same time, the 66th NVA Regiment laid siege to FB-6.

The North Vietnamese planned to attack FB-5 first, so that FB-6 would send relief forces. Then the NVA intended to attack FB-6, forcing the ARVN to fight two independent battles, at the same time.

After FB-6 was captured, FB-5 would be easy prey. The *Stars and Stripes* described it like this:

PLEIKU, Vietnam—A detailed Communist plan to capture Fire Base 6, gain control of Highway 14 and isolate Ben Het, thus opening the way for a sweep through Kontum Province, has been disrupted by South Vietnamese forces around Fire Base 6, according to a high ranking South Vietnamese military source . . . captured documents spelled out how after the 95th NVA Sapper Regt. had taken Fire Base 6, the 66th NVA Regt. was to attack east along Highway 14. This would have given the enemy control of the highway cutting through the heart of Kontum Province, and would have isolated Ben Het.

At this time, the 28th NAV Regt., which was already in position southwest of the camp, was to attack and capture Ben Het.

With control of Highway 14 and all the surrounding territory, the enemy would then be in the position to sweep through Kontum Province, the source said.[2]

In war, battles can be fought technically and mechanically by the numbers, but they are seldom won that way. War is an art form. Active battlefields are confused and chaotic at best. Reports don't get through because couriers get lost or shot. In the middle of a crucial transmission, radios or computers may fail. A decoding device may break down or the encoding clerk may use a wrong code.

The command post's telephones may go dead because a lost tank pivoted over a communication's trench chewing up all the telephone lines. The most sensitive and vital reports don't get sent or received because the unit sending them is in close contact with the enemy and the radios or their operators are blown apart, or the commanding officer steps on a land mine and is dismembered.

Mortar and artillery rounds roar at the enemy, and the enemy reciprocates. Blue-gray smoke clings to bushes, trees, and hilltops, draping itself like a heavy, thick blanket over the hills and valleys of death and refuses to dissipate, obscuring visibility. Sometimes visibility is cut to a few meters penetrated only by rifle and machine gun fire.

Everywhere there is smoke . . . smoke . . . smoke, and noise . . . noise . . . noise, confusion . . . confusion and explosions. On top of all this, the sounds of the wounded and dying cry out in pain or beg for death.

In the middle of this turgid carnage, this plethora of miscues in the absence of any sense of what is actually happening, stand a few men who must make sense of it all and give orders.

Those commanders must make the final decisions alone and bear ultimate responsibility for the battle's outcome. If a commander is ever to master the warrior art form, he has to learn to question most of what he has been told, and most of what he has read. No matter how dangerous or arduous, he must personally go to the killing fields. He must personally see the enemy for himself.

Yet it is not the words the commander hears, nor the sights his eyes see that cause him to draw conclusions. He feels, he anticipates, and somehow he intuitively knows what must be done next and he does it.

Others around him may doubt his decisions or think them peculiar at times. They may believe that the commander has missed it altogether. But he knows better, or at least he hopes he does.

On Monday night, March 29, the North Vietnamese 95th Sapper Regiment probed the ARVN defense of FB-6. Their touch was deft, slow, and careful, like a woman examining a rough patch of skin on her face. Like a caress, the fingers of the NVA reached out to probe for ARVN vulnerabilities, found them, catalogued them, and carefully filed them away for future reference.

Under the cover of darkness, the 95th Sappers dug in, burrowing like badgers. They were fierce diggers and throughout the night and all the next day they pushed their trenches, like mole tunnels, far up the ridgeline toward FB-6.

When they had worked their way close enough, they intended to leap out and assault through the barbed wire protected perimeter, taking on the ARVN in hand-to-hand combat.

Now they were too far down the hill and too wise to get caught out in the open, charging up a bald-faced ridge. They knew from experience that if they showed their faces, the American advisors would call in the U.S. fighter bombers or helicopter gunships and decimate their ranks long before they reached the ARVN perimeter wire.

Instead they spent a second night digging. For now they would wait and conserve their forces. And so, throughout that night and the next morning, they sporadically lobbed NVA Rocket Propelled Grenades and 82-millimeter mortar rounds onto the two fire bases.

The NVA expected to gain little from the firing. Mostly they were checking ARVN reactions. Was this a hornet's nest they were poking a lighted stick of fire into, or was it an inactive beehive? The lack of aggressive response to their probes, and the ARVN's failure to send out reconnaissance patrols or to return fire told them what they needed to know.

Dug in atop FB-6, were an ARVN infantry battalion and artillery as well as a handful of U.S. artillery liaison officers. They were lieutenants from the U.S. 52nd Artillery Group, who unfortunately, had little combat experience.

Should the need arise, they were supposed to arrange for U.S. artillery battalions to provide back up support for the ARVN guns. They kept in touch with the U.S. Artillery's Fire Direction Center by radio.

The one experienced, battle-tested U.S. officer on FB-6—a major, who served as the U.S. infantry advisor, had helicoptered back to Tanh Canh, 10 kilometers to the southeast, for a Monday evening meeting. Each of the other U.S. officers had less than two years of Army service. No one suspected that the void in combat experience would not be filled during the battle for Fire Station Six. In battle, experience is everything.

After his miraculous escape from being surrounded, Captain McNamara had had a few days at Tanh Canh to rest, reorganize, and reequip the battalion he was advising. Since he was in Tanh Canh with me, my interest in the battles raging around FB-5 and FB-6 was professional rather than personal.

When possible, I listened to how the fighting was going over the radio. Occasionally, whenever duties permitted, I drifted over to the command post for the U.S. advisors to get an update on the battle's progress from the operations officer, that is, provided my location—Tanh Canh—wasn't under long range rocket attack, which was often the case. Tanh Canh was the home base for all the ARVN regiments when they weren't out in the jungle fighting the enemy.

The radio traffic I monitored on Tuesday, March 31, 1971, was worrisome. I got the feeling that the reports coming down from FB-6 were more optimistic than they had a right to be. But this was none of my affair, at least not yet. It was the responsibility of the 22nd ARVN Division.

Colonel Dat, the assistant division commander for the 22nd, was in command of the combined ARVN forces at Tanh Canh. There could not have been a worse choice. Five-feet-three inches in jungle boots, and a skinny one hundred pounds, Dat had the restlessness of a hooded cobra. His nervous eyes roved incessantly, and his face read like the cheap huckster he was. You didn't turn your back on Dat, even when he was on your side.

His U.S. counterpart was Colonel Claire Book, a West Point officer of integrity, ability, and decency. Book, my boss, was as straight an arrow as they come. Standing well over 6 feet and weighing about 220, when he and Colonel Dat were together they truly looked like the "odd couple."

As the NVA tightened their noose around the two fire bases, Colonel Dat became more sullen and uncommunicative. It was all Book could do to get him to respond to requests for assistance from the fire bases. Like advisors all over South Vietnam, Colonel Book alternately persuaded, cajoled, encouraged, and threatened Dat until he gave the right order or took the right action.

Evening came, the prelude to a night alive with movement. Under covered of darkness, the NVA forsook their mole holes and trenches and crept upward toward FB-6. Ghostly artillery parachute flares eerily framed the NVA bodies against the outer perimeter's concertina barbed wire. They died where they were uncovered, scythed down by machine gun and semiautomatic rifle fire.

An hour later, they tried again with similar results, leaving their dead hanging on the wire like limp marionettes whose strings had been severed. But they did not give up. The one commodity the NVA had in abundance was men.

At three in the morning, the NVA came at the 600 ARVN defenders again, this time in a human wave assault. Penetrating both the outer and inner perimeters, the NVA overran two bunkers and killed their ARVN defenders. Now the NVA had a toehold on FB-6, but the ARVN still controlled the rest of the base. The deadly minuet for survival began. If the NVA lost their toehold, they could retreat back down the hill and regroup. If the ARVN lost, there was no place for them to go.

Had the experienced U.S. battalion advisor, an Army major, been present he might have coerced the ARVN into recapturing the two bunkers and driving the NVA off FB-6. But he was still in Tanh Canh and only U.S. artillery liaison officers who were inexperienced in combat were left on the hill. They lacked the clout and know-how to make the ARVN fight.

So the ARVN decided to wait until daylight, in the hope that U.S. fighter bombers and helicopter gunships would drive the NVA off the Fire Base for them. A few U.S. aircraft might get shot down, but so what? The Americans loved to fight, didn't they? That's why they were in Vietnam, wasn't it? In fact, some U.S. Army helicopter crews were also on FB-6. Their helicopters had been shot down that day while attempting to resupply the fire base.

Wednesday morning, March 31, U.S. helicopters tried again to resupply FB-6. It was not to be. The fire from Rocket Propelled Grenade Launchers and machine guns was so intense that each time the helicopters tried to fly in, they had to break off their approach and scramble for their lives.

Back at Tanh Canh headquarters, NVA gunners were sporadically firing 122-mm rockets, the size of small telephone poles, into the 22nd ARVN Division command post from positions high up on the hills and ridges. Soldiers inside the perimeter had to wear steel helmets and heavy flak jackets just to move from one fortified bunker to another.

Meanwhile, back at FB-6, the NVA finally dug a trench that linked the two captured bunkers with their forces outside the perimeter. Throughout the day, they jammed reinforcements into the bunkers.

The radio reports from the friendly forces on the hill remained optimistic. "We'll recapture the bunkers by 0900 hours," a U.S. artillery lieutenant cheerfully reported.

That hour came and went but nothing happened. The ARVN refused to counterattack the bunkers held by the NVA. The cheerful American lieutenant called for more U.S. fighter-bomber air strikes. The planes plastered the area with ordnance, but still the ARVN refused to drive out the enemy.

"For certain we'll have the bunkers back by noon," the same optimistic voice reassured the command post at Tanh Canh. Hours passed.

I waited until a rocket attack subsided, then grabbed my steel helmet and flak jacket and hustled over to the 42nd's command post bunker. "How's the war going?" I asked the U.S. advisor.

"It's going pretty well . . . we'll have the NVA out of those bunkers shortly," he replied smiling confidently. "Got a lot of air strikes dropping ordnance all over the place."

"That's what's bothering me," I said. "After each strike someone gives a bomb damage assessment over the radio. Have you noticed how long it takes?"

"Oh sure, but that's war," he chuckled. "It just takes time to assess those things."

I persisted, "I've been listening to the radio traffic on and off all morning. And I have a gut feeling that something doesn't quite ring true. Can it be that FB-6 is in serious trouble, and the people defending it don't know it?"

"If you knew our ARVN like I do, you wouldn't sweat it. Relax, everything's going to be fine," he reassured me. "Just wait and see."

At that moment, another air strike finished. The same voice I'd heard over the radio earlier gave another optimistic assessment of the damage.

"Do you mind asking your man on the hill a question for me?"

"Sure, what's your pleasure?" he responded in a patronizing tone.

"Ask him what pair of 'U.S. eyeballs' saw where those last bombs landed."

"Not to worry, Colonel," he said, confidently radioing up to the fire base and repeating the question.

There was a long silence followed by, "Why, I don't know . . . I'll have to climb out of the bunker and find out . . . be back in a few minutes . . . Wait out," he concluded, a puzzled sound edging his voice.

A few minutes later, he returned to the radio and reported, "No 'U.S. types' saw the bombs hit the target. We're relying on ARVN for the Bomb Damage Assessments."

He sounded less jocular this time.

"Thank you," I said. "Sorry to bother you."

I left and located Colonel Book who was baby-sitting Colonel Dat at the 22nd ARVN command post. "Boss," I began, "I'd like to borrow your helicopter."

"What for?" he asked.

I told him what I suspected and concluded, "If I'm right, we're about to lose FB-6. The NVA will take the ARVN artillery that's up there and fire it straight down our throats. We've got to get an experienced advisor up on that fire base before we lose the entire ridge line."

Book grimly nodded and through gritted teeth muttered, "Let's go together."

Turning to Colonel Dat he asked, "Would you like to join us?"

Dat looked stricken.

"I thought not," Colonel Book said and strode toward the bunker door. Outside, he raised his right arm over his head and rotated it in a circular motion.

At a distance, Book's waiting helicopter crew stopped sunning themselves, snatched up their gear, and scrambled aboard. By the time we got to the helicopter, the rotor blades were slowly arcing from left to right.

As our helicopter climbed to altitude, the radio transmissions from FB-6 grew increasingly desperate. Not only had the NVA successfully reinforced the two captured bunkers, but using them as a base they had dug trenches toward the other bunkers that were still in ARVN hands.

Now U.S. air strikes were coming in almost continuously, an acrid blue gray smoke draped itself over the crest of the fire base like a funeral pall. Still climbing, our helicopter swung west in a lazy arc.

Too late, we arrived on position over the fire base just as the NVA leaped from the bunkers as well as their holes and trenches. With moist eyes, Colonel Book and I helplessly watched the NVA's final, brave assault sweep over the curving hilltop in broad daylight. Even in our helicopter, it seemed that we could hear their victory shouts.

Below us, Lt. Salazar led his two helicopter crews off the mountain accompanied by nearly a hundred ARVN soldiers. It was similar to Captain McNamara's situation of a week earlier. Now, as then, I was little help.

Covering their escape was Lt. Brian M. Thacker, one of the U.S. artillery liaison officers. Armed with only an M-16 semiautomatic rifle, he held off the swarming NVA attackers until Salazar's band made good their escape. Then alone and still firing his M-16, he backed down off the fire base.

Of the four American artillerymen on FB-6 when it was overrun, three were killed. Lieutenant Thacker was listed as missing in action. He would later be rescued and awarded the Congressional Medal of Honor. He deserved it.

26

Charlie Brown

Major General Charlie Brown was in no mood to be trifled with this particular morning. Brown was not a U.S. advisor to the ARVN as were Colonel Book and I. He was the American commanding general of all of the U.S. forces, combat and support, in South Vietnam's Second Military Region.

His command included elite U.S. combat units such as the 173rd Airborne Brigade, Regular U.S. Army Divisions, all the U.S. helicopter units from Medivac to cargo to troop carriers to gunships, plus the supply depots, ports, airfields, and a host of what we called "cat and dog" units.

He controlled the elements of war and logistics that sustained the life of all ARVN units and their advisors. From the South China Sea in the east to the border area of South Vietnam, Cambodia, and Laos in the west, nothing of U.S. origin or character moved without Charlie Brown's consent.

Technically, the ARVN forces fought independent of U.S. Commanders. But in reality, the ARVN forces in the Second Military Region survived at the pleasure of Charlie Brown. This particular day Charlie was mean and angry, and with good cause.

Late the evening before, he had received word that FB-6 had been overrun and had sent a jarring message to the commander of the 22nd ARVN Division: "General, first thing in the morning get into your helicopter, fly west and join me at Tanh Canh!"

Though technically the ARVN commander didn't take orders from General Brown, he was politically smart enough to recognize a summons when served with one. But he wasn't smart enough to get there on time. By the time he arrived, Colonels Dat and Book had told General Brown how FB-6 had been lost. Since then the general had been stomping around the command post like a fire-fighter trying to put out a forest fire with his boots. At six foot four and weighing 230 pounds, he was a force to be reckoned with.

"General," Charlie grumped when the tardy ARVN Division commander finally stepped down from his helicopter, "what is your problem? All you had to do was defend two lousy fire bases—no big deal. I've got the whole Second Region to worry about. I don't have time to go behind you pulling your chestnuts out of the fire; and that's just what I've been doing for the past several months."

The dark-faced ARVN general was short of stature even by Vietnamese standards. He stood at attention staring straight ahead, which was directly into Charlie Brown's brass belt buckle.

Occasionally, he glanced up at Charlie Brown's face. But inch-by-inch during the tongue lashing, his eyes slowly dropped so that now he was staring at the toes of Charlie Brown's highly-polished jungle boots.

His head snapped back up when Charlie's big knuckled right forefinger—pointed like a six-shooter and large as one of the Vietnamese general's forearms—stabbed the tip of his nose.

"You and I are going to get in my helicopter and fly up to that ridge line, and I'm going to explain why you shouldn't have lost FB-6. And while we're gone, my operations officer and your operations officer are going to draw up a little plan."

"When we get back, they're going to brief us on what they've developed. Following which, you are going to execute that self-same plan . . . today! By night-fall, FB-6 is going to be back in your hands."

With each word, Brown's finger ever so slightly bent the end of the smaller general's nose.

"And you are not going to give it away again, General . . . ever! Now get in my chopper."

By the time the helicopter returned from their prolonged reconnaissance, Colonel Book, Colonel Dat, and the U.S. and ARVN Operations Officers had worked out the details of the plan. It was simple, as successful military plans usually are.

The South Vietnamese, reinforced by all available U.S. artillery fire support, would first pulverize the fire base with high-explosive artillery shells. This softening up would culminate in an intense saturating salvo of tear gas.

As the last artillery rounds carrying tear gas exploded, soldiers of the First Battalion, 41st ARVN, wearing gas masks, would combat assault by U.S. helicopters directly onto the fire base.

Meanwhile, the remaining three battalions of the 41st ARVN Regiment, reinforced by one battalion from the 44th ARVN, were marching six miles through the triple-canopied jungle to fight their way up the ridge line to FB-6. They would link up with the First Battalion, which by the time they arrived would already be in place.

All this was privately explained to the ARVN general before he entered the command post so that he could digest it and compose himself before facing his assembled commanders and staff. It was a wasted courtesy. Not only would he not agree to the plan, he refused to execute it.

"You expect us to do too much," the brooding ARVN general protested, "The North Vietnamese are too strong for us. We are only South Vietnamese . . . it is very difficult for us," he whined.

But Charlie Brown would have none of it. He was in a hurry to get on with running the war in other sectors. "General, now that you've had time to reconsider, you like the plan very much. In fact, you feel confident that you can recapture FB-6 today."

General Brown's eyes bored through the resistance of the ARVN general. "Here's why you are so thrilled with your plan, General, so thrilled that you can hardly wait to execute it." He loudly emphasized the word "your."

"You are going to order your division to recapture that fire base because if you don't, this is what is going to happen." Charlie's voice dropped an octave in pitch. "Your division will get no more support from U.S. Forces. Effective immediately we won't Medivac your wounded in our helicopters; we won't resupply your units with food, water, and ammunition; we won't provide gunship and fighter-bomber support; we won't fire artillery to back up yours; we'll just leave you and your men out here under the boiling sun for the snakes and the NVA to feast on your carcasses."

The ARVN general's shoulders sagged and the cigarette he'd clutched in his teeth all this time drooped, then dropped to the ground. With a small foot he toed it into the sand. Taking off the dark aviator sunglasses he always wore, he folded them resignedly and tucked them under the flap of his left fatigue shirt pocket.

"I understand," he muttered pathetically, "I will give the order."

Like a good actor in a play, he regained his composure, straightened his stooped shoulders, plodded down the rough wooden plank stairs that led to the 22nd ARVN Division's command post bunker, which was sunk deep into the red clay. Awaiting him were his assembled 22nd ARVN Division staff and commanders.

Soon the briefing was over, the details coordinated, and the goodbyes said. The ARVN commanders, staff, and advisors quickly scattered to put action to the plan. For me, there remained one last detail that I had to address. It could neither be delegated nor avoided.

When I was a young infantry second lieutenant, I'd been taught that "pointing" is not the same as leading. At Fort Benning, Georgia, the motto of the Infantry School isn't "Follow Me" for nothing. Some things a combat leader does himself.

Twenty minutes later, on a sparsely green hillside hot with sun, Captain Larry McNamara and I found ourselves sitting across from each other with a fold-up wooden military campaign table between us, slowly sipping bitter Vietnamese tea.

My other advisors silently sat apart by a clump of pine trees, watching us, though they pretended not to be. They cleaned and oiled their weapons preparing for combat. Occasionally, their eyes darted toward us. They had been briefed on the regiment's mission and could guess what Larry and I were discussing.

A week before, Larry had been deserted and left to die by the Fourth Battalion Commander, Major Uy. Larry's returning alive was an embarrassment for Uy. If Captain Mac had died as Uy intended, Uy could have fabricated a heroic story saying that the fighting had been so intense that he and Mac had been forcibly separated and that he had endangered his own life trying unsuccessfully to save Captain McNamara.

But because Larry had defied all the odds and come back alive, Uy was forced to explain why he had deserted Captain McNamara on the battlefield. According to his version of events, he had become so deathly sick that he was unable to lead his battalion. So while his unit was fighting for its life, Uy made his way to the rear to find medical help.

Most of the other ARVN officers and senior sergeants had followed him. That's why Larry had ended up surrounded by the enemy and in command of a remnant of 40 ARVN soldiers.

Today was Captain McNamara's moment of truth, as well as mine. I broached the subject by saying, "You've studied the plan. You know we've committed every battalion."

"Yes. You want me to go out with Fourth Battalion again," he said without blinking. "It's still commanded by that coward, Major Uy."

"We must commit your battalion this afternoon," I confirmed.

"Colonel, you know as well as I that at the first shot fired, Uy will turn tail and run. The battalion will fall apart, just like it did last week." He was stating a simple, unemotional fact.

"True," I acknowledged.

After a long pause, Larry said, "If I go, I won't come back."

I felt drained, empty.

"This fight won't end like last week," he continued. "The North Vietnamese aren't going to let me get away twice."

"I know," I replied looking away, pain in my heart. "Do you want me to go in your place?" I asked.

"No," he countered sharply. "You've got your job to do, and I've got mine. I'll go this one last time."

Simultaneously we pushed our metal folding chairs back and slowly stood. I held out my hand. Larry took it in both of his and muttered, "Goodbye, Colonel. We won't meet again. Not in this life. Write my wife. Tell her I love her."

I nodded and he was gone. The lump stuck halfway down my throat throbbed and pained. I couldn't dislodge it.

27

Fighting by the Rules

The ARVN attack to recapture FB-6 jumped off on schedule. An hour's artillery bombardment pulverized the fire base, the bombardment ended with canister shells laying down a dense concentration of tear gas.

Helicopters from the 52nd U.S. Army Assault Helicopter Battalion, stationed at Pleiku, bravely slammed down their ships directly on top of the NVA and disgorged the First Battalion, 41st ARVN. Blinded by tear gas, the confused and demoralized NVA were killed, captured or forced to retreat back off the ridge.

At the command post in Tahn Canh, the 22nd ARVN Division commander, his eyes shining with excitement, radioed to General Brown and triumphantly proclaimed, "FB-6 is back in friendly hands!"

"Now comes the hard part." General Brown reminded him. "Keeping it."

Choosing which battalion would assault by helicopter directly onto FB-6 was easy. It had to be First Battalion, commanded by Major An.

An was slight of build, strong of heart, a born leader and fighter. His battalion was head and shoulders above the other battalions in the regiment. If South Vietnam had been led by the likes of Colonel Vy and Major An, the NVA would have been soundly defeated years before.

Major An's U.S. advisor was one of the Army's best, Captain John R. Seiss. John was a knowledgeable, brave, no-nonsense, combat-smart veteran who was on a voluntary second tour as advisor to the 41st ARVN Regiment.

Though he did not intend to make the military a career, John represented what was best about young Americans who volunteered to fight in Vietnam: patriotism, dedication, hard work, sensitivity to the suffering and pain of the South Vietnamese people, and a willingness to risk his own life over and over again to help them secure their freedom and a peaceful and prosperous future for their children and their country.

It was remarkable how the First Battalion, under Major An and Captain Seiss, routinely acquitted itself bravely in battle, while at the same time its sister unit, the Fourth Battalion, commanded by Major Uy, seemed to search out excuses not to fight, or looked for opportunities to flee or surrender. The Second and Third Battalions were more reliable than the Fourth, but not much.

The difference was the leaders. It did not matter if you were making world-class automobiles or providing quality education for the nation's youth, or winning wars, the leaders made all the difference. Someone once said, "When men die, and in war some must, you don't manage them to their death, you must lead them there."

Grimly, the Second, Third, and Fourth Battalions pushed through the jungle and fought their way up the ragged ridge line toward FB-6. They would not reach it until early the next morning, after bitter fighting. For one two-hour period they would lose over a man a minute to enemy fire.

At the Infantry School at Fort Benning they teach that the commander should physically establish his tactical headquarters where the bulk of his fighting forces are located. But as is sometimes the case, the purist or school solution is not always the best solution, or so Colonel Vy was about to teach me. As soon as the fire base was back in friendly hands, I quickly secured my equipment and prepared to helicopter up to FB-6 where I assumed Colonel Vy would be relocating his command post, where he could personally take charge of the base's defense.

"Colonel Curry," Vy patiently explained, "in the American Army a commander goes where his troops go. This is not the case with the South Vietnamese Army."

Gently, he took my hand in his. "Colonel Curry, you saw what happened to the regiment holding FB-6 before it was overrun by the NVA. What help did they get from the 22nd ARVN Division?" he scornfully asked.

"Very little," I agreed.

"That is precisely the point. Your U.S. advisors did more to keep our ARVN soldiers from getting killed than did my own division." His face darkened, his words were framed in profound sadness.

"If the two of us fly up to FB-6 and set up our command post there, as we should, we will sign the 41st Regiment's death warrant. Do you want to be responsible for getting my soldiers and all your advisors killed?"

Silently, I nodded, "No." The smell and taste of hot, red dust hung in the air.

"Trust me, Colonel Curry," he said slowly, forcefully. "Do not insist that you and I go to FB-6. We must remain here, where we can influence the outcome of the battle. On FB-6 we can influence the immediate fighting, but not the regiment's ultimate survival. Back here, we can do both. Do you understand, my friend?" he begged.

"It is difficult, but I think I do," I said, thinking of how little I understood the ways of the South Vietnamese Army.

Having suffered major losses as well as having been embarrassed by the ARVN, the NVA did not go gently back down the ridge into the jungle. For 12 hours, they regrouped and refitted. Then they swarmed out of the jungle and back up the mountain toward FB-6.

Colonel Vy's and my job was to use the 12 hours to try to secure the fire base against the NVA assault that we knew was imminent. Part of that requirement was to get the U.S. artillery registered so that the artillery could provide backup fire support to the ARVN on call and without delay.

Vy and I helicoptered northwest along Route 214 and had the pilot land on the Dak To emergency airstrip located in the valley due north of FB-6. Standing on the pierced steel planking of the short runway, and peering through binoculars, we could easily make out the fire base in the distance. A senior officer from the 52nd U.S. Artillery Group, whose helicopter had landed at the same time as ours, joined us.

"We'd like to register your guns, and assign concentration numbers as soon as possible," I said matter-of-factly.

"Can't be done, Colonel Curry," he replied. "You know we have to agree upon procedures. My group's stated mission is to reinforce the ARVN artillery fire. Until they have fully engaged their own artillery, I can't fire a round."

"By the time they're fully engaged, it will be dark," I countered. What I really wanted to do was to punch him out, but there were too many witnesses. "If we do it your way, the fire base will be under heavy NVA attack before your unit fires a shot. In the middle of a fire fight and in the black of night we can't ask the enemy to stop attacking for an hour, just so you can register your artillery. When the time comes, and it will come tonight, we need to be able to call on you for instant artillery support and get it immediately. We can only do that if you register your artillery now, while it's light, while we have time, and while there's no fighting."

At a respectful distance, a young artillery liaison officer silently listening to us argue.

Though I argued as forcefully as I knew how, the senior officer from the 52nd Group was adamant. If the ARVN didn't ask him directly, he claimed regulations made him powerless to do more.

I knew that if the ARVN asked for help now, before the battle had even begun, in the Oriental mind that would be admitting that they could not defend the fire base without U.S. help. They would "lose face."

I busied myself with other matters. Finally, the 52nd Group officer, tired of making small talk with his lieutenants, got back into his helicopter and flew off. I could hardly wait for him to leave.

As soon as he departed, the young artillery lieutenant liaison officer hurried over to me and said, "Sir, I've been listening to you and my boss and I've got two buddies who are flying up to FB-6 right now. Are you saying that if we don't register the U.S. artillery now and that if there's an all-out attack tonight, my two buddies might not be alive tomorrow?"

"You got it, Lieutenant," I acknowledged. "That's exactly what I'm saying."

He thought for a moment, and then conspiratorially whispered, "My job as liaison officer involves routine things like registering artillery concentrations all the time. The officers in the Fire Direction Center are my friends. They'll do anything I ask. And they wouldn't mention it to headquarters if I told them not to."

I smiled broadly. The lieutenant was a fast learner.

"Colonel, if you gave me a direct order to register the artillery, I guess I'd have to obey."

"Lieutenant," I said smiling, "this is a direct order. Register the artillery concentrations now!" Turning to one of the operations sergeants standing nearby who had overheard our conversation, I asked, "Did you hear me give your lieutenant an order?"

The sergeant was a big, hard man with a shock of salt and pepper hair and a no-nonsense air. "Yes, Sir," he said, looking up from posting the tactical situation on his map. "You just gave the lieutenant a direct order to register the artillery. When the time comes, I'll swear to it," he added obliquely, measuring me with careful eyes.

Grinning, the lieutenant saluted and ran for his radio. I went looking for Colonel Vy.

That night, the NVA launched an all out attack against FB-6. As expected, the ARVN artillery needed all the help U.S. forces could give them. The 52nd Group's artillery tubes weighed in without missing a beat, right on target. The NVA were defeated and driven off with heavy losses.

Until Major Elrod, advisor to the Third Battalion radioed me, we had no idea that the 1200 ARVN of the Second, Third and Fourth Battalions were facing two NVA regiments of two to three thousand men each. Intelligence had wrongly concluded that the NVA force was only about two battalions.

Major Elrod was a tall, gangly, professional, and a determined fighter, as good a U.S. Army officer as there was. "Colonel, we're in deep trouble," his voice crackled over the radio.

"What do you mean?" I asked, "You aren't even in contact with the enemy. A shot hasn't been fired in hours."

"Doesn't matter. We just stumbled over one of their communication lines. This isn't a two-strand telephone line, it's a full-fledged communications cable. There must be a couple dozen or more pairs of wires."

Startled, my mind racing, I said, "Cut a large section out of it so they can't repair it."

"Will do," Elrod chuckled. "But today isn't going to be much fun. This communications cable probably indicates an NVA infantry tactical command post for a 12,000-man division." *A division! We were way outnumbered.*

Then over the radio I heard the chilling chatter of semiautomatic weapons fire. The battle had begun.

Quickly, I told Colonel Vy and notified Colonel Book. Vy and I ran for the waiting helicopter.

All of Vy's battalions were now encountering stiff enemy resistance. Continuous, heavy, accurate mortar fire rained in on their positions. Helicopter gunships were unable to silence the deadly mortar fire.

The Third Battalion tried to break and run but I was later told that Major Elrod fired his M-16 semiautomatic rifle in the air and threatened to personally kill any ARVN officer or soldier who tried to desert, including the ARVN battalion commander.

Then over the radio came the words every commander dreads hearing.

"I'm hit!" It was Captain McNamara's voice screaming in pain.

"How bad?" I shouted back into the microphone.

"Real bad . . . both legs . . . can't walk."

Severely wounded, Larry lay three-quarters of the way up the side of the jungle ridge leading to FB-6.

While I was still in anguish over Larry, a transmission came in from Elrod. "We're up on line and assaulting . . . the ARVN look great . . . my God! I'm hit!"

At this the ARVN commander of the accompanying 44th ARVN Battalion deliberately turned his unit 90 degrees away from the fighting and assaulted in the wrong direction. For four days he and his battalion sat on top of a hill west of FB-6, completely out of the action. Later they would skulk back to Tanh Canh without firing a shot.

"The ARVN are deserting . . . leaving me to die . . . can you do anything? Or are you fresh out of miracles, Colonel?" Captain McNamara radioed.

If I had ever been in possession of miracles, I was certainly out of them now. But still I prayed for one.

"Talk fast, Colonel, the ARVN are jerking the radio out of my hand." His words came in torn fragments.

I had to level with him. "Larry, it's impossible to get a helicopter to you in that dense jungle . . . and we can't get there in time on foot." My insides were churning in frustration.

"Yeah, that's what I figured," he answered bravely. "Well, let's just say that I called to say good-bye. Elrod's being laid beside me right now. He's in bad shape . . . and an ARVN soldier is trying to jerk the radio away from me."

"I'll pray for you both," I said lamely. Years before I had done the same while watching my son die.

"If you pray for us, Colonel, everything will be all ri—gh—t!" Larry screamed as the ARVN soldier finally succeeded in wresting the radio handset from him and left him to die.

I wept.

28

The Lieutenant from KSU

And so the fighting continued, fierce, bloody, and deadly. Casualties escalated sharply on both sides. For now, FBs 5 and 6 remained under ARVN control.

On April 6, 1971, *Pacific Stars and Stripes* wrote:

SAIGON—The fire base was surrounded as of mid-afternoon Sunday, and no helicopters could get in or out . . . The toll of Communist dead in five days of fighting at the base 49 miles northwest of Pleiku rose to 1,546 . . . *Stars and Stripes* correspondent Sgt. John Mueller said he counted 10 Communist rockets Sunday afternoon when they exploded near (Tanh Canh) the command post of the 22nd ARVN Div.[3]

Day blurred into night, then into day, and back into night. Sleep came whenever and wherever we could catch it: sprawled on our backs in a jungle clearing or slumped on the side of a hill; propped up in a Jeep seat bouncing along some badly rutted, long-deserted dirt trail that pretended to be a single lane road; or sagging down and dozing off in a canvas helicopter jump seat.

Hour after bloody hour advisors struggled with the ARVN, jointly planned, offered advice, wheedled, cajoled, flattered when it helped, and, as a last resort, threatened. Casualties continued to mount. Up the valley to the northwest near Dak To airstrip, located halfway between Tanh Canh and Ben Het, is where Colonel Vy had established the 41st ARVN's forward tactical command post. It was not on the fire base itself, but close to the fighting and it provided excellent radio transmission and reception. But it was also vulnerable to enemy attack.

Fighting seemed to break out everywhere. The 22nd ARVN Division, though continuously propped up by the sweat, blood, and bodies of U.S. advisors, artillery, and helicopter support units, was slowly coming apart. It was like a garment unraveling not just at the hem and buttonholes, but at the main seams. It was stretched so taut that daylight shone through between the pieces of fabric.

General Brown and his boss back in Saigon, General Weyand, knew that the 22nd ARVN Division had to have help, or all was lost. They prevailed on the ARVN high command to divert some of their strategic reserve, made up of elite Airborne and Ranger units, from Saigon to the highlands.

One day, Colonel Book sent a helicopter out to pick me up at the 41st command post and bring me back to Tanh Canh for a meeting. Afterwards, I managed to steal away for a badly needed shower. The facilities weren't much by American standards. But considering how badly I smelled, it was as good as being at the Four Seasons in Georgetown.

Clutching a borrowed towel at my now skinny waist, my right hand carrying a borrowed canvas toilet kit, I clunked down the narrow concrete walkway in someone else's wooden shower clogs. The shower building was made of corrugated tin, had a concrete slab floor, and reminded me of a small, damp, empty warehouse. Along one wall, opposite the six shower heads, were two wooden benches. I dropped my towel and toilet bag on one of them and walked over to a shower head.

I had just lathered up when the door creaked open. A tall U.S. Army first lieutenant, wearing artillery brass on his jungle fatigue shirt collar, slipped in with the caution born of living with danger. He looked too old for his years and in his right hand he carried a loaded Colt .45 automatic.

Quickly he shucked his clothes and boots, got naked, and cranked the handle on the pipe two showerheads down from me. He shifted the .45 to his left hand and lathered up with his right.

I'd never seen anyone carry a loaded gun into a shower. Either the lieutenant was scared senseless, was crazy, or a touch of both.

Uncharacteristically I let my curiosity get the better of me. "I'm Jerry," I offered, rinsing off the last vestiges of soapy foam and moving toward my towel, "I'm the senior advisor to the 41st ARVN—the guys who are holding on to FB-6."

"Glad to meet you," he said, offering his hand. It was strong and rough with a lot of calluses.

"My artillery battery is providing some of your ARVN backup fire support. I'm the commander. I managed to hitch a ride in for a quick clean up." He stood six-two, a stringy, lean 180 pounds, and was serious of mind.

"Thank your men for me," I said. "Without their help we'd have been run off that ridge a week ago."

"Glad to be of service." He shifted the automatic back to his right hand.

"It's really none of my business, Lieutenant," I said, toweling dry. "But I've never seen anyone shower holding a loaded .45 before."

"Oh," embarrassed, he ducked out from under the shower spray and tossed the .45 on top of his clothes. "It's a habit . . . forgot I had it. Have to carry it everywhere I go: to the mess tent, the toilet, chapel services, I even sleep with it." He ducked back under the water, "Lot of fragging going on."

Duty with the ARVN as a U.S. advisor was so remote that I'd forgotten how dangerous it was to command an American unit.

This was 1971. Drug use had spilled over from the U.S. civilian population and had infected U.S. military units worldwide, even here in Vietnam.

GI drug pushers openly sold drugs in some U.S. units, and secretly sold them in just about all the others. In a few cases commanders who stood up to the criminals were "accidentally" blown away during a battle. Occasionally a commander was "fragged." It was easy to do.

The term came from *fragmentation* hand grenades. The drug pushers or enforcers waited and watched until the commander was asleep or inattentive. Then they pulled the pin on a grenade and rolled it under the officer's cot or desk. It exploded, fragmenting into dozens of pieces of steel.

Once a drug pusher successfully intimidated or silenced the unit commander, the junior officers and sergeants pretended not to see anything. It became a vicious, endless, deadly game. If the commander played along with the pushers, he lived. But many of his men became addicts or died unnecessarily in combat because they were high on drugs.

Fortunately, most of our youthful sergeants and officers, like this lieutenant, stood firm. But in doing so, they paid a terrible personal price. When they returned to the U.S., it angered me to see them vilified and spat upon by the war protesters—some of whom were drug pushers themselves.

Drying between my toes, I half asked, half stated, "You must be a career officer?"

Throwing back his head, he laughed hard. It was probably the first laugh he'd had in a long time. "I'm ROTC from Kansas State University. I'm only in for three years, then I'm splitting," he said, as he turned the shower handle off.

Shifting the .45 from the jumbled pile of clothes, his hand dug into the tangle for a towel. "Never wanted to be in the military," he said without looking at me.

"I'm surprised," I said, wrapping a towel around me and preparing to leave, "that you're not a professional military officer."

"This man's army will never appeal to me. I guess I'm just a country boy at heart."

"Since you're a Reserve Officer, you don't have to risk your life by volunteering to command and find yourself fighting both the enemy and your own men. You could easily serve on staff, back in the rear.

"I know. I volunteered to command, OK? And, yes, occasionally drug pushers have tried to kill me. It is scary sometimes. But I've sent quite a few of them to prison. Maybe next time one of them will get me, but until they do, everyone knows that my artillery battery is a drug-free zone."

He continued, "It's a stupid war. Anyone can see that our government has no intention of winning it. Many of my peers think I'm crazy, but they're wrong," he said. For a minute he stared off into nowhere.

"I didn't volunteer to fight in Vietnam because I agreed with it. I'm here because the country, for whatever dumb reason, decided to fight over here. And that automatically makes it my war. When this is over, if I make it back alive, I'm getting out of this dumb Army and going back to farming." Sitting down on a bench, he pulled on his socks and jungle boots and started lacing them up.

I nodded and left.

What the young lieutenant didn't mention was another problem he faced, one equally as deadly as drug pushers. Racial tension was boiling over in Vietnam just as it had in Schweinfurt, Germany. The difference was that in Vietnam, the militants had ready access to loaded weapons.

That year, in the Americale Division in Vietnam, there was a race riot in the 198th Infantry Brigade. Two hundred black soldiers seized the headquarters and threatened to turn it into a war zone, which they would have done had it not been for the dynamic action of Major General Fritz Kroesen, the division commander. He calmed the troops by personally assuring that all racial allegations were quickly and thoroughly investigated and fairly resolved.

As an advisor, I was spared such racial problems. There were only a handful of U.S. advisors, embedded in the Vietnamese Battalion, so we had to get along to survive. We lived and worked so far out in the jungle that we had few visitors. In one year, my advisory unit had one visit from a chaplain, plus a visit from four USO girls who played cards with my men for about an hour before helicoptering on.

In the end, it was not the 22nd ARVN Division but the strategic ARVN Ranger and Airborne Battalions, recently deployed from Saigon to Pleiku, that took the pressure off Tanh Canh and the two fire bases. Without their insertion and support, the 22nd Division would have lost the battle and the Vietnamese highlands.

Using FB-5 and FB-6 as anvils, the ARVN Airborne and Ranger units swept up the mountain ridges, flushing the NVA before them. Generals Weyand and Brown's staffs coordinated the nightly B52 strikes that wiped out the NVA headquarters and supply depots.

As the NVA attack ran out of steam, the crisis atmosphere subsided. Incoming reports became more favorable. From an eagle's-eye view, things were working out quite well. But at my worm's-eye level, we still had days of bloody combat before us. One day I arrived back at the 41st tactical command post in the field just as intelligence warned Colonel Vy to expect an attack on the command post near FB-6 that night.

The lowering sun threw long shadows at us. Soon it would touch the horizon, grow brighter, slowly blink, and then step down out of sight. Once again we set about shoring up our defenses and preparing for an all-out assault on our position. Other than me, the only Americans at the tactical command post were my assistant operations sergeant and a communications specialist.

The operations sergeant was a square-shouldered man of medium height. His hips were lean, his waist small, and his physical condition superb. My communications specialist was one of the happiest, most decent men I've known. He had a long-jawed face and his body moved with masculine grace.

Clearly our command post could not hold out against an all-out attack, and for tactical reasons the 41st could not move the command post to another location. Since we might be overrun, I thought it best to minimize the loss of American lives.

Calling my two sergeants together, I briefed them on the intelligence report and ordered them to pack their gear and radios and get back to Tanh Canh. They were unwilling to leave, but finally I persuaded them that there was no sense placing all three of our lives in danger.

From a cynical point-of-view, only one American life needed to be sacrificed to show that U.S. forces had not abandoned the ARVN during a crisis. Fortunately, the intelligence report proved wrong. The 41st enjoyed a quiet and peaceful night.

Early the next morning, Colonel Book sent his helicopter out with word for me to get on it and report to him as soon as possible. When I arrived back at Tanh Canh, I was stunned to find that the main command post for our 41st ARVN no longer existed. Nothing above knee height was left standing. Everything was a maze of splintered wood, twisted tin, smashed equipment, blood, and dried bits of flesh.

The evening before while my two sergeants were still unloading their equipment, a NVA 122 mm rocket hit the 41st ARVN command post at Tanh Canh dead center. My communications specialist and the ARVN soldier who was helping him carry in equipment, died instantly. My operations sergeant was severely wounded. They had begged me not to send them back to Tanh Canh. They had said, "Let us fight and die with you." By trying to save their lives, I had caused them to be killed. It still haunts me to this day.

The news media were also there. While a medic administered lifesaving assistance to my sergeant, a reporter pushed him out of the way so his TV cameraman could get a shot of him dying. Luckily Major Paul Emmitt, one of my senior battalion advisors, was also present and decked the newsman with one punch.

Unfortunately in Vietnam, journalists often got too caught up in the role of "aggressive reporter determined to get a story at all costs" and forgot their responsibility to help save a fellow American's life. Although my operations sergeant was evacuated, he later died from his wounds.

A few days later, I was making my way from the 41st's new main command post to my Jeep when one of my sergeants ran out of the building toward me shouting. He was a brusque, square-shouldered man who allowed no half measures. Waving both arms, he yelled, "Sir, they've found Captain McNamara!"

I froze mid-stride, and stared at him. The sun was pressing down hot upon Tanh Canh's red soil. Perspiration had already stained my fatigue shirt dark gray under the arm pits, even though noon was hours away. *Could it be true?*

"Sir," he persisted, "they've picked up Mac. He's alive!"

Stunned, I turned back to the command post. On the radio was the commanding officer of one of the Army's aviation gunship platoons.

"Are you certain it's Captain McNamara?" I asked, desperately wanting to believe, but unable to make the leap of faith.

"Roger, we've got him on board. It's a positive ID. I repeat again, it's a positive ID. He's in bad shape, but I think he'll make it."

"How? Where did you find him?"

"An ARVN airborne battalion sweeping down the ridge line cleaning out pockets of NVA resistance stumbled across him. Their U.S. advisor called for an emergency Medivac, and we happened to be in the area, so we kicked some gear overboard and made room for him."

"Tell me more about his condition?" I pleaded.

"Sorry, don't have time. A lot's going on right now . . . got to change radio frequencies. We'll drop him off at the U.S. Army Hospital in Pleiku."

There was no time to rejoice, for just then I heard the "wop-wop-wop" noise that Huey helicopter blades make when air pops out from under them during a descent. The string of Hueys pass-ing overhead sounded like a freight train.

The helicopters arched away in the usual elliptical pattern and then descended for the landing at Tanh Canh. Flaring to break their descent, they slapped down on the dirt airstrip that had been hacked out of the top of the hill.

The 22nd ARVN Division commander had decided to replace the 41st troops on FB-6 with newly arrived reinforcements. Once off the mountain, the regiment was released from its commit-ments and free to return home across the mountains to Landing Zone Crystal.

We couldn't send the relief plan and coordinating instruc-tions up to FB-6 over the radio. The enemy would intercept the transmission and ambush the ARVN forces as they picked their way down the mountain. Someone had to go to FB-6 and brief our people face to face.

29

A "Lovely" Visit

There was never a good time to fly into FB-6. The North Vietnamese surrounding it sat and waited, knowing that helicopters had to resupply the base at least once a day. When the choppers flew in, the NVA shot at them like clay pigeons.

The temperature was so high that the ARVN soldiers defending FB-6 were always in danger of becoming dehydrated. Water became more important than food. The ARVN didn't eat canned "C" rations like the American soldiers. In addition to ammunition, medical supplies and sacks of rice, the helicopters that resupplied them had to bring in five gallon cans of water. Cooking the rice required lots and lots of water.

There was only one helicopter route in and out of the landing zone on FB-6. Though the helicopters tried to vary their approaches, there was no room for deviation once they got on short final approach. It was a little like landing in the middle of a shooting gallery.

That day, in addition to the supplies, the only passengers on the helicopter resupply run were my South Vietnamese radio operator, Sergeant Lee—a different Lee than the one who drove my Jeep—and me. Lee was skinny, slender boned, and very nervous.

Lee and I scrambled aboard the lead cargo helicopter and flopped down on the hot metal cargo floor wedged between boxes of supplies, near the open cargo door. This helicopter belonged to the ARVN and a pinched-faced ARVN crew chief threw me a radio headset.

I jammed it over my ears while cradling my steel helmet between my legs. There were no canvas jump seats or safety belts. The helicopter wasn't rigged to carry passengers.

Its rotor blades started turning faster as the pilot wrapped up the engine to its full operating limits. Sighting back along the line of cargo helicopters, I saw all their rotor blades cone upward, straining and fighting for enough air to lift them and their cargo off the ground.

It was late in the afternoon and the air was muggy. My jungle fatigue shirt collar was drenched with sweat. Wearing a heavy flak jacket didn't help.

Slowly all 11 helicopters got light on their landing skids and one by one staggered off into the heavy air. Soon, we were strung out in a loose "daisy chain" formation, about three rotor-blade lengths apart.

Flying in a straight line, the trip to FB-6 took 15 minutes. But because the mountains were high, rugged, and steep, we flew a long, circuitous route so that the overloaded helicopters could gradually climb to an altitude high enough to clear the ridge.

Finally we were high enough and started angling west toward the ridge and FB-6. Sergeant Lee was shaking like a leaf. When we got to FB-6, I knew I'd have to keep a firm grip on some part of his body or he wouldn't jump off the helicopter with me. He'd stay on board and ride back to Tanh Canh leaving me without radio communications.

Bright, white muzzle flashes from enemy AK-47s and machine guns that were dug in around the fire base winked a hostile greeting to us. Both the door gunner and crew chief returned fire with their swivel mounted M-60 machine-guns.

Soon the ARVN gunships flying alongside both flanks of the cargo helicopters opened up with rocket fire. I don't know how effective it was, but it made me feel good.

Absently, I fingered the right front pocket of my jungle fatigue shirt feeling for the worn New Testament that I knew would be there. I called it my "Combat Bible." It was as much a part of my uniform as the silver lieutenant colonel's leaf pinned on my shirt collar. In it I had underlined favorite words and passages and had written all sorts of notes to myself.

As we drew near FB-6, I looked down from the helicopter onto a landscape so pockmarked and cratered by the fierce struggle taking place on it that it had taken on the look of an eerie lunar landscape. Its charred earth, and wind-whipped, sun-baked rocks were burned black; in a few places they were a mottled reddish-brown color.

Everywhere the military fortifications were surrounded by heaps of dry burlap sandbags. They lay rotting in the sun or were ripped open by lethal pieces of exploding steel. As a result, in many places the guts of the bags had spilled out and fallen into the erosion-gnawed foxholes and trench lines they were meant to protect.

Dramatically placed here and there, for artistic effect it seemed, were twisted metal helicopters. But their bent frames were melted by the searing heat and force of fiery explosions instead of an artist's welding torch.

Reaching out, I got a firm grip on Sergeant Lee's left arm and dragged him over to the doorway. Side-by-side we sat on the Slick's floor, our legs dangling out the open side cargo door.

The helicopter flared, slowed, skidded over the ground at about three feet and we jumped. That is, I jumped and dragged Lee with me. The crew chief and door gunner kicked boxes of cargo out behind us.

Before I hit the ground, something slammed into my chest, momentarily knocking the wind out of me. Lee and I crashed into the ground, rolled, ate dirt, and scrambled for cover. A number of empty slit trenches and foxholes were scattered around the landing zone. Finding one to roll into was not a problem.

With shaky hands, Lee checked out the radio. It was still working. While he was busy, I examined my chest. A piece of shrapnel from a North Vietnamese mortar round had torn through my right front shirt pocket and imbedded itself into my combat Bible. The amazing significance of this miracle did not sink in until much later, but to this day, I still have the Bible that saved me. As soon as the cargo helicopters cleared the landing zone, most of the enemy firing stopped. Miraculously, the entire string of helicopters ran the gauntlet successfully and made it back out safely. I hoped they would return later to pick us up—provided we were still alive.

Now we were inside the thick barbed wire that formed the defensive perimeter around the fire base, but we were still a long way from the command post at the top of the hill. Up there the headquarters bunker was embedded deep in the ground. Lee and I started climbing.

As we struggled toward the final roll of interior concertina barbed wire and toward the safety of the internal trenches, Lee dropped farther and farther behind. About 20 meters past the last wire, I looked back. The razor-sharp barbs of the concertina had deeply embedded themselves in his fatigues and webbing. He was caught fast.

Nothing would do but to crawl back down the hill, unbuckle the radio, jerk it off his back, throw it up the hill, then pry him loose. Fortunately, we were just about out of the range of enemy small arms fire. Still, an occasional spent AK-47 rifle round kicked up dust near us. Keeping Lee close to me this time, I clawed my way up the last one hundred meters or so of hillside.

My U.S. Advisors, whom I hadn't seen in two weeks, were overjoyed. For security reasons, I hadn't been able to alert them that I was flying in for a social call. The senior advisor was Major Paul Emmitt, a tall, solid American of unusual dedication and professional ability. He was ably assisted by Captain Cardin, who had volunteered for the mission, and, of course, the indomitable Captain Seiss.

Four brave and heroic U.S. Army sergeants were with them, helping coordinate the fighting and the ARVN defenses. They were Jefferson, Kyzer, Miller, and Thompson. With me at Tanh Canh had been Lieutenant Adler and Sergeants Culp and Jiles, brave men all. In spite of the horrific ordeal my men on FB-6 had lived through these past weeks, they were still in fairly good shape. Only one of them was wounded, but not seriously.

Ragged clouds drifted over the ridge and drenched the fire base with a sudden sheet of rain. As quickly as it started, it stopped, and the clouds moved on.

Unfortunately, intelligence wasn't clear about how much enemy resistance remained in the area. If the amount of firing at the helicopters was any indication, there were still a good number of NVA lurking about.

I shared with my advisors that tomorrow morning an ARVN Airborne Battalion would helicopter in and relieve them on position. At the same time several ARVN Airborne and Ranger battalions would start fighting their way up the hill to the fire base.

One of our battalions would get on the Vietnamese helicopters and fly out. The other two battalions would have to walk out. Of course, as our battalions picked their way down the mountain toward McNamara's rope bridge, they still might get blown away by an enemy ambush. Or then again, they might encounter only light NVA resistance.

Spreading out my map on the ground, I explained the route the battalions must take. I went over what they needed to remember and passed on all the intelligence as to the location of suspected enemy units. Half an hour later, we said our goodbyes.

The ARVN officers and my advisors were smiling as we shook hands. Their difficult ordeal was nearly over. In 24 hours, they'd be off FB-6, or would they?

Where it once had been difficult to get Sergeant Lee to climb the hill, now he led me all the way down to the bottom. With water up to our ankles from another sudden heavy rain shower, Lee and I crouched low in a foxhole on the uphill side of the landing zone, and awaited the return of the cargo helicopters. The NVA were unaccustomed to helicopters flying into the fire base twice in one day, so the return caught them by surprise. As a result, enemy fire was light and sporadic.

Several helicopters skidded over the landing zone as their crews kicked out supplies. One slowed and touched its skids lightly on the ground like a humming bird hovering at a bird feeder. The crew chief beckoned us to hurry.

Ten quick steps and Sergeant Lee and I dived through the open helicopter door and skidded across the hot metal floor. Abruptly, the helicopter popped up into the air and at the same time banked sharply to the left. Its turbine engine screamed in protest as the pilot wrapped in all available power and streaked toward our home base at Tanh Canh.

The next morning, Colonel Book loaned me his helicopter to fly to Pleiku to visit Captain McNamara. It was another hot day, as were all days in South Vietnam, except during the monsoon downpours when humidity blanketed the heat.

The wood and cement block field hospital wasn't much to brag about by U.S. standards, but the wards were clean. An overworked Army nurse, with stringy hair and bags under her eyes, wearing unpressed jungle fatigues, led me to Larry's bed.

He was lying on his back with tubes taped to his arms and face. Weak, tired, and dehydrated, he looked as all soldiers do when they have suffered too much, been scared for too long, and been tested beyond the limits of human endurance.

"Sir," he said, thinly smiling through cracked, swollen lips, "thank you for praying. I made it!"

Gripping his hand I said, "A lot of people were praying for you and still are." Then I patted his shoulder reassuringly. "I'll be talking to your doctor shortly," I said. "Has he given you any word?"

Slowly tears trickled down his face. "I've got gangrene in both legs. I'm going to lose them," he said, embarrassed by his tears but unable to hold them back.

Quickly changing the subject, I asked, "How did you manage to stay alive?"

"Well, my legs were useless. So I had to drag myself along with my arms. I hid in gullies and ravines. The North Vietnamese knew I was somewhere in the area, and they looked hard. They got as close to me as five meters once, but passed by without seeing me." Painfully, he continued, "The hardest part was getting water. Thank God it rained every day. Water got trapped in the tropical plants and banana trees where the large leaves form a sort of cup with the stalk. I dragged myself from plant to plant. I never gave up."

"What about Major Elrod?" I asked.

"He was bad off . . . lost too much blood. With my bad legs I couldn't help him much. After a while . . . he just died."

Upon her return, the exhausted nurse insisted that I leave. Reluctantly, I turned to go.

"Sir," he said, "when the ARVN left me to die, they stripped off my watch, wedding ring and stole my wallet. Please try to get them back for me."

"You bet," I said hoping my bitterness wasn't showing.

On the way out, I talked to Larry's surgeon. He was a bone-weary Army major who had operated on too many wounded for too long.

"In the captain's case, both legs have to go," he said matter-of-factly. "The guy's lucky to be alive. One leg gets cut off above the knee. The other gets cut below the knee." He shrugged.

Before shuffling away to see another patient, he added, "That's the way it is, Colonel. There's nothing you or I can do about it." Sad, weary, and more than a little dejected, I trudged back to the helipad.

Back at Tanh Canh, I reviewed the plan for my U.S. Advisors to fly out of FB-6 on the helicopters—that is, they would all fly out except one. Captain Seiss, my most savvy and combat experienced advisor would accompany the ARVN on foot. If everything went wrong and the two battalions were lost to the enemy, John would make it out alive, if anyone could.

Hours of waiting and radio silence again gnawed at my insides. Once more, Colonel Vy and I stood at the steep approaches to the same muddy river where Captain McNamara had previously escaped from the clutches of the enemy. Finally, in the distance we heard the sound of soldiers' boots pounding the hard earth. Soon there were hands raised in salute and greeting as the two battalions wearily emerged from the primeval forest on the far side of the river.

Once again there were ecstatic embraces and warm greetings. Captain Seiss piled his weapons and gear in the back of my Jeep and we began the long, dangerous drive back to Tanh Canh.

For the 41st, the war in the highlands was almost over. When the regular NVA troops retreated, the VC guerilla fighters disappeared from the Tanh Canh area. Like the NVA, they too had been badly mauled.

After the Paris Peace Talks ended the war, a senior North Vietnamese officer commented to a senior American officer that the U.S. Armed Forces had never lost a major engagement to the NVA. From the DMZ in the north to the delta in the south, not a single VC battalion was still able to fight as a unit.

Colonel Nguyen Don Tu of the NVA put the war in perspective when he said, "Your military victory was irrelevant, since we North Vietnamese won the peace negotiations." He was right. Our armed forces won the fighting war; our peace negotiators lost the peace negotiations.

The following day, Captain McNamara's surgeon told me over the radio telephone that Larry's recovery was bordering on the miraculous. As a result, he would only have to amputate one leg and that below the knee, not above it.

Strangely, the surgeon chose to wait another 24 hours before operating. The next day, he reported continued progress and said that Larry would probably only lose a foot.

The following day, I telephoned the hospital again to check on Larry. I was told that he had been flown back to the United States and that the amputation would be performed there.

Several years later I met Major Lawrence V. McNamara in Bremerhaven, Germany. It was during NATO war maneuvers. He was newly posted there and both his feet and legs were functioning fine. Oh yes, I did manage to locate his wedding ring, watch and wallet and mail them to him.

The action on that ridge and how we reacted to it became part of who we are. We American advisors are eternally welded together with FB-6 by what happened there. In the same way we are all part of our country and its history and culture, part of our place of origin, part of our ancestors, and the heritage they passed on to us.

Just before I left Vietnam in the fall of 1971, Colonel Vy asked me this question after a long and introspective dinner conversation, "How does America make people like you and your advisors?" It's a question worth pondering.

30

Pentagon Bound

My return to Colorado Springs from Vietnam was uneventful; the reunion with Char and the children was happy and joyful. But as soon as I got home, we had to immediately relocate the family—an added stress that made the adjustment all the more difficult for all of us. Quickly we packed our household goods, shipped them off, and once again drove across the country. This time, our destination was Washington, D.C. There, in Carriage Hills, a suburb of Vienna, Virginia, we found a house that suited our needs and rented it.

It is never easy for a family to adjust to living without the father for a year, and then suddenly make room for him again, no matter how much they love him, miss him, and want him to return. The adjustment is particularly difficult when the father is coming back from fighting in a war.

On top of that adjustment, the children had to once again give up old friends in Colorado and make new friends in Virginia. For the children, being uprooted was never easy, and having an absent father suddenly thrust back into their lives added to the difficulty.

It wasn't easy for me either. It was months before I no longer reflexively dove for a "foxhole" when startled by a loud noise. It took even longer for me to enjoy a deep sleep, since failure to sleep lightly in combat can be the difference between life and death.

Two weeks after we got settled in Vienna, and the children were enrolled in school, I headed to the Pentagon, with orders in hand. Once inside, I stopped an officer walking down the hall and asked, "Can you tell me where this organization is located?"

He looked at my paper and his face soured, "Oh, you're one of those. Go down the hall, turn left at the second hallway, and it's the third or fourth door on the right."

I followed his instructions, then handed my orders to a secretary, who took me into an inner office and introduced me to the colonel in charge. He stood up, smiled warmly, extended his hand and said, "Welcome to the Office of the Assistant Vice Chief of Staff of the Army. People on the Army staff call us AVICE," he stressed the letter A. "The old joke is that if you have to be in 'vice,' choose AVICE."

He chuckled alone at the inside joke, then walked me around and introduced me to my fellow laborers in the vineyard. I was assigned a desk in a windowless cubicle complete with chalkboard walls, chalk, erasers, and an electronic calculator.

My fellow officers were bright, energetic, busy, tough, and—like me—clawing their way up the corporate military ladder. All had graduate degrees in subjects such as operations research, mathematics, engineering, or physics.

"What's your graduate degree in?" someone asked.

"International Relations," I said. Judging by the looks on their faces, liberal arts degrees were not highly esteemed by AVICE.

It seemed no one could talk without a piece of chalk. To emphasize concepts or make a point, they wrote equations or mathematical squiggles on the chalk board walls. After awhile it rubbed off on me, no pun intended. I still like to talk with chalk or a magic marker in my hand.

The book of Proverbs says that even a fool will be considered wise if he keeps his mouth shut. I did, but it wasn't easy. *What great sin have I committed,* I asked myself, *that merits such punishment as being assigned to this office?*

The answer came in the form of Major General Herb McChrystal, boss of the Office of Programs, Plans and Analysis which is now called PA&E. Herb was a slender, sensitive, down-to-earth fellow with a great sense of humor and an extra portion of humility. To know him was to like and respect him.

One day he called me in for a chat, "Have you noticed," he began, motioning me to a chair beside his desk, "that all your fellow staff officers have hard graduate degrees?"

"Yes, Sir," I painfully admitted.

"Good. Now the reason you are here, and I selected you myself, is because your personnel file says you have a lot of common sense."

"So?" I mumbled glumly.

"Cheer up, Jerry. There are two people in this organization who have liberal arts degrees: you . . . and me."

He watched my face closely for a reaction. I didn't disappoint him.

"Now your question is probably, 'what's a nice, liberal arts lieutenant colonel like you doing in a place like this?'" He leaned back in his chair enjoying himself.

"Yes, Sir," I agreed. "I would like to know why I'm here, because right now I feel like a duck out of water."

"Well, it's like this. AVICE is overflowing with ambitious, hard-chargers." He clasped his hands behind his head. "There is one thing lacking, an abundance of common sense. I selected you because I believe the Army is too important to leave to technicians, engineers, mathematicians, and scientists. Your job is to try to make sense out of what's going on around here." Standing up and coming around the desk, he took me by the arm and moved me across the room.

"I want you to keep your eyes and ears open and become involved in everything you can. Anything that doesn't make sense to you, say so. If they won't listen, come to me. I'll see to it that they do pay attention. Any questions?"

"Not right now. But there may be some later," I said.

"Fine, come back at any time," he eased me out the door.

Herb knew, and I was soon to learn, that when you assemble two hundred plus of the Army's brightest, most aggressive, most relentlessly ambitious officers together in one organization, they bear close watching. They were so talented that when a problem arose requiring only a simple solution, for the sheer joy of seeing the problem-solving process at work, they would complicate it.

By habit, someone would pick up the omnipresent piece of chalk and start squiggling on a wall. They loved elegant processes, and it became both fun and exhilarating to work with them. From them I learned a lot, including what not to do.

Of course, learning what not to do didn't just apply to my military work. It also applied to Charlene's and my effort to learn how to broaden our Christian lives. For example, one day, Charlene and I were invited to speak at a Full Gospel Businessmen's meeting. It was a Christian group, which met in a hotel in downtown Washington. After the meeting, we were asked to pray for the sick.

Over the years, both of us had spoken to church groups, and I had occasionally taught Sunday school. And though we had always been devout Christians and believed that Jesus still healed the sick just as the Bible described, we had never publicly prayed for anyone to be healed.

The first person we were asked to pray for that day was a man whose doctor said he was dying of cancer. A man pushed him toward us in a wheelchair; his head had fallen lifelessly to one shoulder. Char and I looked at his condition, the expectancy in the eyes of his friends, and knew that we were wasting our time. We weren't Jesus, and God wasn't about to heal this man based on our weak prayers.

To our amazement, after stumbling through a most ineffective prayer, the man's head slowly raised itself to an upright position. A few minutes later, he stood up, stretched his legs, and walked out of the room with a friend following behind pushing his wheelchair. Years later, a woman came up to me in a hotel lobby and asked, "Did you once pray for a man in a wheelchair who was dying of cancer?"

"Yes," I replied.

She smiled, "I was there in the room when you did. I was a skeptic and didn't believe in praying for the sick, but I was curious as to what would happen. So I pressed in close to see what kind of gimmick it was. In fact, when he walked out of the room, I followed him and even got on the garage elevator with him and his friends, because I knew it was all a fake.

"I got the name and phone number of his friend, the man who was pushing the wheelchair, so I could follow up on the scam and expose it. But as God would have it, he and I started dating. We were later married, and are still happily married today. The other man, the one in the wheelchair is still in good health. Thank you, for leading me to my husband."

But most of my time was spent working in the Pentagon. And though professionally my Pentagon assignment was career enhancing, Charlene and I often wondered where my career was heading—if anywhere! Ex-enlisted men who became officers usually topped out at about the rank of lieutenant colonel. A few officers with enlisted backgrounds are selected for promotion to full colonel. Fewer still attain general officer rank.

So one evening, we convened a family meeting around the large dining room table that had been handmade for us by the Pennsylvania Dutch. I reminded the children that I had entered the Army as a young private, and though the U.S. Army had been good to me and though I'd worked hard, it would be highly unusual for those whose career paths followed mine to rise much above my current rank. It might be smart to think of retiring and taking up a civilian career.

Charlene was enthusiastic about how great it would be to live together as a family with no more separations and wars for me to fight. The children shared similar feelings and we prayed that God would help us know what we should do. As it happened, God was preparing a very different answer to our collective prayer.

A month later, as I walked along a Pentagon hallway, an excited major enthusiastically congratulated me, "Congratulations for making the full colonel's list."

"What? I'm not even eligible to be promoted."

"Here it is, in the *Congressional Record*," he waved a copy at me.

Going back to my office, I phoned Big John McCleod who was now working in Army Personnel. "John, just saw a copy of the *Congressional Record*. It's got my name on the promotion list, but I'm not in the zone to be considered for promotion. Is this some kind of sick joke?"

"Jerry, you know that after we select from among people who are in the zone of eligibility, we're allowed to pick another five percent from those who are junior but are considered truly outstanding. Why don't you thank me instead of bawling me out? This is no joke and no mistake, that's really your name. You've been selected for promotion to full colonel even though you're below the zone."

The following month brought another surprise. A letter from John's office notified me that I had been selected to attend the U.S. Army War College in Carlisle, Pennsylvania. At the college, students are immersed in courses on military affairs, international relations, economics, and domestic matters. Officers from sister military services, as well as top-level civilians from the State Department, CIA, and other government agencies also attend.

My career had taken an unexpected, but delightful upturn—and the good things were just beginning. Midway through the War College year, my name appeared on the Army's first selection list for brigade commanders. It was an Army truism, at that time, that for an infantry officer, all roads to general officer rank led through brigade command.

About this time our oldest daughter, Charlie, who had been attending community college in Harrisburg, was admitted to the dental hygiene school at the University of South Dakota. There she met and married Doctor Raleigh Vantramp, who was then a student. Later, they established the Dove Family Dental practice at Federal Way in Washington State.

On June 11, 1973, the day after graduating from the War College, I stood at attention while Colonel Hal Barber, the War College Chief of Staff, pinned two of Hal's own silver colonel's eagles on one of my shoulder epaulets. Charlene pinned on the other.

Once again the Curry family, minus our daughter Charlie, boarded a jet for Germany. There I became commander of the 2500-man Third Brigade, Eighth Infantry Division, located at Coleman Barracks near Mannheim. The division was ably commanded by Major General Fred Davison, America's first black division commander. If I did well as a brigade commander, I would be in competition for promotion to general.

When my tour as brigade commander ended, further career opportunities didn't look promising. In fact, my next assignment seemed to portend the worst. I was posted to V Corps Headquarters in Frankfurt, to a job created just to give me something to do.

There was no office available, so the headquarters commandant took a large closet with no windows, painted it and moved in a desk and telephone. In place of a wall painting, I had a telephone junction box to look at.

Lieutenant General Bill Desobry, developer of the M-1 Abrams tank that twice proved its worth in Iraq during combat operations, was the corps commander. Bill was one of the Army's great generals, an officer and gentleman of the first rank. He and his wife,

Jackie, set a standard of personal conduct for us all to emulate by showing us how to care for our troops and their families.

Occasionally after a few drinks at the Officer's Club, the other colonels in Corps Headquarters would razz me about my telephone junction box office. "Boy, you must have really fouled up your brigade command to end up in that closet," they would say.

Several months later, Char and I hosted a dinner party at our home. After dinner, General Desobry announced that I had been selected for promotion to brigadier general. He then made me V Corps Chief of Staff. This meant that all the colonels who had previously razzed me, now worked for me.

Some years later, I met General Jack Faith, who had been on the promotion board that had selected me.

"You know, Jerry," he confided, "a year later you might not have been selected."

"Why not?"

"Normally the Army chooses those who have the right background, to be selected for flag rank. You know . . . those who have been aides to generals, or to the Secretary of the Army, or whose father or grandfather was someone important, or those who have the right kind of officer efficiency reports. Being a West Point graduate also helps. You didn't have any of that. In addition, you were an ex-enlisted man and an African American who had graduated from college by spending years attending night school.

"I particularly enjoyed reading one of your early efficiency reports. It said, 'If this officer had more ambition, he'd make an outstanding officer.'

"Fortunately for you, the war in Vietnam had just ended and successful combat command was at the forefront of everyone's thinking. The promotion selection board was instructed to give weight to those who had commanded in combat with distinction and had demonstrated outstanding leadership abilities. Those instructions got you selected. The next year, that window of opportunity closed. Selections reverted to being based on more traditional criteria. I, for one, am glad we selected you."

* * *

One day I learned that the military's Frankfurt Junior High School had been singled out for an award of excellence. A group of educators had traveled from the United States to Europe to evaluate various schools. Of the hundreds of military overseas schools evaluated, Frankfurt was the only one to qualify for the award. My job as chief of staff also made me superintendent of military schools, so I made an appointment to visit and congratulate the principal.

"General," he began, waving me to a seat in his cramped office. "It is good of you to come by. To what do I owe this honor?"

"The honor is mine. I came to congratulate you for winning such a prestigious academic award."

We talked of many things that day, and finally I leaned forward and asked a question I had been wanting to ask someone for a long time.

"Tell me, what makes for an excellent school, like yours?"

He leaned back in his chair and said more to the open window than to me, "You'll never find a good school with a bad principal or a bad school with a good principal."

Of course, he was right and his comment applies to most organizations and institutions. *Leadership is everything.*

Toward the end of my tenure as chief of staff, a terrorist planted a bomb in the cloak room of the Terrace Officer's Club near V Corps Headquarters. It exploded, destroying the dining room. My 15-year-old daughter, Toni Rene, was eating lunch there. Fortunately, she escaped injury.

Unfortunately, V Corps was about to undergo something much more serious than a terrorist attack.

31

The New Corps Commander

One day the Army announced that V Corps was getting a new commander—he was a lieutenant general who had been newly promoted to three stars. His orders took him from Fort Hood, Texas to Washington for two weeks of Pentagon briefings, and then on to Frankfurt, Germany.

At Fort Hood he had been an armored division commander. Officers at V Corps Headquarters who knew him mentioned a darker side to his character, which manifested itself by intimidation of subordinates. But he was also well known for his willingness to carry out orders at all costs. "Give him a job to do, and he gets it done," the senior generals fondly said.

When his name was circulated among the Army four-star generals, the "College of Cardinals," as they were called, gave their blessing. But not all of the four-star generals supported his selection. General Bill Knowlton not only strenuously objected to it, but tried to prevent it. Most of the four stars elected not to support Bill's efforts. They later came to regret their decision, but by then the damage had been done.

As a West Point cadet, he had flunked out, twice. Doggedly persistent, determined to be an Army officer, he enrolled in a civilian college ROTC program. After graduation, he was commissioned a second lieutenant.

He then successfully navigated up the promotion channels with the determination of a spawning salmon. Now he was about to take over an Army corps, a choice general officer assignment.

It seemed a fortuitous coincidence when I was ordered back to Washington to attend a two-week new-general-officer "charm school." I thought that being in Washington would give me a great opportunity to meet and greet the new corps commander before he came to Germany—especially since I was going to be his chief of staff.

At the meeting I warmly began, "Sir, I've canvassed the senior generals in Germany and have several items to brief you on, which may be of interest to you."

"I am already the best-informed, best-prepared general ever to be assigned to Germany," he exploded, jutting out his chin. "I know Europe!" he boasted. "I know Europe! So don't try to tell me about Europe! I have no interest in what other generals think!"

I looked at him. He was a heavy-set, broad-boned, man with hard eyes. It is easy to summarize the results of my later inquiries at the Pentagon concerning him. The concensus was that he was ruthless, driven, and utterly unforgiving of anyone who crossed him for any reason. I flew back to Europe troubled in spirit.

It is customary for the outgoing and incoming corps commanders to have a joint ceremony, complete with marching troops and a military band playing rousing marches. When I broached the subject to General Desobry, the outgoing V Corps commander, his face clouded. "Under no circumstances will I appear with that man on the same reviewing stand!" he said.

So we had two identical ceremonies, separated by a two-week period. The first was for the corps to say goodbye to General Desobry, the outgoing commander. The second was to welcome the new incoming commander.

Intuitively, I knew that the general and I could not peacefully coexist. Still, like a broken record, I kept repeating to myself one of my pet management theories, *A true professional can work for anyone*. But deep inside something kept saying, *This isn't going to work out . . . it really isn't!*

It seemed to me that he would change facts to suit his mood. He was so skillful at shading the truth that even those who knew better were persuaded to believe his version of it.

A case in point was a meeting with the new corps commander, the deputy commander, Major General Herb Wolff, a senior administration official, and me. Later, while Herb and I were listening to the commander brief the Corps' Staff, Herb whispered to me, "Evidently we were in a different meeting. That isn't even close to what was said."

Herb was a true infantryman who had taught bayonet fighting at Fort Benning and firmly believed in our nation. He was also an excellent linguist.

One of the commander's favorite ploys was to convene a meeting of subordinate commanders and staff officers, and ask them to report on a subject such as, "How ready is your unit for combat action?"

He would then pressure subordinate officers into publicly reporting that the combat readiness of their units was much better than it actually was. This made V Corps look good in the Pentagon's eyes, at least on paper.

Once an officer surrendered to his badgering, the commander would indifferently shrug his massive shoulders and say, "Well, I'm not telling you to change your report. That's entirely up to you."

Although he compromised the integrity of many officers in this way, in others he inspired a type of "German Führer" hero worship. They strained to emulate his swagger, his blunt talk, and his short-cut methods of getting instant results. For them he became a hero.

One Wednesday morning, he called me into his office and gruffly instructed, "General, I'm calling a meeting of the top commanders and staffs in the corps. Set it up for Saturday at noon."

"Yes, Sir," I replied, "But all month they've been working 12 and 14 hour days including most weekends. Can we schedule the meeting for Friday or Monday?"

"Are you contradicting me?" he shouted, reddening.

Naively I thought, *He'll settle down later in the day. By then I might be able to get him to change his mind.* So I quietly went about my duties.

I knew the time-honored rules for success that most general officers follow. Essentially, it was a policy of see-no-evil, hear-no-evil, and speak-no-evil, especially about or to another general officer. Be respectfully moderate at all times; be conservative in your decisions and actions. Never offend; never contradict unless it can be done in a self-effacing manner. Always shift blame away from yourself and avoid responsibility whenever possible, especially with anything controversial. Take credit for successes and express measured concern when there is a failure.

I suppose many generals-to-be tell themselves that when they finally claw their way up to positions of great responsibility and power; they will become strong, decisive decision makers. The truth is that by the time they get there, some of them have so compromised themselves that their conscience has gone limp. It has been so long since they stood for anything, they no longer know how to stand firm.

That afternoon, I knew I was overstepping the bounds of propriety when I sent my boss a small typed memo suggesting that with 50 or so people giving up their Saturday afternoons; perhaps we could reschedule the meeting to take place on a weekday.

He zinged the memo back to me with handwritten comments scrawled across the top of it, "The meeting will take place on Saturday. See that everyone is in attendance!"

My duties as chief of staff included suggesting options, but the commander always had the final say. So I set up the meeting. Besides, I rationalized, the corps had worked so many weekends that one more wouldn't matter.

Saturday came and the commander was in fine form, marching across the stage for the benefit of the assembled commanders and staff. Then turning toward me, he said, "You all know I am opposed to requiring anyone to work on a Saturday."

He paused for affect, then continued, "I did all I could to prevent calling you here, but my chief of staff insisted that this meeting take place today."

He turned and looked at me, then smirked and said, "If I had my way, you would all be at home enjoying your families."

My response was to stand up and slowly walk out of the room. Back at the office, I directed that packing boxes be brought in. I began to take pictures off the wall and remove mementoes from bookcases and pack them for shipment.

Half an hour later, General Wolff walked in, saw me packing, and asked, "Jerry, what does this mean?" He gestured toward the empty walls.

"Herb, if this is what it takes to wear general officer's stars on my collar, the price is too high. I'm quietly leaving the Army. No press conferences, no dramatic gestures. I just want out."

Shock registered on his face. He started pacing back and forth, then turned to me and said, "Stop packing. Dismiss the idea that you can run away from this. You and I and the corps commander have got to talk."

Reluctantly, I agreed.

"Don't do anything more until I get back," he directed and left.

Soon he returned, followed by the corps commander. Only later would I learn that Herb had forcefully collared him and insisted that he apologize to me.

"What is this General Wolff is telling me about your wanting to leave?" the commander began.

"I don't respect you personally or professionally," I began. "To me you are devious and dishonest."

"This is ridiculous," he laughed, enjoying the spectacle. "Never in the history of the United States Army has a junior general like you said such a silly thing to a senior general like me. Don't you know who I am?" he asked rhetorically. "You obviously don't understand how to get along as a general officer." He laughed, "But because I am a very understanding man, I'm going to overlook your insubordination."

After a lengthy monologue, he stepped to the door, turned and offered an afterthought, "Look, Jerry, I like you. I want to see you get ahead. You're the youngest general officer in the Army. Now if you cooperate with me, do everything I say exactly as I tell you to do it and quit being a problem, I guarantee that you'll be promoted within 12 to 18 months." In a threatening, yet patronizing voice, he added, "If you don't, you're going to embarrass your race and your family by being discredited and thrown out of the Army."

As my heart thudded against my rib cage, I said, "Sir, I believe that you are the one who doesn't understand."

Grunting, he turned and stomped from the office, slamming the door behind him.

Herb Wolff gave me some sage advice, "An abrupt retirement may seem justified to you, but in the eyes of the Army it will signal that you did something terribly wrong and got yourself fired. Like it or not, you have to stand your ground by coming to work every day, no matter how distasteful you find it."

He squeezed my shoulder with his large hand and added. "It will take time for the Army to assess this situation. You've got to hang in there until they do."

Later, the commander sought out General Wolff and gave him a scathing lecture about loyalty, closing with the words, "If you report this to higher headquarters, your career is ended along with Jerry's."

Herb was not easily intimidated, "Failure to report this will inevitably lead to an Inspector General investigation or worse. We owe a 'heads up' to General Blanchard, our boss in Heidelberg. It would be better if you did it, but I'm prepared to do it myself if you won't."

With any organization, when there is an irreconcilable conflict between the boss and a subordinate, the boss usually wins and the subordinate gets fired. So I expected that when this crisis was over, the commander would still be in charge and I'd be retired. In the meantime, as Herb Wolff reminded me, life and work must continue.

Because I was the commander's chief of staff, every morning I had to report to him at the daily staff meeting. We talked over the activities of the preceding day, discussed the current day's proposed activities, and planned for the future.

Before the confrontation, Char and I had been one of the most popular couples in the corps. Now others reacted to us as though we had social leprosy. Our home phone, which usually rang day and night, fell silent.

If I was in a room full of officers and the commander entered, people scooted away from me. Few officers were willing to be seen talking to me in his presence. Life became difficult, lonely, and silent, not just for me, but for the whole Curry family. Other wives didn't want to be seen with Charlene. They feared that when I was decapitated, some of my blood might splash onto their husbands' careers.

At school the other children pumped our children for information. They asked our children how Charlene and I were holding up under the ordeal. Undoubtedly the parents of those children were using their kids to find out how we were doing.

The real man in the middle was General Wolff. He had done nothing, but as second in command, he was thrown into the impossible role of middleman. With integrity, honesty, and great personal courage, he carried on with his duties. He also tried desperately to help the general be a successful corps commander.

In spite of Herb Wolff's best efforts, it was not to be. The corps commander's actions became more erratic. Soon even German Army generals and high-ranking civilians started noticing his unpredictable behavior.

As was our custom in the military, we regularly attended the base chapel and supported its activities. But this year was different. The old chaplain departed for an assignment back in the United States and was replaced by a nice-looking, articulate young major who seemed to feel that it was his calling in life to socially and politically reeducate the less enlightened.

From the pulpit, he told us that God the Father was really God, the Mother and Father. Supposedly Eve was created at the same time Adam was created, so Adam was not the first person God created. In his sermons he worked hard at neutering and feminizing the Bible. I tried to engage him in a dialog about his sermons, but he seemed to feel that laymen had no right to question his theology.

With all of the difficulties I faced contending with my boss on a daily basis, I needed some spiritual encouragement and nourishing. So for the first time in nearly 25 years, Charlene and I started attending an off-base church.

It was located on the edge of a lovely green park and was called Christ the King Anglican Episcopal Church. The services were high church and in English. We joined the choir. For us Christ the King became an oasis in the desert. Since then, we have usually attended Episcopal churches, though we are troubled that the Episcopal Church of America has strayed so far from its biblical roots.

Three long months passed . . . then four. Day-to-day living and my military duties got lonelier and became more wearisome. There is nothing quite like a terminal career crisis to help concentrate one's thinking.

The phone call came just before Christmas, on a bleak European day in 1975. A few weeks before, General Wolff had briefed me that General Blanchard had instructed him to be prepared to assume command on short notice.

Over the phone, the voice of U.S. Army Europe's Chief of Staff said, "General Blanchard wants you to know that a decision to relieve the corps commander has been made."

I wasn't aware of how crushing the weight of the situation had become until it lifted. The months when my family and I had been ostracized had been traumatic. When I realized the gravity of what was going to happen, I felt a heavy sadness. The happy ending that I had almost not dared to hope for had come, but there was no joy in it.

"What's the next move?" I asked.

"Well," he continued, "General Blanchard would like the commander to enjoy one last Christmas holiday season in the Army, without knowing that he will be relieved of command shortly."

Little by little, all the pain and agony my boss had caused me over the past months dribbled away. "I understand and agree," I heard myself saying.

"Thank you, Jerry," he answered, then graciously added, "General Blanchard will be most appreciative." Then he hung up.

The Christmas season is always joyously celebrated in the military. But this year it had a special significance for Char and me, probably even more so for General Wolff and his wife, Billie. In our hearts there was truly peace on earth and good will toward men.

A few days after New Years, on a soggy, cold German morning, the second phone call came. "General Blanchard will relieve the corps commander today. Have him report to Army Headquarters in Heidelberg at half-past noon."

"It will be done," I promised, echoing the V Corps motto with a heavy heart.

After making my way through the narrow, private passageway that led directly from my office to the commander's, I quietly told him, "Sir, General Blanchard would like you to be in his office at half past noon today."

"That's great," he exulted. "I've been looking for an opportunity to tell him about all the wonderful things the corps has been doing. He lunged to his feet and with a spring in his step, skipped around the huge oak desk, then bent his head and peered out the window.

"It's raining too hard to take a helicopter," he said, more to himself than to me. "So I'll go by sedan. My wife and daughter can ride down with me and go shopping while I'm talking with General Blanchard."

Bubbling over with enthusiasm, he departed for Heidelberg. I never saw him happier. For me it was bittersweet.

Standing in front of the Abrams Building that housed V Corps Headquarters, I watched the general's military sedan splash off in the ice-cold rain. As he motored away, I saluted him for what was to be the last time. I never saw him again.

An hour later, the drizzle stopped, the clouds thinned, and patches of blue appeared overhead. Then, like an omen of goodwill, the cold smell of rain faded, and bright January sunshine bathed Frankfurt.

Finally, the phone call came, "The commander has been relieved of command of V Corps. He is on his way back to Frankfurt by sedan. His orders are to drive directly to his private residence and stay there. The Corps Headquarters building is off limits to him."

"Have his aide pack his office and household goods. He is to depart Germany as soon as arrangements can be made, but under no condition will he stay in Germany longer than one more week. Do you understand, General?"

Chief of Staff Blanchard's voice had that cold, clipped tone that the military reverts to in times of crisis or grave danger, "Is General Wolff in the Headquarters building?"

"No, he's in a helicopter flying to Fulda."

"Get him on the radio and have him return. Tell him he has just assumed command of the corps."

"It will be done," I answered.

As was to be expected, the Army chose an honorable and exceptionally competent officer to replace the relieved commander, Lieutenant General Don Starry. Sooner than anyone thought possible, memories of the short-term commander faded.

The boxes in my closet were unpacked and pictures rehung on the walls. The Corps began functioning as it was designed to function. Don Starry was fully and decisively in command of us all.

Once again Charlene and I became socially acceptable. Our friends—or were they just acquaintances?—returned. In a few months, we found ourselves more popular than ever, socially in great demand.

But there was a price to be paid. Major General Wolff was blamed by the senior generals in the Army for not having "saved the career" of the relieved corps commander and was denied his third star.

In my next assignment, General Dutch Kerwin, who was my endorsing officer, refused to render an efficiency report on me. He just scrawled, "Noted," across his portion of it. That delayed my next promotion for another year.

Char and I wanted to remain in Germany, but the Army felt that we had worn out our welcome, which was probably true. So we were returned to the United States.

32

America's Bicentennial

Late in the spring of 1976, America's bicentennial year, we drove to Frankfurt's Rhein/Main Airport for another flight back to the United States. In Frankfurt the chill of the European winter had unexpectedly returned. People walked briskly along the sidewalks clutching their buttoned-up overcoats at the throat.

My new assignment in the United States was deputy commanding general of the U.S. Army's Military District of Washington (MDW), headquartered at Fort Leslie J. McNair in southwest Washington. Fort McNair was activated as a military post in 1791, and is the nation's second oldest continuously-active military installation.

Also located at McNair is the Inter-American Defense College, home to many Caribbean, Central, and South American officers of all services. Fort McNair is the place where the conspirators who assassinated President Lincoln were imprisoned, tried, and hanged. The gallows were located on the present site of tennis court #4, near the officers' club.

My new boss, the commanding general of the MDW, was Major General Bob Yerks. Bob was a tall, slender, classy, unselfish gentleman who was a superb officer and a great American patriot. He and his honest, hardworking, unpretentious wife, Iris, became lifelong friends.

"Jerry," Bob said shortly after my arrival, "you couldn't have come at a better time. The entire world is coming to Washington to help us celebrate our two hundred years as a free nation. Nineteen seventy-six will be a great, historical extravaganza that you and Charlene will never forget."

Bob was right. Everywhere we went that bicentennial year, the air was electric with excitement, and there was a spontaneous outpouring and celebration of joy. The floodgates of freedom and reminders of the blessings of liberty and American citizenship poured through the nation's capital like a torrent.

When George Washington was sworn into office as the nation's first President, the Congress directed that the U.S. Army provide the necessary logistical support. Two hundred years later, the process remains essentially the same.

Every four years, the Army puts together the nation's Presidential Inaugural Committee. The other armed services contribute personnel to the Army's effort and several sub-committees are formed.

One subcommittee plans the inaugural parade. Another handles the swearing-in ceremony; another is placed in charge of invitations and the certification of guest lists for the official inaugural balls, galas, receptions, and functions. Still another subcommittee is responsible for inaugural logistics and transportation. And still another subcommittee works on special events such as folk and art festivals, dinners, parties, and public celebrations, which take place during the inaugural week.

Since Governor Jimmy Carter of Georgia had been elected president, our military inaugural committee briefed Carter's inaugural team on the arrangements to date. Then we helped Carter's people put his personal stamp on the inaugural plans and events.

The principal cochairman of the Carter Inaugural Committee was Bardyl Tirana, a prominent Washington lawyer. His father was an Albanian economist, who worked for the United Nations. Bardyl's sensitivity for political nuances and his ability to work with just about anyone, including the news media, made all our jobs easier.

Various Carter staff members such as Gerald Rafshoon and Carter's son, "Chip," sat in on the joint meetings of the Civilian and Military Inaugural Committees. As often as possible, General Yerks made room in his demanding schedule as Commander of the MDW to be present.

The sergeants-at-arms of both the House and Senate requested an invitation to meet with us. They arrived, we briefed them on the details of the swearing-in ceremony, and a dispute broke out over a matter of protocol.

One of the sergeants-at-arms chided, "Gentlemen, the President doesn't inaugurate the Congress! By law and the Constitution, the Congress inaugurates the President!" That calmed things down a bit, but not for long.

A few minutes later one of the sergeants-at-arms stood to his feet and announced in a tone of voice reminiscent of the one used when introducing the President to a joint session of Congress, "The leaders of the House and Senate have asked me to express to Governor Carter their congratulations for his being elected President of the United States. They also cordially invite the Governor and his wife to come inside the Capitol after the swearing-in ceremony and have lunch with them."

The Carter people conferred in whispers, and then their spokesman said, "We appreciate very much the kind and generous offer of the leaders of the House and Senate. However, Governor Carter will be unable to accept the invitation."

"Perhaps the Carter people didn't understand the invitation from the leaders of the House and Senate," I said, underscoring the words, *leaders of the House and Senate.* "Perhaps you'd like to rephrase your response?"

"We understood it the first time," the Carter man said cavalierly. "The answer is still the same."

A chill invaded the proceedings, the remaining business was completed swiftly and the meeting adjourned. After the two sergeants-at-arms left, I collared the chief Carter "lieutenants" and ushered them into my office.

"Look," I began, my voice rising, "these are the people you're going to need to get your legislative programs through Congress. I'm just a dumb general," I continued, "but it seems to me you might want to pick up the phone, call over to Capitol Hill and say that you didn't understand the invitation you just turned down . . . and you need to do it before they get back to their offices."

"General, don't you think this is none of your business?" one of Carter's men began. "Governor Carter doesn't intend to sit down to lunch because it'll take too long. By the time the parade starts, it will be so late that the last 30 minutes of the parade will pass by the presidential reviewing stand after dark. That means that some of the states won't get to see their people march by on TV," he lectured.

"I agree it's none of my business," I said still pressing. "But every president inaugurated this century has had a sit-down luncheon with congressional leaders."

"General, when we need your advice we'll ask for it," was the reply.

"This seems almost like show business," I protested.

"General, this is show business!" he retorted.

The Carter administration's relations with congressional democrats never recovered from that disastrous meeting. It was no surprise to later read in Tip O'Neill's book, *Man of the House*, the following: "Although I barely knew him, I was terribly excited when Jimmy Carter was elected. *Here*, I thought, *was a guy who knew how to get things done.* What I hadn't realized, and what almost nobody knew in Washington at the time, was that Carter's greatest political achievement was already behind him."

I briefed Bob Yerks on the meeting and my subsequent conversation with the Carter folks. He shook his head in disbelief.

But the Carter myopia didn't adversely affect the inauguration and swearing-in ceremony. The Army's job was to make it happen, and we did, in spite of subfreezing weather.

Inauguration day, January 20, was one of the bleakest, coldest inauguration days in memory. Too quickly it was over, the music, the swearing-in, the speeches, and the pomp and ceremony. Charlene and I didn't know it then, but this was not to be the last Presidential Inauguration we would attend.

Six months later, our tour in Washington was over. It was back to troop duty for me. Char and I were delighted. Quickly we said goodbye to the political whirl and I got back to driving tanks, firing artillery, and flying helicopters.

We didn't suspect that one day we would return to Washington where politics would become part of our life. At the time, we only thought about our next troop assignment.

An old V Corps friend, General Fritz Kroesen, had seen to my reassignment to Fort Carson, Colorado, as assistant division commander of the Fourth Infantry Division. Fritz was a tall, lean, bright general officer with lots of savvy and experience.

For Charlene and the children, returning to Colorado was a rare treat. They remembered joyfully their previous stay there while I was serving my second tour of duty in Vietnam.

At Fort Carson, Toni, our third child, married her childhood sweetheart, David White. Our son, Jerry, was in college at Penn State. Natasha had just entered high school and was the only child left at home to move with us to our new assignment.

The year at Carson passed rapidly. All too soon it was time to leave. The end came when I was promoted to major general. In the fall of 1978, a second star was added to the single one on my shirt collar. New orders arrived assigning me as Commanding General of the U.S. Army's Test and Evaluation Command (TECOM), headquartered at Aberdeen Proving Ground in Maryland.

Generally speaking, it was TECOM's job to put the U.S. Army's equivalent of the "Good Housekeeping Seal of Approval" on all Army equipment such as electronics, computers, Jeeps, trucks, tanks, missiles, airplanes, helicopters, artillery, and munitions.

33

Press Secretary

In Babenhausen, Germany, lives an internationally renowned big game hunter. One room in his home is designed to resemble a hunting lodge trophy room. Emblazoned across the mantle of the chest-high stone fireplace are the words, "Experience Is Everything."

My assignment to TECOM at Aberdeen Proving Ground was a case in point. A military "proving ground" is a place where equipment and ammunition are tested against specific criteria to determine whether or not it measures up to Army specifications. For example, a main battle tank may be designed to drive through a swamp. At Aberdeen, it will be driven through swamp-like conditions to prove whether or not it can successfully operate in swamps.

As a field commander, I had first-hand experience with all sorts of new equipment. Most items were first-rate, a few were dogs. For years I had wondered why. So I asked Ben Goodwin, TECOM's chief scientist, "Why does the Army sometimes buy junk?"

Ben, a tall, dignified engineer whose thinning hair was fast graying, had been testing Army equipment since the 1940s. His understanding of technical engineering problems was unequalled.

"Well," he slowly answered, "TECOM's mission is to test equipment, to detect and record flaws and to make recommendations on how to improve performance. But we aren't permitted to make a recommendation as to whether or not the equipment we test should be adopted."

"Give me some examples," I challenged.

Ben went to the files and pulled out reports detailing faults with several items of older Army equipment. Sure enough, the TECOM findings matched the complaints I'd heard from troops I'd commanded in the field, or what I had experienced using the equipment myself.

That day, Ben and I set a new policy. In the future, TECOM would routinely comment on whether or not piece of equipment should be given to the troops, even though our purview did not include evaluating its usefulness.

* * *

Early in the hot summer of 1979, TECOM's chief of staff, Jerry Simmons, sauntered into my office and said, "General, the Army wants to send you to a two-week seminar at Harvard to study national and international security affairs."

Jerry was a stocky, serious, highly-intelligent officer of medium height who had a distinguished military career. The seminar he was describing included some highly-classified fieldwork that could not be discussed.

"Do I have to go?" I asked.

"Yes, Sir," Jerry replied, smiling. "Headquarters is being nice about it, but the underlying message is clear. They're not asking." Again he smiled, probably thinking that he'd be rid of me for two weeks.

"OK, schedule it," I barked and went back to work. But later as I thought about it, I warmed to the idea. A two-week sabbatical would probably be good for me.

For the most part, the faculty members at the John F. Kennedy School of Government were first rate. The 50 or so students who attended the course with me represented a significant cross section of the federal government including the Department of Defense.

Doug Johnston and Ernest May seemed to be the driving forces behind the seminar, which covered such subjects as history, communism, international relations, economics, and the news media. Hugo Uyterhoeven was particularly effective in teaching economics, and the class on the news media, taught by Arthur Miller was a delight.

The self-critique sheet they asked me to fill out at the end of the seminar showed me that I was seriously deficient in only one area of study—press relations. That was probably because I was wary of the press, a caution I'd developed during my tours of duty in Vietnam. Whatever the case, Arthur Miller's delightful seminars convinced me that I had much to learn about working with the news media.

Meanwhile, back at TECOM, Jerry Simmons had important news, "Tom Ross, the press secretary to Secretary of Defense Harold Brown, has asked for you to become his Military Deputy Secretary of Defense for Public Affairs."

"You mean deputy press secretary? Working with the press on a full-time basis?" I asked incredulously.

"That's it."

I laughed. "Jerry," I said, unable to control my voice, "I just failed Professor Miller's news media seminar at Harvard. This must be a joke."

"Sir," Jerry insisted. "This is no joke."

He was right. It was no joke. Three months later I was transferred back to the Pentagon. There I became the military deputy to Tom Ross, Press Secretary to the Secretary of Defense and the Pentagon spokesman. Tom was responsible for briefing the national press, and fielding their questions concerning the Carter administration's defense policies. A consummate professional, he taught me most of what I know about the news media and press relations.

Tom could handle reporters one-on-one, or in a crowd. He alternately massaged their backs or minds—whatever was needed. He understood them, and they understood him.

"Jerry," he said, waving me to a seat on an overstuffed chair in his cavernous office located on the Pentagon's famous "E" Ring, "Journalists should build their stories upon accuracy, fairness, objectivity, balance, and completeness. You and I are expected to help them do just that.

"As my military deputy, your job is like a street cop on a ghetto beat. To do it well requires dedication, a wary eye, and swift reactions. A somewhat jaded outlook comes with the territory."

"My knowledge of how to deal with the news media borders on the Neanderthal," I said.

"No matter," Tom rejoined. "I'll teach you all you need to know." He did so by conducting a running seminar just for me.

"Journalists have a built-in skepticism and a negative news bias," he said. "They forget that all stories have both good and bad aspects. Only when you put the bad and good together in a balanced piece do you have news. Without that coupling, you only have information or opinion. Just as it takes both a positive and negative charge to make electricity, it takes a positive and negative perspective to turn information into news."

Those were challenging and educational days. With fascination I watched Tom handle Jimmy Carter's Iran hostage crisis, including the failed hostage rescue attempt at a pitch-dark refueling site named Desert One.

One of the most reliable, irreverent, and irascible members of the Pentagon Press Corps was Fred Hoffman of the Associated Press. Fred was an honest, professional craftsman who loved his country more than his profession. He did his research well; when Fred put a story on the wire, it was usually accurate. If he wrote that an event happened, it had. When he quoted someone in the Department of Defense, the quote was trustworthy. He was a newsman we could trust.

Fred never put a negative or undeserved spin on a story. And I knew he would not draw an unwarranted conclusion. Fred's reporting was reliable, though there were days when I wanted to strangle him.

Not everyone was like Fred. In my experience, some of the journalists wrote unreliable stories, with elements of fiction. Their reports would have glaring omissions or they would sensationalize them.

A year passed. One day I was sitting in the Pentagon newsroom prognosticating with the reporters about the upcoming 1980 Presidential elections. It was a month before the vote and most of the newsmen favored Carter. Only a few were for Reagan. The consensus was that the election was too close to call, but leaning toward Carter.

"No way," I said, perhaps more boldly than I should have, "Reagan will win by a significant majority."

There were a lot of guffaws from the newsmen. The polls seemed to justify their skepticism. The closer voting day came, the closer the election seemed to be. Seventy-two hours before the voting, the pollsters forecasted it to be a dead heat.

A week later I was back in the newsroom and someone shouted out, "How did you know that Carter would lose to Reagan by a landslide, Jerry?"

"I didn't predict a landslide, only a significant majority," I corrected.

"Quit splitting hairs," someone else piped in. "Just tell us how you did it."

"Quite simple. Part of my job last year was traveling around the country explaining defense policy. I listened to private American citizens a lot, and learned that even in the President's native Georgia, most people perceived him as a loser. When Americans go into a voting booth, they'll vote for an unknown before they'll vote for a loser."

"Nuff said," the first reporter concluded. They turned back to their cluttered cubicles.

Shortly after the election, Tom Ross asked me to take over the duties of formally briefing the Pentagon Press Corps.

"Once the press becomes accustomed to your acting as the Pentagon spokesman," Tom conjectured, "the transition from the Carter to the Reagan Administration won't be too difficult."

As usual, he was right. The press treated me just as irreverently and irascibly as they had Tom. Like him, I tried to respect them professionally. After a while, they learned to respect me a little, I think.

In January of 1981, a chastened and saddened President Carter exited the White House, and President Reagan entered. Quickly he revitalized our demoralized nation. At defense, Harold Brown was replaced by Caspar Weinberger. I became his press secretary and the Pentagon spokesman.

A man of immense talent and humility, Weinberger quickly took control of the Department of Defense, pursuing a policy of peace through strength. "Peace without freedom is slavery," he often said. In my humble opinion, Cap Weinberger was one of the finest secretaries of defense this nation has ever had. As a team, he and President Reagan got the job done. U.S. Military preparedness and prowess became second to none and freedom's greatest enemy, the Soviet Union, was dismantled.

In my new job, I enjoyed frequent telephone conversations coordinating White House and Defense Department press strategy with Jim Brady, President Reagan's press secretary. Suddenly, on March 30, 1981, a few seconds of gunfire altered life dramatically. President Reagan recovered from his gunshot wounds; tragically, Jim only partially recovered.

Brady would be difficult to replace, but fortunately, Lyn Nofziger stepped into the breach at the hospital and handled things like the pro he is. Back at the White House, Larry Speakes and David Gergen took over. And as it always does, government life continued.

All new administrations have their initial crises with the press. President Reagan's was not an exception. Early on, Secretary of Defense Weinberger routinely responded to a reporter's question concerning the "neutron bomb."

"The Reagan Administration will reexamine the Carter Administration's decision not to produce the enhanced radiation warhead, otherwise known as the neutron bomb," Weinberger simply said.

The answer was no big deal at home, but overseas it had major foreign policy ramifications. At that time Europe was highly sensitive to the subject of nuclear weapons. Weinberger's remarks caused political protests and demonstrations across Europe.

In the United States, liberal dissidents in the State Department decided to use these events to sabotage the new Secretary of State, Al Haig. So they leaked a false story through the *New York Times*.

The next day the *Times* carried the story, which alleged that Secretary of State Haig was so upset by Weinberger's statement concerning the enhanced radiation warhead, that he had sent a classified cable to all U.S. embassies, instructed them to ignore Weinberger's remarks because they had not been cleared with the Department of State and did not represent Administration foreign policy.

The story named no source. After reading it, I hurried down to the newsroom, cornered the *Times* Pentagon reporter, and heatedly explained that the *Times* had gotten the story wrong.

He later came to my office and assured me that the *Times* reporter at State, who had written the story, would call me shortly. The call never came. I followed up with three calls of my own, but none was returned.

Ike Pappas was covering the Pentagon for *CBS News*. When I walked into his cubicle, he was on the phone to the CBS newsroom in New York. Ike was built, walked, and talked like a bear.

When he paused for air, I interjected, "Ike, the *Times* story is untrue."

"Hold on," he growled into the phone. "Jerry, what do you mean? The *Times* carried it this morning. Since then the wires have picked it up!"

Weinberger's credibility was at stake, so I took a risk. "Here's the message Haig sent," I said shoving it in front of his face.

"All it says is for the Ambassadors to be aware of the Weinberger statement. If they get any queries from reporters or foreign governments, they are to refer them directly to Weinberger's statement!"

"Well?" I asked.

Uttering an expletive, he turned back to the phone. "We don't have a story," he growled. "Kill it."

I could only hear Ike's part of the conversation with CBS New York. But they seemed to be insisting that he was becoming part of a Pentagon cover-up.

Irritably, Ike shouted, "I'm holding the classified cable in my hand! The *Times* story isn't true. It's not even close to being true. Do you want to go with a lie?"

CBS dropped the story.

But Ike was not pleased, "This was a good story . . . a good story, Jerry. And you ruined it. You owe me."

In May of 1981, President Reagan's political appointee, Henry Cato, was confirmed by the Congress and replaced me as press secretary. Henry, a former Central American ambassador, later became ambassador to the Court of St. James in London.

34

Jubal Diggs, A Citizen

In the summer of 1981, I became commander of the MDW. It was a kind of a homecoming for Charlene and me. It also meant that we could continue to live at Quarters Two, one of the gracious homes along General's Row at Fort McNair nestled on the banks of the Potomac River.

Our job was to take care of the needs of the soldiers, officers, and military families who lived and worked in the National Capital Region. This included providing pay, health care, goods, and services, and supervising the administration of military communities such as Fort Myer in Virginia and Fort McNair in southwest Washington.

Arlington National Cemetery, the famous resting place of the late President John F. Kennedy and his brother Robert, as well as the Tomb of the Unknown Soldier, also came under our coordination. Ray Costanza, a splendid, dedicated American patriot was director of the cemetery.

The "Old Guard" of the Army, the Third Infantry, coordinated the ceremonial troops of the other military services. It could always be counted on to represent the nation with dignity and perfection.

We also oversaw the Army Band, known as "Pershing's Own," which was directed by Colonel Gene Allen, a great musician and

American. Providing music for marching troops, concerts, and coordinating special musical events for White House affairs was all part of Gene's portfolio.

We also were in charge of White House ceremonies. No one in the nation was more trusted and knowledgeable about protocol and state events than Paul Mueller. He had designed, rehearsed, and coordinated ceremonies for American Presidents and foreign heads of state since the end of World War II. During that war, he had served on the personal staff of General Eisenhower. Nation-wide when anyone needed a definitive word, including the President's Chief of Protocol, they phoned Paul.

It is the MDW who sees that the speaker's stand on the south lawn of the White House is in its proper place when a foreign dignitary such as a president, prime minister, or king visits. They also position the ropes that channel the crowds and mark the grounds at the White House to show where the dignitaries are to stand.

When a head of state departs Blair House by sedan, his or her movements are exactly timed for the drive to the West Executive entrance. Entering the gate, the sedan loops south around the White House grounds, then turns north to arrive at the south door of the White House at the precise second.

As the sedan stops and its door is opened, the last note of MDW's Herald Trumpets' fanfare still hangs in the air. The music doesn't perfectly conclude at this exact instant by accident. It takes much hard work and many rehearsals.

Ambassadors and their staffs attending these functions carefully note the content of each ceremonial event and the honors rendered to each head of state. They compare them to those honors accorded their own country's dignitaries. Any omission or oversight can result in a perceived diplomatic slight.

Often I've been asked, "What does a king or queen or president talk about when you are escorting them through a ceremony?"

It goes like this: "Sir, about three steps ahead of you is a loose flagstone that we discovered during rehearsal this morning. If you step on it, you may fall flat on your face. So move a little more to the right. There, that's fine. Now turn your head a little to the left, the TV cameras don't have a good angle on you. Just a little more . . . hold it right there, Sir."

Sometimes the dignitary wants to talk. For example, during a state visit, King Juan Carlos of Spain was so impressed with the massed array of our nation's 50 state flags that he stopped the ceremony to inquire about each of them.

One of the most amusing conversations I had with a foreign dignitary took place at Arlington National Cemetery. At the climax to an elaborate ceremony, President Diouf of Senegal was to place a wreath at the Tomb of the Unknowns.

President Diouf, who is just under seven feet tall and speaks little English, insisted on conversing in my almost forgotten French, without an interpreter.

The ceremony took place on the east side of the Tomb of the Unknowns, which offers a sweeping panoramic view of the city of Washington, which lies directly across the Potomac River from Arlington. The ceremonial setting is a glorious one of green trees, manicured grass, flagstone walks, and marble stairs.

That day the soft sky was bright blue, and fluffy white clouds with no sharp edges had come down wonderfully close to the earth. A gentle breeze stirred the leaves.

Slowly we two mounted the stairs, alone. It was a little like being in a football stadium, with the bleachers full of quiet fans and only two people moving about the playing field.

At the top of the stairs is a landing too narrow for a ceremony. There is always the possibility that the dignitary will make a misstep and tumble back down the stairs.

So as we climbed I cautioned, "Mr. President, when we get to the last step, stop there. Do not go any farther. The landing at the top is quite narrow. You will feel my arm touching your back to remind you not to back up. Remember, it is important that you stop on the last step."

Slowly, majestically we climbed the stairs, our footsteps perfectly synchronized. From his great height, President Diouf obliquely glanced down at the top of my head and said softly, "My dear General, thank you very much for your concern for my welfare. However, when you are the President of a country like mine, your government can be quite fragile. Any step could be my last step. On which one of my last steps would you like me to stop?"

"Mr. President," I responded, struggling to keep from laughing out loud, "in this case, I am able to choose the last step for you. I assure you it will be quite safe."

One of the more curious things happened one day when I was escorting President Kenneth Kaunda, President of Zambia. After we had completed the ceremony at the Tomb of the Unknowns where President Kaunda showed his respect for America's honored dead, he bowed toward the monument and softly sang a full verse of Amazing Grace. I was shocked. He was revered all over Africa, the "Nelson Mandela" of the 1950s, and he was singing Amazing Grace! Later I asked him where he had learned the hymn. He told me that at one time he had attended a Christian missionary school.

Commanding the MDW was unique in many ways. For example, we had the Army's only authorized horse unit, the Caisson Platoon at Fort Myer. The platoon provides the matched black and white horses used for burials in Arlington Cemetery and for state funerals. Its red brick stables, though quite old, are among some of the cleanest and best maintained in the world.

The MDW is also a treasure trove of history. Prior to World War II, cavalry parades at Fort Myer were led by General George S. Patton, Jr. It was in the Caisson Platoon's red brick stables that the horse was quartered that General George Marshall, then Chief of Staff of the Army, was riding on December 7, 1941, when news reached Washington that Pearl Harbor had been bombed by Japan.

After the war, Dwight Eisenhower took up residence in Quarters One at Fort Myer. It was there that he dictated the book *Crusade in Europe.*

One day, I unintentionally uncovered a forgotten piece of history. It was in the spring of 1983. I was riding along the north wall of Arlington National Cemetery with my deputy, Colonel Don Bills. Don is a dignified, lean, serious officer, a first-rate cavalryman, and one of the Army's finest gentlemen.

The last sting of winter had departed. As always, spring in Arlington County, Virginia was handsome. The valleys had quietly turned a lush emerald green. Fruit trees were breaking out into redolent pink and white wafer-like blossoms. Hungry insects were crawling from their winter hiding places. Long deprived birds, hoping to vary their boring winter diet, marked the insects' resurrection with keen interest.

Just inside the north wall, Don and I noticed a marker stone with the words "Jubal Diggs, A Citizen" graven into it.

"Why the inscription 'A Citizen,' Don?" I asked, reining in my horse, Travis. "Isn't everyone buried here a citizen?"

Turning the head of his mount toward me, Don replied, "I've no idea. Tomorrow I'll ask the cemetery's historian to dig into the archives. Maybe he can find an answer."

He did. The story begins with President George Washington, who adopted his wife Mary's grandson, as his own son. He and Mary had no children. The son was named George Washington Park Custis.

When Major Custis, as he was later known, got married, President Washington gave him a farm in Arlington, Virginia, as a wedding present. That farm is now Arlington National Cemetery.

Before his death in 1799, President Washington directed that all of the slaves owned by his Mount Vernon estate be freed upon the death of his wife, Mary. Mary did not wait to carry out his wishes. She freed them the same year that he died.

Late in 1799, Major Custis moved north from Mount Vernon to the farm in Arlington and built a farmhouse that is now the Custis-Lee Mansion. He and his wife had one child, a daughter named Mary. She married General Robert E. Lee of Civil War fame.

Major Custis died in 1857. In his will he followed President Washington's example and directed that all of the slaves on his Arlington farm be freed within five years of his death. He also directed that they each be given a 50 dollar bonus.

Before the five years passed, the Civil War began. General Lee, who now owned the farm, prepared to ride south to join the Confederacy. Before he left, he honored his father-in-law's wishes and freed the Arlington slaves. Unfortunately, he couldn't afford to pay them their 50 dollar bonus.

During the war, Lee's farm was confiscated and turned into Arlington National Cemetery. One of Lee's freed slaves, Mr. James Parks, was employed by the cemetery. He helped build what was known as Freedman's village, a village for freed slaves. It extended along the east side of the cemetery, from Section 27 north to the Tomb of the Unknowns.

Prior to this, free Negroes and escaped slaves had lived in a ragged camp across the river from Arlington in the District of Columbia. Living conditions were wretched, and diseases such as smallpox and typhoid fever ravaged the camp. The construction of Freedman's Village on General Lee's Arlington farm was supposed to provide "pure country air" for them.

Families received plots of land to farm and 10 dollars a month from the federal government, which in return charged them three dollars for rent. The village was self-contained with a carpentry shop, smithy, school, store, and hospital. There was also training in job skills. About 1890, the government bought back the land so that Arlington National Cemetery could be expanded.

Buried in this area, Section 27, along with Jubal Diggs are more than 5,000 U.S. Colored Troops who were killed in combat during the Civil War, as well as the dead from Freedman's Village.

The words "A Citizen" were chiseled on some of the gravestones to proclaim that those who were buried here were no longer slaves, but full-fledged American citizens.

* * *

Another bright, cheerful spring day, I donned my rumpled gardening coveralls, slipped a pair of pruning shears and gloves in my back pocket, and headed for Quarters Two's rose garden to perform my weekly "groundskeeper's duties."

A short time later, a large delivery truck chugged up the street along General's Row. A tall African American driver was hunched over in the driver's seat peering out the rolled down window as if looking for a house number.

When he saw me, he smiled, pumped his air brakes, stopped, stepped down from the cab, and sauntered across the lawn. I stopped pruning and walked over to meet him.

"These people nice to work for?" he inquired, extending a heavy calloused hand.

I pulled off my gloves and we shook a greeting.

"Yes," I said, "they're very nice to work for. Very considerate."

"How long you been working here?"

"A little over two years."

"Uh-huh," he took off his baseball cap and wiped his sweaty forehead with his shirtsleeve. "I used to work all up and down this street, just like you. Everybody treated me real nice. These are fine people."

I nodded in agreement.

Satisfied that things hadn't changed much from the time when he had worked as a groundskeeper at Fort McNair, he again shook my hand, ambled back to the truck, stepped up into the cab, started the engine, gently meshed the gears, and pulled away.

I didn't tell him that I was the commanding officer of the base. I just went back to pruning roses.

Then, in the fall of 1983, Charlene and I were once again reassigned back to Germany.

35

Charlene's Kidnapping

Over the West German plain webbed with canals and autobahns, solid gray layers of clouds had stagnated for nearly a week. Now, high up in the stratus, the wind slowly herded the clouds east across the shameful barbed-wire border, studded with landmines, that halved Europe from the Baltic to the Adriatic.

The day before, a cold drizzle had begun a steady tattoo. When the soaked earth could swallow no more water, hollows turned into tiny lakes. Little streams turned into larger streams. Then Poland and Russia beckoned and the clouds moved on, the rain laying silver on the cobblestone streets.

Grumpy men, hardworking women, and chastened children shivered in the wet streets and damp apartments. On this cold, soggy morning with the bite of frost in the air, Charlene and I stepped back onto German soil. We had lived in Europe for so many years that Germany had become a *Zweite Heimat*, a second home for us.

Returning to Frankfurt as deputy commander of V Corps was nostalgia personified. In 1951 I had begun my military career in Europe in the Seventh Army as a private. A year later as a corporal, I had been selected, by a board of officers meeting in this same corps headquarters building, to attend Officer Candidate School at Fort Benning, Georgia.

Now I was returning as the Deputy V Corps Commander, with offices in the same building. In addition to performing normal military duties, the deputy was directly responsible for providing for the health, education, and welfare of the U.S. military, civilians, and their families in military communities extending from France and the Low Countries in the west to the East German border.

I coordinated life in the military townships—the operations, maintenance, and development of their police forces, fire departments, hospitals, and airports. I was also superintendent of nine military school districts. Daily, I had to coordinate with German city and state governments, as well as keep German federal agencies happy.

It was a tense time to be an American in Europe. In 1980, a few years before we arrived, 80 people had been killed when a Red Brigade terrorist bomb detonated at the Bologna railway station in Italy. Later that year during Oktoberfest, the Red Army Faction and the remnants of the Baader-Meinhof Gang set off a bomb that killed 12.

The following year, 1981, the U. S. Air Force's Ramstein Air Base was bombed. Later that year, a rocket was fired at an Army sedan in which General and Mrs. Fritz Krosen, the Seventh Army commander, were riding on their way from their house in Heidelberg to Army headquarters.

Then in December, the military community faced another attack in Verona, northern Italy. Brigadier James Dozier and his wife, Judy, were in their sixth floor apartment preparing to attend a community meeting. The doorbell rang and two "plumbers" asked to come in to try to locate the source of a water leak in the apartment below.

Once inside the apartment, the "plumbers" whipped out pistols with silencers, they handcuffed and gagged Jim and knocked Judy to the floor. Two more men entered the apartment with an empty refrigerator packing case into which Jim was thrown. He was taken down the elevator and the case loaded onto the back of a rented van.

The terrorists drove to another city, dragged the packing case into an apartment and forced Dozier into a tent, which had been pitched in the middle of the living room. Dozier was chained to a bunk at the ankle and wrist for 42 days. He was finally rescued after one of the most massive police manhunts in Italian history.

Jim's capture inaugurated a period of intense terrorist activity throughout Europe, which lasted for years. Americans were targeted by the terrorists—particularly generals and their families.

So it came as no surprise to me when in November of 1984, my aide, First Lieutenant Alexander Ilic, burst through the office doorway and blurted, "Sir, pick up the phone. It's urgent."

Alex was a lean six feet, mustached, and fluent in several languages including Yugoslavian, the tongue of his ancestral homeland.

"General Curry," I said into the handset.

"Sir, this is the Provost Marshall. I'm at your quarters. Mrs. Curry is missing. Military and German police have sealed off the housing area. Please come at once!"

Adrenalin surged through my nervous system; my heart hammered against my chest wall. "The indications?" I demanded.

"We found the garage door up, the kitchen door leading into the garage open, the lights on, the television playing. Your wife's car is still in the garage."

"Any signs of a struggle?"

"None."

"How were you alerted?"

"The German police responded to a duress alarm that was activated in your house. They arrived in less than five minutes. But by the time they got here, Mrs. Curry was gone."

"I'm on the way," I said slamming down the telephone.

Alex had already taken my general officer's leather pistol belt from the closet. I buckled it on, repositioning the .45 on my right hip. Lieutenant Ilic, who had already strapped on his .45, handed me my hat and camouflage field jacket as we hurried through the suite of offices and down the hall.

"The car and driver are waiting out front," he told me.

Rushing out the main entrance of the Abrams Building, which housed V Corps Headquarters, I now regretted that Charlene and I had not remained in the United States.

Sergeant Dexter, my driver, had the engine running and was holding open the door of the armored BMW. He too was wearing a pistol belt with a loaded .45 in the holster. Swiftly and expertly, Dexter steered the heavy sedan through Frankfurt's noonday traffic.

How things had changed since I first arrived in Frankfurt as a private. Back then there had been few cars on the streets, aside from those owned by the Americans, British, or French. Most Germans could only afford bicycles and motorcycles.

These days the roads were jammed with Mercedes, Volvos, Volkswagens, Audis, Porsches, Fords, Opels, BMWs, and occasionally Japanese cars, and as well as a few motorcycles and bicycles.

Gothic stone churches were still familiar, with their bell towers and their cathedrals with ornate stained glass rosettes. Somehow small shops, kiosks, butcheries, and bakeries had survived. Side streets were still paved with ancient cobblestones.

In Europe, apartments, shops, and store buildings are connected end-to-end so that an entire block melds into one continuous stucco building, though the color may change from light gray to off-white to cream. The gray slate roofs are accented with red tile capped chimneys. Scattered across the roofs are farms of TV antennas of all shapes and designs.

Where is that storybook land I first saw in 1951? I asked myself. I missed the slow, leisurely pace of the European cities of the fifties and sixties. It was afflicted with the same busyness as most major cities of the world.

Back in the fifties, Charlene and I had strolled hand-in-hand along these same streets. Now I was being chauffeured through them in an armored car with my driver, aide, and myself carrying loaded weapons.

In my stomach a knot tied, untied, and tied itself again as I reflected back over the 32 years Charlene and I had spent together. There had been many tough and difficult days, as well as many dangerous ones. And we had traveled together over much of the earth and found it wonderful and rewarding.

Smoothly and powerfully the armored sedan purred along. Now we turned into the housing area where Char and I made our home. Dexter swerved the BMW around the hastily erected German police barricades.

I remembered that Charlene had asked me to retire instead of accepting this tour of duty. Now I regretted not having listened to her.

For several years we had felt stifled in the military. It had been a great life, and we had been more than amply rewarded for our sacrifices while serving the nation. But within us was a feeling of restlessness, a desire to move on to new things.

I identified with General George Washington who said that when he put on the military uniform, he did not take off the civilian. Like him I reveled in the challenges of military duty; like him, I longed to return to private life.

Sergeant Dexter stopped the sedan in front of my house. The grounds were awash with German police carrying submachine guns and accompanied by guard dogs. German and U.S. military police had searched the immediate area and the houses on either side of ours and were now in the process of expanding the search to the rest of the neighborhood.

Suddenly, the door of a house four doors down the street burst open. Charlene popped out and called, "What is all the commotion about? Why are all those men trampling my rose bushes? Jerry, why aren't you at work?"

Charlene, who had been watching television, had decided to pop in on her neighbor on the spur of the moment. For some unexplained reason, rather than use the front door, she had decided to go through the garage, intending to be gone only for a minute.

But the conversation became interesting and she had forgotten that she had left the garage door open. As things would have it, the duress alarm system short-circuited itself and sent out an emergency signal. The German civilian police and U.S. military police responded en force.

I had mixed feelings. On the one hand, I was delighted to see Char alive and well. On the other hand, her hurried departure from the house and the false alarm had given us all quite a scare. Even the stoic German police were out of sorts.

Most importantly, the affair had a happy ending. Emotionally drained, I went back to work and somehow dragged myself through an unproductive afternoon.

When I returned home from work that evening, there was the usual fire burning in the fireplace. Hors d'oeuvres were tastefully arranged on a Meissen china dish placed on the end table by my favorite easy chair.

"You know, Jerry," Charlene said, sweetly helping me off with my combat boots. "I don't believe we really need this. Isn't there some other line of work that would interest you?"

The next morning I informed a stunned corps commander and staff that I was taking early retirement effective the following month. We had been in Germany just over a year. Before Christmas 1984, for the last time as a member of the United States Army, Charlene and I sorted out our household goods and supervised their packing. Then we had our car driven to the port at Bremerhaven, attended a splendid round of both German and American farewell parties, and left Europe to begin a new life as private American citizens.

36

Politics

Though Europe and Germany had become second homes to Charlene and me, they could never replace America in our hearts. Right or wrong, with all its warts, liver spots, and racial hang-ups, America remains our beloved land.

After retiring from the military, Charlene and I traveled across the United States and got reacquainted with our magnificent nation. We took our time visiting family and friends along the way.

In February, 1985, Pat Robertson of the Christian Broadcasting Network unexpectedly phoned and asked if I'd be interested in coming to Virginia Beach to set up a public policy "think tank." The phone call was curious because I'd shaken hands with him only a few times over the years, and once, I think, we had dinner together. Other than that we hadn't spoken.

As president and publisher of the think tank, he promised that I'd be free to produce papers on any aspect of national or international policy that interested me. He kept his word and CBN provided the start-up money.

At the end of our first week at "The Beach," as the locals referred to the city of Virginia Beach, Virginia, Pat invited us to dine with him and his inner circle. He lived in the chancellor's mansion at Regent University, a delightful Williamsburg-style building. The university is first rate; I can't say enough good things about it. The buildings and the campus in the early Federal style are impressive.

After dinner and small talk, Pat turned to Charlene and me and loudly asked, "Well, what do you think of the idea?"

Mystified, we asked, "What idea?"

"Haven't you seen the cover of the *Saturday Evening Post?* What do you think of my running for President of the United States?"

We were stunned. Evidently we had lived in Europe too long. I only managed to mumble an innocuous reply.

"Well, Jerry, one of the reasons I wanted you to join us here at Christian Broadcasting Network was so that, in your spare time, you could put together my Presidential campaign."

Everyone else at the table seemed to know all about Pat's interest in running for president and were highly enthusiastic about the idea. Without waiting for a reply from Char and me, there was a chorus of congratulations. It seems I was to be appointed campaign manager by acclamation.

At first, I was so busy getting the think tank off the ground that several months passed before I was able to get around to campaign planning. My first hire at the think tank was Greg Rotelli, a recent MBA graduate of Regent University who was exceptionally bright and had a lot of common sense. Together, we named the think tank The National Perspectives Institute (NPI).

Later, with the help of others, Pat and I mapped out a campaign strategy and started exploratory work. For Pat, political campaigning was a bit of a come down from having his own TV show—the 700 Club. Our first visits to New Hampshire and Iowa, were interesting. By the end of our second political trip, Pat had taken to campaigning better than a mallard takes to Chesapeake Bay. Of course, Pat was no stranger to politics. His father had been a U.S. Congressman for many years, and later became Virginia's junior senator.

From the beginning, it became painfully obvious that Pat and I were incompatible. We had a definite personality conflict that wasn't going to improve with time. Also, we didn't always agree politically.

We parted company mutually disillusioned with one another in May of 1986. I wished him well, and continued to follow his campaign from afar.

* * *

About that time, the state Republican Party Chairman, Don Huffman, asked me to run for the seat of Virginia's Second Congressional District, which encompassed the cities of Virginia Beach and Norfolk. So in 1988, I ran against a Democratic incumbent in a predominately Democratic district. Though I lost, I am glad I ran because it made me think through my positions on local and national issues, including the problems in our inner cities.

I also learned that candidates are put under a microscope when they run for election. Every word is pounced upon, and often twisted or misquoted. From that experience, I learned to have a healthy respect for politicians and what they endure to serve the public.

Both the incumbent and I ran a gentleman's campaign with no mudslinging on either side. We only debated the issues. I lost magnificently.

37

The National Highway Traffic Safety Administration

In late March of 1989, President Bush nominated me to be the Administrator of the National Highway Traffic Safety Administration (NHTSA), part of the Department of Transportation. That fall, the Senate confirmation hearings went smoothly and a Democratic Senate unanimously approved my nomination. This was primarily due to the efforts of Senators Warner of Virginia, Bryan of Nevada and Gorton of Washington State.

The NHTSA had never had a high-level minority political appointee, let alone an African American administrator. Rumors concerning my appointment ran rife throughout the agency. Some said I would be bringing a political staff made up of only minorities. Others insisted that because I had worked with Pat Robertson for a year, I would use my office to indoctrinate the agency with far right-wing Christian beliefs.

At the time, Char and I were members of Saint George's Episcopal Church in Arlington. One Sunday morning, an agitated member of the congregation approached me waving a newspaper article. In it the reporter had written several unflattering paragraphs about me and concluded with what should be expected from me because I kept company with religious extremists.

"Since when do we, the congregation of Saint George's Episcopal Church, qualify as religious extremists?" she angrily demanded. I tried unsuccessfully to mollify her.

At St. George's, Char was a lay reader and we both sang in the choir, which was wonderfully and masterfully directed by Jane Tavernier. I also served as a vestry member. The style of worship was liturgical and although we tend to prefer a more spirit-filled atmosphere, we nevertheless loved our time there.

* * *

The career government employees in NHTSA were some of the finest I had ever worked with in the federal government. For the most part, they were intelligent, motivated, and consistently put the good of the nation first. Yet in some ways, I think I disappointed them. They were expecting major changes, someone more colorful, more sensational, and perhaps even a little outrageous.

I am proud of what we accomplished. During my tenure, alcohol-related traffic fatalities decreased. Total fatalities on the nation's highways dropped from 47,000 annually in 1988 to 39,000 in 1992, even though the total number of licensed drivers and the number of motor vehicles operating on our highways increased. Seat belt use and mandatory seat belt laws increased sharply throughout the 50 states and territories.

I made family vans, pickup trucks, and sport utility vehicles match the same safety standards as passenger cars. Side impact safety regulations were adopted and, even though I was a Republican in a Republican Administration, more safety regulations were enacted during my administration than by any other administration in the agency's history, except perhaps during the agency's first few years.

This was not because I believed in more government regulation; I didn't then and I don't now. In fact, I believe in less government. It happened simply because these regulations were technically feasible and they saved lives. When lives are at stake, political ideology shouldn't get in the way.

We even cut the time it took to process petitions related to traffic safety matters. Even Democratic controlled committees of both the House and Senate praised the agency for the progress made under President Bush's Republican administration.

Despite all we accomplished, my work was not without controversy. I got into conflict with several senators over CAFE or Corporate Average Fuel Economy legislation. We were under tremendous pressure to increase car gasoline mileage. Back then, in the late 1980s we didn't have the technology to dramatically increase fuel efficiency. The only way to get a sizable increase was to reduce the weight and size of cars.

This meant that the size of all cars would have to drastically shrink. In the Army I learned that when a tank crashed into a Jeep, the occupants of the Jeep lose. So when a heavier car or pickup crashed into a little new car, the occupants of the little car are often killed or seriously injured. I was unwilling to raise mileage requirements if it was going to cost lives. This got me into all kinds of conflict with the media and certain special interest groups who wanted to reduce foreign oil imports more than they wanted to protect the lives of our citizens.

I also got into conflict with a number of consumer special interest groups who seemed to be bent on finding problems with automobiles so they could sue the manufacturers. Several of these groups had reported that the Audi 500 was prone to sudden acceleration where the car sped away out of control because the gas pedal would suddenly, on it own, hit the floor. This was covered by *Consumer Reports* as well as *60 Minutes'* and *Dateline.*

At the NHTSA, we put the Audi 500 though extensive testing but did not find a problem. Meanwhile, lawyers for Audi were able to establish that, for its TV special, *Dateline* had forced the gas pedal to depress by drilling a hole in the car's transmission and attaching a hose leading to a tank of compressed air or fluid. They did this so they could film it. It angered me that a perfectly good car's reputation was savaged, forcing Audi dealership franchises out of business and U.S. workers employed by Audi to lose their jobs.

It seemed like car manufacturers were being sued in situations where it was hard to imagine how they could be at fault. In 1994 the driver of a Suzuki Samurai, an SUV, fell asleep at the wheel. The car drifted off the road, crashed and flipped over. The highway patrolman covering the crash cited the driver for failure to maintain control of her vehicle. This should have been the end of the matter, but it wasn't. The driver sued Suzuki Motor Corporation—and won!

Another car manufacturer was sued when a trailer hitch not made by the manufacturer—indeed the hitch had been purchased at a flea market—failed, leading to a series of events where a woman died.

I had not intended to be an activist administrator, but I felt that justice was being usurped. I had to make a stand and as a result, I was vilified in the media and hated by consumer interest groups. But I was not the only one who thought things were getting out of hand.

In September of 1989, 50 career civil service employees of NHTSA's Office of Defects Investigation wrote a letter to the executive director of an auto safety organization, saying, "the career, non-political staff of the Office of Defects Investigation want to go on record that we believe your organization frequently goes beyond legitimate disagreement with the program and may, in fact, be seriously undermining it." This was an unprecedented action that has never happened in the Department of Transportation—before or since.

I was confident that the two most important motor vehicle safety problems the nation faced were drunk driving and people not wearing seat belts. This was where I thought we should focus our efforts.

A major unreported aspect of the Princess Diana tragedy is that had she and her boyfriend buckled their seat belts, they might still be alive today. The rear seat in any car is the safest place to be in a crash. Since the bodyguard in the front seat, a much more dangerous location, was wearing his seat belt and lived, it is highly likely that the princess and her boyfriend would also have survived this tragic accident had they buckled their seat belts.

I thought that this was a splendid opportunity for the news media to preach the message that buckling seat belts saves lives. In reporting the story they could have stressed that these two beautiful people should have taken advantage of the lifesaving protection available to them. But they did not.

I thought that the media should cover such stories, and be a force for good in society by helping change driver behavior. I knew this would save more lives than all the Federal Motor Vehicle Safety Standards combined.

The first week in June of 1992, I resigned from the Bush Administration. Sam Skinner, White House Chief of Staff, phoned me at home to say how sorry he was that I had chosen to leave the administration. In the months that followed, I began full-time work as a consultant. At the outset, I spent my time encouraging legislatures of the 50 states to pass stronger seat belt laws. Later on, I began doing consulting in traffic safety and federal regulatory matters.

As with our decision to retire from the Army, withdrawing from the federal government was a happy time for Char and me. We had both worked hard, had served the country well, and could look back on our accomplishments with satisfaction.

Once more Char and I were private citizens facing new and different challenges. God blessed us so that we could buy 10 acres of land atop a mountain ridge in northern Virginia. There we built a very small French-style chateau.

38

Singing Opera

In the fall of 1994, Char and I transferred our church membership from St. George's in Arlington to Saint Paul's Episcopal Church in Haymarket, a 15 minute drive from our new home on the southern face of Bull Run Mountain. As was our custom, we became chalice bearers, lay readers, and choir members. I also began teaching the adult Sunday school class, and a weekly Bible study.

Construction of the chateau, with an art studio to accommodate our painting avocation, was completed in March, 1995. Unfortunately, we didn't have enough money to build the music conservatory, but sketched out plans for one to be added at a future time.

Shortly afterward, our household goods were delivered, filling all the rooms with stacks of boxes waiting to be unpacked. We lacked the energy and courage to begin such an ordeal just then, so we locked the door, flew to Maui with our oldest daughter, Charlie, and her husband Raleigh, for some much needed respite. A week later, rested and refreshed, we arrived back in Virginia ready to face the problems all new house builders have. We solved most of them, postponed some, surrendered to others, unpacked boxes, and for the next year, filled the house with purchases of old furniture, paintings, etchings, engravings, tapestries, and odds and ends.

In the middle of 1996, I decided to fulfill a lifelong ambition of mine, to become a better choir singer. I tried to interest Charlene in joining me, but she had other diversions of a higher priority. So I spoke to Sheila and Jim Todd the co-choirmasters at church. Sheila, in addition to playing the violin, had a delightful, classically-trained singing voice.

"How serious are you?" she asked.

"Very serious, but I'm also very busy and only have time for a few lessons."

"Well, in your case there's only one person that I'd recommend. His name is Michael Warren and he lives and teaches in New York, but every three or four months he comes to Washington for a few days. Some of his students sing in major opera houses around the world, including the Metropolitan Opera in New York.

"Many opera singers in the Washington area take lessons from him. He'll be here in a few weeks. I'll phone his office and ask whether he can see you. You'll like him and he'll do wonders for your voice . . . but he's not cheap."

A few weeks later, I drove to a private home in Bethesda, Maryland for my first voice lesson. Michael was friendly, polite, and professional. For an hour, he played and I sang. We talked some and he suggested several vocal exercises for me to practice.

Three or four months later, he came back and I again sang the scales and vocal exercises he had given me to practice. When the hour was over, he said, "Jerry, you have some decisions to make."

"What decisions?" I asked, puzzled.

"You have to decide whether or not you want to sing on stage at the Metropolitan Opera."

Though I'd loved opera since I was a teenager, and though I had sung with church choirs and folk groups most of my life, I had never seriously considered pursuing an operatic career. I didn't think this was the time in life when one takes to the opera stage.

Both Pavarotti and Placido Domingo were younger than I, and both were scaling back their performances.

"There are no guarantees," Michael continued, "but you have a world class voice and I feel certain that with intensive study and practice, in two years you could be ready."

"But I thought that once you passed a certain age your voice was shot."

"Not necessarily. Genes have a lot to do with it. If you have the vocal equipment and develop the proper singing techniques, you should be able to sing at the highest professional level for many years to come. The oldest person I know who signed with the Met was 70. But you will have to move to New York and take regular voice lessons."

For the fleetest of seconds, I savored the idea. Twenty years earlier I might have even traded an in-law or two for a chance to sing at the Met. But that time had come and gone. Char and I had become more than comfortable inhabiting our little chateau and with our private sector lives. We were not struggling artists willing to sacrifice all for the sake of "Arte."

Secretly I thought Michael had lost his mind. True, I had a pleasant enough voice, but not one good enough to compete at the level of world-class opera. Through lessons and hard work it is possible to stretch and improve any voice, but world-class voices are a gift from God. If you aren't born with one, you'll never have one. So I had to tell Michael, "No."

About that time, October 18, 1997, The Revered Mercer Marion Curry, my beloved mother, died. She had been born in 1911, at Steele's Tavern, Virginia. Mom Curry, as she was known nationally and internationally, preached the Gospel message of Jesus Christ all over the world including, within the last two months of her life, teaching a week and a half seminar to the largest Christian gathering ever held in northern Finland. For 20 years, Mom's ministry included annual visits to the National Capital Region where she spoke to standing room only Bible studies at the Pentagon, and to numerous other Christian groups and churches in the Washington area.

A few days before her funeral, my brother Bob and I were whiling away the time at Mom's house when I mentioned my voice lessons. Bob, who has a wonderful baritone voice, and is an accomplished pianist and composer, erupted. He enthusiastically encouraged my operatic efforts and said that if I ever decided to record a CD, he knew just the place. It was called Life Studios, owned by a man named Asaph Borba, and was located in Porto Alegre, Brazil.

I thanked him, told him I never intended to make a CD, and that if I ever did I would make it in the United States.

He smiled. The conversation ended.

In the meantime, whenever Michael came to Washington, I took a lesson from him and my singing continued to improve. Occasionally I sang solos in church. Not too many churches today embrace opera singers, but our local congregation seemed to tolerate it fairly well.

In the spring of 1998, Michael mentioned that he'd like me to come to New York for a week in August, for what he called a Summer Intensive. Students from all over the east coast converge on his studio at that time of year to study voice, attend seminars, and participate in master classes. At the end of the week there is a recital at which selected students sing.

After thanking him for the invitation, I pointed out that my consulting business did not allow me to give up a week's work. Secretly it didn't make sense for someone who didn't want a stage career to fly to New York and stay in a hotel for a week just to feel good about the little voice they had. That year, Sheila Todd and her husband Jim, who both teach music, went and reported back that it had been a wonderful experience. They strongly recommended that I attend Michael's seminar the following year.

In the early spring of 1999, Michael Warren again suggested that I participate in his Summer Intensive. This time I halfheartedly mentioned it to Charlene. To my surprise, she said, "I think you should go. You never do anything for yourself and you're always quick to spend money on others or buy me things. I think for once you ought to be selfish. You have nothing to lose but a little money and it'll do you good. While you're away, I'll drive up to Pennsylvania and spend the week with my mother."

That's how I came to spend a hot, sweaty week in August 1999 in downtown Manhattan. About 40 to 60 students met at Cobi Hall, a tiny concert hall directly across the street from Carnegie Hall. The third day of the intensive study seminar, I was scheduled for a master's class. Being the only student with no professional music resume caused me to feel inferior, mostly because I was.

The song I chose to sing for the other students at the end of the Master's Class was a schmaltzy German love song entitled *Dein Ist Mein Ganzes Herz*, taken from the Franz Lehar operetta *The Land of Smiles*. The operetta debuted around 1920; Richard Tauber sang the tenor lead.

In the operetta, Lisa, the daughter of an Austrian diplomat, is introduced to Prince Sou-Chong of China who has been posted to Vienna. They fall in love and he sings this song to her. Even for a schmaltzy love song, the words are quite exceptional.

"I am like the flower that fades unless it is kissed by the sun . . . You cause my love to explode . . . Wherever I go, I feel you near me. . . I want to inhale your breath . . . I beg you to let me sink to my knees at your feet and worship you . . . Your voice is like music . . . You are my entire life. I must always be in your presence." This is my translation, Lehar is not to blame.

To my surprise, when I finished singing, the other singers rose to their feet and applauded. I overheard one young lady say to another, "Forget Pavarotti."

The standing ovation, the shouts of "Bravo," and that offhand Pavarotti comment, probably said in jest, had a profound affect on me. Until then the notion that anyone would compare my singing to "The Three Tenors" seemed absurd. But now I had to ask myself whether Michael Warren had told the truth when he said that I had a world-class voice?

Returning from New York, I was humbled and perplexed. Finally, I phoned Michael, confessed that I had been converted, and asked what the next step was. Without hesitation, he said, "You either go on tour or you make a CD."

"Why?" I respectfully asked.

"Because you need a challenge to push you to the next level of performance. Only singing concerts or recording a CD will do that—at your expense," he added.

I was not convinced, but I had been wrong before and Michael had been right. So this time I decided not to second-guess him. When I mentioned the conversation with Michael to Charlene, she surprised me again by saying, "Go for it."

We decided to record a CD as opposed to the concert route. It would be expensive, but it would save us the rigors of an extended tour. I phoned my brother Bob in Oregon, ate the requisite serving of humble pie, practiced a little grovel 101, and told him I'd decided to make a CD and would like to accept his offer of recording it in Brazil, if the offer still held. He was gracious as always, said he was traveling to Brazil in a few days, and would make the arrangements.

Soon I had a phone call from Asaph Borba, the owner of the recording studio, sketching in the details of a recording session. He reminded us that when he was a teenager, Bob had arranged for him and his friend, Don Stoll, to visit Charlene and me when we had been living in Colorado. It sealed the deal.

I didn't have any inkling of what I was getting into when I agreed to produce the CD. Had I known, I would have run, not walked away from it.

In addition to honing my singing voice, I had to choose which songs were to be recorded. I prayed a lot, scanned hundreds of pieces of sheet music, read dozens of books, listened to audio tapes and CDs ad nauseam, and plodded my way through what seemed like every music store in northern Virginia.

I must have faxed a dozen proposed recording programs to Asaph. But I got very little feedback, primarily because he knew that it's the producer's job to choose the songs to be recorded. And I was the producer.

Finally, I settled on a formula. The recording would be about 40 percent Christian-Gospel songs since most of my solo singing had been to church congregations. One of my loves was opera, so another 40 percent would be operatic arias. The remaining 20 percent would be ageless popular "feel-good" songs with an operatic quality. In practice it didn't work out that cleanly, since some songs fell into two or three of the categories.

Also, I decided to write a hymn and include it on the CD, because as a youth in church I had sung from a hymn book. Back then many congregations routinely sang all four musical parts: soprano, alto, tenor, and bass. For the past 30 years, there has been a decided drift away from the old hymns toward "praise" songs, catchy music with little harmony, where everyone sings the melody.

Young church congregations grow up seldom hearing rich alto, tenor or bass harmony. I wanted to write a hymn with definite down beats and simple harmony, one that whole congregations could sing in parts and enjoy. I recognized that young people might not appreciate the hymn, but I was paying for it . . . so I wrote an old fashioned hymn, which I titled *Before The Throne*.

As producer, it was necessary to purchase musical scores and get copyright permission to record. Since the recording was made in Brazil, we probably didn't need U.S. copyright permission because the recording studio had already arranged for international copyright and publishing rights. But I felt that it didn't hurt to go the extra mile.

Then, I phoned an old family friend, Ed Elliott, in West Chicago, who owned Domain Communications. He put me in touch with his staff and we agreed on a price to have them manufacture, package, and shrink-wrap the CD.

Next, Char and I drove four hours to Virginia Beach to visit our youngest daughter, Natasha, her husband John, and their two children. The real purpose of the trip was to do a CD cover photo shoot with Eva Fryess. She is an internationally recognized photographer and a christian friend, whom Char and I had known for many years. The shoot went smoothly and she promised to have the finished photos ready in time for our first trip to Brazil.

Both Char and I wanted to record a German song because we had lived much of our young lives in Germany, had learned to speak a little of the language, and still have many German friends. That's how *Dein Ist Mein Ganzes Herz* made its way onto the CD. I wanted a French song because I had studied French and still managed to speak a little of it without too much of an American accent. *Pourquoi Me Revellier* was the result.

Italian was a no-brainer because it is the language of opera. If Italians didn't invent opera, then opera must have invented Italians. My African heritage is responsible for the selection of the American Spiritual *Deep River*. Similarly, the Irish on my mother's side mandated *Danny Boy*. I regret Mom isn't alive to hear my version of the old standard.

Finding piano, vocal, and orchestral scores sounds easy, but isn't. I phoned all over the country trying to buy various pieces of music. Persistence pays off, and finally I had copies of all the scores except *Dein Ist Mein Ganzes Herz*. No matter how hard I tried—and I had several research agencies helping me—I was unable to locate the music.

To this day, I don't understand why it was so difficult to locate the music here in the U.S. As popular as the song is and as many times as it's been recorded, I'd thought any music store could have simply ordered it. But it didn't work out that way.

One night, Char and I had dinner, as we often did, with Bob and Gisemunde Kramer. Bob was a United Airlines captain and Gisemunde was a United flight attendant supervisor. Bob's roots are German and Munde's are Austrian. They are wonderful, down to earth, honest-to-goodness real Americans.

It was spring and we were reminiscing about how tasty the German and Austrian *spargle* (white asparagus) is, and wouldn't it be wonderful if we could sit down to a mountain of it as we used to do in Europe about this time of year? The more we talked, the more mouth watering the idea became. Before the evening was over, we had talked ourselves into flying to Europe for a *spargle* dinner.

So a few weeks later it was wheels up on a United flight to Munich. There, we rented a car and made the lovely, leisurely drive up the Alps to Saltzburg, Austria. Checking into the Lichenskyhof Gasthouse, we unpacked our bags and headed for the dining room and *spargle*. That and the *wiener schnitzels* made the trip more than worth while.

And since we were now in the land of Lehar, we decided to try to find the music score to *Dein Ist Mein Ganzes Herz*. In Saltzburg, the four of us plodded from music store to music store without any success. The store clerks brightened when I mentioned Franz Lehar's name, but none of the stores had the song in stock. The last store was the largest. A clerk took us to the basement, tried unsuccessfully to locate the music, finally gave up in frustration and said irritably, "If it's here, it's on that long shelf." Then she marched back upstairs.

We all looked, but to no avail. I was thinking about deleting it from my program when Bob said, "We've come all the way from the United States and if the music is in this store, we're going to find it." With that, he started at the far left end of the 12-foot-long shelf the clerk had pointed to and methodically worked his way toward the right looking in every book, at every page, examining every piece of sheet music.

Somewhere about 50 inches toward the middle of the shelf he triumphantly uncovered, buried deep within the maze of music books and sheet music, the conductor's score for *Dein Ist Mein Ganzes Herz.*

39

Compliments from Leontyne

Mission accomplished, we flew back to the United States and finished preparations for the CD recording session. Michael Warren had some unsettling parting words of wisdom for me just as Char and I were about to board the plane for Brazil.

"Jerry," he said over the phone, "it is unfortunate, but when you record opera, those who listen to it have listened to every song you are singing a hundred times before. They have heard the best operatic voices in the world sing those same arias. They won't say, 'Well, he's just starting out, and for a beginner it's a very good recording.'

"As soon as they finish listening to your track, they will pop in Pavarotti or Domingo or Caruso and compare you with them. In short, your competition is a hundred years of operatic singers, not new recording artists like yourself. If you can't record a track on the CD that favorably competes with operatic history, don't record it. For the rest of your life you will hear critics say how poorly you sang that particular aria. It isn't fair, but that's the way it is."

Had I not put so much effort and money into preparing for the recording session, I might have quit right then, but by this time there was no turning back. We boarded the plane in October 1999, Charlene and I flew from northern Virginia to Miami, changed planes, and seven hours later landed in Sao Paulo, Brazil.

Bob and his family had gone ahead of us, and we spent a few days with them and their Brazilian friends. Brazilians have got to be some of the friendliest people on the globe, and we loved Brazilian food! Then, it was back on the plane for a two-and-a-half-hour flight to Porto Alegre.

The next morning, we were in the studio early, met Asaph and his staff, got briefed, established working rules, and began recording. Bob did the translating. Without him the recording sessions would have been a disaster. Two and a half very long weeks later we returned home to the United States physically, mentally and emotionally drained, but knowing that all had gone well.

Production work on the recording continued at the studio through the Christmas holidays, and the second week of February we flew back to Brazil for the final mixing and shaping of the CD. Two exhausting weeks later, on February 24, 2000, we returned to Virginia elated. All agreed the quality of the CD exceeded expectations. We believed it was a product of which we need not be ashamed. Would others agree?

I had brought back a dozen plain CDs and gave them to family and friends; one went to retired Army General George Price. Also, I made a few audiotapes and sent them to other friends. Some phoned back to thank me and comment, most did not. All who did comment loved the CD. Some said they cried; others said the singing gave them goose bumps.

The afternoon of March 10, George Price phoned from New York. He was at the apartment of his sister, opera diva Leontyne Price, and had just played the CD for her. George said, "Jerry, I want you to hear these comments from the source." Then he handed the phone to Leontyne.

"Bravo, General," she began. "Bravissimo. Your recording is absolutely superb. You must continue on with your singing!" After we spoke for several minutes, she passed the phone back to George, who promised to talk more with me when he returned to his home in Columbia, Maryland.

Leontyne didn't know it, but she had made my year. All the hard work, all the frustration, all the expense, all the self-doubt fell away. Here was someone who had sung with every major tenor in the world and in every major opera house in the world, who knew what a great recording sounded like, who knew how much hard work and how many disappointments there are before someone can sing at such a high level, and she was encouraging me.

Obviously, she could pick out the flaws in my voice and singing technique. But she, one of the finest singers of the century, was willing to set all that aside and applaud the overall musical effect. I was humbled and ecstatic at the same time. In the future, no matter what music critics and others say about my singing, they can never take away the joy I experienced from Leontyne's phone call.

Since then I have continued to take voice lessons with a new teacher, Dr. Medea Rudhadze-Lamoradze who immigrated to the United States from Georgia in the former Soviet Union. Medea was an opera diva in Georgia and Russia. But when an opportunity came to relocate to America and to apply for citizenship, she literally leaped at the opportunity. I, for one, am very thankful that she did.

For Charlene and me it is now a time of transition. We are grateful for all the opportunities this great nation of ours has given us, and we have tried to make the most of them. We look forward eagerly to what the future may have in store.

Looking back over the past years, and forward toward new sunrises, I think more and more on the wisdom, character and sacrifice of those who founded this great nation. I pray that their ideals, hopes and aspirations will continue to be ours forever. Our ancestors founded this great nation on immutable biblical principles, which produced clarity of thought, precision of words and courageous deeds. These alone define the true character of the American people, and reveal the true nature of American hopes and dreams.

Today all over the world, America's valiant, fearless youth unselfishly put their lives at risk in service to our nation and to all the civilized world. For them, uncommon valor remains a common virtue. Family members and loved ones still meet their coffins at the ocean's edge.

Shouldn't all of us keep faith with our honored dead and their families by conducting ourselves in ways that are worthy of the heroic sacrifices these young men and women make?

So, then, let us dare to preserve, protect, and defend America's historic moral values, based on the faith and conviction of our forebearers. If we are successful, the benefit of their heroic struggles and their lofty words and deeds—those values and principles written with iron, in the blood of our history—will continue to live and prosper.

NOTES

[1] Excerpt from *Pacific Stars & Stripes*, Monday, April 5, 1971

[2] Excerpt from *Pacific Stars & Stripes*, Monday, April 19, 1971

[3] Excerpt from *Pacific Stars & Stripes*, Tuesday, April 6, 1971

Generally Singing

OPERA FOR THE PEOPLE

Selections by Jerry R. Curry

Musically, opera has been Jerry's first love since childhood. Before the Korean War came along and his life in the military began, he seriously considered pursuing an operatic career. Over the years he has been able to sing with myriad church choirs and choral groups. But only in the last few years has he found time to pursue operatic studies. Jerry has sung in Europe, the United States, the Far East and Brazil.

SONG TITLES:

Praise Ye The Lord	*O sole mio*
Vesti la giubba	*Pourquoi me reveiller*
Danny Boy	*Mattinata*
I'll walk with God	*Recondita armonia*
Dein ist mein ganzes herz	*Before the throne*
Una furtiva lagrima	*E lucevan le stele*
Deep River	*Psalm XXIII*

Available from Amazon.com

Charlene Curry

THE GENERAL'S LADY

God's Faithfulness to a Military Spouse

Charlene Curry recounts all the joys and challenges of being a career military spouse and how she triumphed over difficulties by relying on a source of spiritual power that transformed her life.

Fern C. Willner

WHEN FAITH IS ENOUGH

A Safari of Destiny that Reveals Principles to Live By

A faith-inspiring story of a missionary wife and mother of seven relying completely on God in the heart of Africa. *Accompanying workbook also available for discussion groups in 2007*

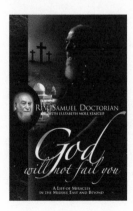

Rev. Samuel Doctorian
with Elizabeth Moll Stalcup, Ph.D.

GOD WILL NOT FAIL YOU

A Life of Miracles in the Middle East and Beyond

The miraculous life story of Rev. Samuel Doctorian, the renowned evangelist used mightily by God in the Middle East and around the world.